Books by Joseph E. Garland

An Experiment in Medicine
Every Man Our Neighbor
Lone Voyager
To Meet These Wants
That Great Pattillo
Eastern Point
The Gloucester Guide
Guns Off Gloucester

GUNS OFF GLOUCESTER

The Battle of Gloucester, August 8, 1775

GUNS OFF GLOUCESTER

Joseph E. Garland

ESSEX COUNTY NEWSPAPERS, INC.

Gloucester, Massachusetts   1975

First edition

Library of Congress Catalog Card No. 75-21650

GUNS OFF GLOUCESTER was written with the support of a grant from The Cape Ann Bank and Trust Company, Gloucester, Massachusetts.

Typography and design by Richard Cook and Barry Parsons

Layout by Robert W. Perrigo, Jr., and Elizabeth Rizzotti

Cover illustration by Margaret Garland Spindel

Printed by The Cricket Press, Manchester, Massachusetts

For
A.K.G.

If we are compelled to make the last appeal to Heaven, we will defend our resolutions and liberties at the expense of all that is dear to us.

Gloucester Town Meeting
December 15, 1773

CONTENTS

MAPS

ILLUSTRATIONS

FOREWORD

One of the interesting things about Joseph Foster in these days of preoccupation with the artificial projection of personality called image is that he is *not*, for a change, a figure larger than life on the unrolling diorama of the American Revolution. He was of the colonial New England yeomanry, not greatly better nor worse than the other fellow. He went to sea as a boy, climbed to the quarterdeck in the West Indies and European triangular trade out of Gloucester, and as a captain and merchant was caught up in events which were pushing and hauling Britain and her colonies to the breach, issues of trade regulation, monopoly, competition, revenue-raising and representation.

Foster rose in politics, but not as a skyrocket. He was a leader in the home guard, but no military genius. He sent his townsmen privateering and then tried it himself, but took no prizes of which he left a record. He prospered, but not by profiteering. His actions speak louder by far than his words, which are limited to a few cryptic account books and two letters of military instruction, literate but unrevealing of the man.

Colonel Foster stands still shadowy, although distinguished from that vast silent majority of his Revolutionary contemporaries. He was a leader to be sure, one of many, not precisely a hero, not exactly an anti-hero, not ordinary by most standards, nor unworthy of the chronicling. The man was typical of the untypical American, able, enterprising, crude, streaked with a strain of frontier ruthlessness, principled and courageous. His life deserves the telling and the tale. There is much in the record of it to bear out one's intuitive sense that his maritime and mercantile interests, and his actions in forwarding and defending them, exemplify the irrepressibly expanding American nationalism which the imperative of history demanded must branch from the mother stem and blossom forth on its own. Too, his military and political adventures during the interminable and terrible years of the Revolution reveal him as one of that staunch and stiffnecked lower echelon of leadership without which the war would not have been won. He was a rough frontier Yankee from Chebacco Parish who could make a saw cut and a ship sail. A hard man, it must be admitted.

That Joseph Foster should have been given, or taken, such a hand in shaping the subtleties of the archetypal Constitution of the Commonwealth of Massachusetts adds the more to the paradox of him. And that he should have taken exception to the ambiguities with which that remarkable document pretended to guarantee sectarian religious freedom, and won his point and made his mark on the road to the separation of priest and politician, all deepen the mystery of him.

The scarcity of material about Joseph Foster makes it the more necessary to range over the context of his times, specifically to reexamine the era between 1760 and 1800 on Cape Ann in the new light of documents and manuscripts which were not available to John J. Babson when he published his incomparable *History of Gloucester* a hundred and fifteen years ago. They show, for example, that possession of Gloucester Harbor, and by extension Cape Ann, was considered of the utmost importance by General Washington, and no less so by his adversaries, Generals Gage and Howe and Admiral Graves, during the pivotal Siege of Boston. And if the Siege had failed by Cape Ann's falling into the hands of the British, and they had thereby held and extended their New England foothold, what then might have befallen the American cause?

These newly dredged sources, many of them from the United States Navy's staggering bicentennial project, *Naval Documents of the American Revolution,* add detail and color to the North Shore beginnings of the fishing schooner flotilla launched by George Washington...to *Falcon's* ferocious confrontation with the patriots of Gloucester...to the town's subsequent hairbreadth escape from draconian retribution...and to the hitherto unrealized extent of the privateering effort put forth by impoverished Cape Ann. Other data such as Captain Foster's vessel accounts and British Admiralty records tell us on a whole new level of documentation about Gloucester's surprisingly busy foreign commerce during the late colonial period and after the Revolution when American ships were again caught in the tired old European rivalries being played out in the bloody Caribbean.

Newspaper publication during the Revolution was erratic; furthermore, Cape Ann had to depend on Salem and Newburyport papers for word of the world, and of its own doings, until the appearance of the *Gloucester Telegraph* in 1827. It makes slim pickings for the gleaner after the mundanities in this isolated community in those hardest of times. Out of local records, diaries, the *Naval Documents,* odd newspaper items and a scattering of sources I have tried to get across some feeling of the intensity of the suffering, its endless grinding overlaid with epidemic smallpox, and deprivation that frequently skirted starvation, eight years of it, and its long aftermath. This was but a part of the price paid by the people of Cape Ann for their pledge to defend with their lives their resolutions and their liberties.

For two hundred years history has bypassed Cape Ann's important and possibly crucial part in the early months, especially, of the War of Independence, its suffering, its contributions to the beginnings of American commerce--and as an arena of struggle--to the definition of religious freedom. This work is offered, this year of the Bicentennial, as a start on the way to redress.

To former president Charles E. Kendall of the Cape Ann Bank and Trust Company I express my appreciation for his imaginative approach to Gloucester's history which led to the preservation and restoration of Joseph Foster's landmark colonial house and to the generous grant which made possible the research and writing of this book. To Philip S. Weld, president of Essex County Newspapers and the neighbor across Gloucester Harbor with whom I share the ghostly lapping of *Falcon*'s wake upon our respective shores, I fire a broadside of thanks for making publication possible. And of my dear wife, R.C.G., once again I beg indulgence for so many hours and so many groans in the labor thereof.

J.E.G.

Eastern Point, Gloucester
April 1975

GUNS OFF GLOUCESTER

GLOUCESTER: AUGUST 8, 1775

Leaving the parched pasture of Ten Pound Island on their quarter, the three armed boats from his Majesty's Sloop of War *Falcon* knifed through the blue of the harbor toward the town. The cool Atlantic breeze had borne their ship in from the sea and now helped them toward their destination. As each bow was lifted by the brawn of each pull of the oarsmen, it clove away a dash of spray that fell back into a widening wedge of wake.

It was early on a Tuesday afternoon in the fifteenth summer of the reign of George the Third of England, and seven weeks and three days after the bloody victory of his ramrod regulars over a hastily assembled force of rash and raw American revolutionaries who the night before had made the costly mistake of fortifying Breed's Hill on the heights of Charlestown under the impression that it was the more tenable Bunker Hill to the northwest ... and the fatal mistake of being there at all.

The ship's boats surged on, almost soundless save for the click-clacking rhythm of the sweeps in the oarlocks, the audible gurgle of their hulls, the swish of dripping blades on the backswing. A pageantry in red and blue. A royal bristle of bayonets. A parliamentary proclamation of brass in buckles and buttons. A ministerial menace of cold English steel, glinting in a hot New England sun.

A half a mile from the nearest wharf, between Stage Head on the western shore of the harbor and Ten Pound Island to the east, *Falcon* lay at anchor, high-tailed and blunt-beaked. A springline to her cable held her all but motionless off the wind, her wings of canvas clewed and yards aback, displaying her three towering spars, the thousand threads of her rigging, the pretty flutter of her ensign, and the bared talons of her broadside to this unimportant fishing outport of his Majesty's rebellious province of Massachusetts.

Having nothing better to do since lobbing cannonballs amongst the Yankees from her station in the Mystic River that famous day in June, *Falcon* had given chase to a brace of inward-bound West Indiamen this morning. Capturing one, the swift warship pursued the other into Cape Ann Harbor, where she came to anchor, brought the town under her guns and put over a landing party to go in for the prize.

Onward and inward rowed *Falcon*'s boats, into the narrows between Rocky Neck's stone-studded pasture, fluffed with placid sheep, and Gloucester's old grassgrown fort, relic of happier days when every loyal yeoman loved his liege. Now they were in the calm water of the lee, coursing easily through the tide, past the mouth of Harbor Cove where the crude vessels of the colonists crowded in the docks. The wharves looked to be deserted. Ahead, a few strokes on, the fleeing schooner had fetched up flying on the Five Pound Island flats and bilged. Her sails were in a heap on deck. No sign of her crew. Up in the town, the bell in the white, spiking steeple of the church pealed insistently, incessantly.

At his quarterdeck rail, lean and handsome and as haughty as an admiral, Captain John Linzee squinted through his glass at the progress of his landing force. *Falcon*'s gun ports were open. Carriage lashings were cast off and tampions stowed. Powder cartridges and ball were properly stacked on deck. Gunners stood ready at their stations, and all eyes were intent on the three paired sets of flashing oars, almost a mile up in the harbor. The seven six-pounders of their broadside, all aimed and quoined, pointed seven black muzzles where the wood frame of Gloucester was the thickest.

Onward rowed the Royal Navy, into the deepest pocket of the second deepest harbor in Massachusetts Bay, three thousand miles from home, to administer a small lesson in large obedience. Not a bloody Yank in sight. A covey of cowards. A quail shoot.

Now the three boatloads were abreast of stony Duncan's Point. Just ahead, almost under their plowing bows, the loot lay helpless on her keel.

At that exact moment the stocky figure of Joseph Foster, sea captain, smuggler, politician and patriot, rose up in silhouette against the August sky. He slashed the air and bellowed to his fishermen and his farmers, and from behind those silent rocks and wharves the flintlocks and fowling pieces and the one rusty old swivel gun of his first ambush barked and roared.

The mouse had turned and sprung upon the lion.

From his rail Captain Linzee saw the white puffs of battle-smoke, and then the crackle of gunfire reached his ears. As he watched, his three boats rounded the bend of Duncan's Point, and the firing increased.

Proud *Falcon*'s commander knew now that he had sent his men into a trap, though of the trapper he knew naught. And he knew he must act, and do it quickly. Gloucester lay before him. If the town possessed a single cannon, which he doubted, it had not fired it. He glanced at his gunners.

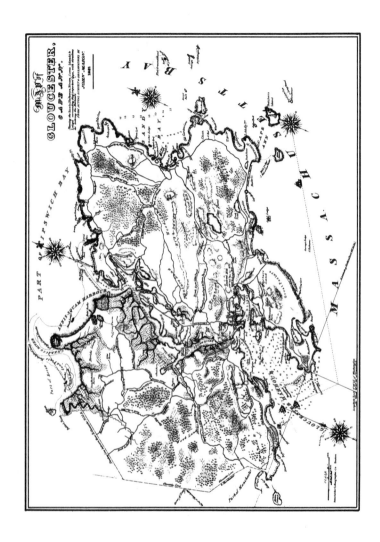

MAP OF
GLOUCESTER,
CAPE ANN.

FROM ACTUAL SURVEY & OBSERVATIONS BY
JOHN MASON.

MASSACHUSETTS BAY

IPSWICH BAY

PART OF

1

THE RASP OF THE SAW
AND THE SONG OF THE SEA

When they knew the midsummer tide would flood at dawn in their part of Ipswich called Chebacco and now called Essex, it is a fair chance that Joe Foster and one of his brothers had laid their plans the night before to roll out of bed with the first glow in the east, dress, pack a loaf of bread, jug of water, clam fork and handlines, and in a couple of minutes to be at the landing downstream of their father's sawmill where the Chebacco Falls meet the farthest inland reach of the tidal Chebacco River.

Toss grub and gear into the dory, drag her down the mudbank into the stream, jump aboard, shove off, take to the oars and stroke along the winding waterway, brushing the tall grass on either side that nearly hides the higher landscape.

The birds of the wetlands would peer curiously at the boys gliding by, no sound but the spatter of the oarblades. Fish crows flapped and croaked about their business overhead. A distant rooster cock-a-doodled up the day. Swallows skimmed and whirled above. A gull wheeled by with a whoosh. The retreating current of the ebb wafted them along, easy work at the oars, and in no time they had covered the mile through the marsh to the causeway, where the road between Gloucester and Ipswich spanned the stream, and were flicked under the low bridge in a gurgle and a rush. By now the flaming sky ahead proclaimed the coming of the sun.

Past the stocks of the shipyards the outgoing tide carried them. Along here were built many of the vessels of the

Gloucester fishing fleet and launched into the twisting channel. The chips and sawdust on the bank were a hundred years thick. A Chebacco boat in frames, unplanked yet, was outlined high above their heads against the rosy dawn ... the stubby skeleton of a frail creature for a man to trust his life to. The shipwrights were gathering ... dubbers, plankers, caulkers, finish men ... sizing up the day's work; a couple of them noticed the Foster boys oaring by and gave them a casual wave of recognition.

The sea was still six miles on. When the shipyards and the village and their sounds were behind them, the brothers changed off at the oars. The river broadened, and they gathered speed between Conomo Point and the drumlin of Cross Island, and then they were in Chebacco Bay, a mile across and yet a mere tidal puddle filled and drained on a plain of sand. The dazzle of the beaches all around them brought tears to their eyes, squinting in the forenoon sun. They headed for the bay's entrance from the sea, made by the sea itself, which had cast up twin barrier reefs of sand, Castle Neck of Ipswich, three miles long on the west, and the Coffin family's mile and a half of snowy beach and dune on the east, in Gloucester, anchored by the rock pile of Two Penny Loaf.

Out beyond was the Atlantic.

The tide was two hours gone. The boys beached their dory on the wet flats where the channel dropped off, dug in their heels, bent their backs, and soon had forked out of their hiding places in the sand enough bait clams to catch a boatload of fish, which was the object of the day. They pushed off, waded out and hurdled back in.

It seemed as if the whole of Chebacco Bay was rushing toward the sea in impatient rips and eddies under their bottom. The sensation produced a profound excitement, an anticipation of commitment of the smallness of their boat and themselves to an overwhelming force as the slow semidiurnal drop in the level of the ocean sucked the tide out of this pocket in the land and them with it, in a rush across the entrance bar. The clutch was so powerful there was no rowing against it, no bucking it, no turning back, only submission.

So clear, for all its depth and agitation, was this outpouring of pale green water that they could very plainly see sand dollars and sea urchins and starfish on the white sand four fathoms below, and even a flounder here and there, queer little snouts nosing into the current. Then they were through it as through a sluice, on the deep, and the guiding rower rested for a moment on his oars.

Out here on great Ipswich Bay, on the heaving sea, the water was the richest blue, the sky strangely less so this hot and windless morning.

They rowed out a ways and shipped the oars. Smashing clams, baiting hooks, dropping lines over, jigging, hauling in a fish, curling the hook through a fresh clam, again the plonk of the sinkers over the side in an otherwise unspeaking, hypnotic routine ... the sun was high overhead when they realized that time had slipped by and that they too were slipping and sliding over some dozens of glassy-eyed and gasping codfish, haddock, hake and slithery flat greysole.

They were munching on their bread when Joe pointed to a ruffle of wind on the sea toward Gloucester's Halibut Point, and clouds piling up high above the horizon. Yes, it would breeze up southeast, likely. Time for a last bait-up. A bite, a pull down deep there somewhere ... yank hard ... a big one on the hook. The line came furiously alive. Together they grabbed it and hauled in, hand over hand. The gunwale was down two strakes in the water with their straining .. ah now ... easy ... he broke the surface in a frenzy of thrashing and splashing ... up and over the side with him in a shower of spray, a fine ugly chicken halibut, all of forty, perhaps fifty, pounds. Whack him on the nose and let's beat the breeze.

It was dead low water, as they had figured, when the Foster boys rowed back through the now narrow channel into Chebacco Bay, and it could blow a gale for all they cared; they had left the sea behind and were back safe in the lee of the West Parish hills of Gloucester. Again the brothers beached out, stripped and dashed into the icy water this time, screaming with the shock of it. A dozen numbing strokes were enough before racing back for the beach, blue, shivering, chattering at the teeth. With their shirts they scrubbed away the goose pimples, dried their tanned bodies in the sun and the wind, dressed and shoved off.

The tide was with them, thrusting now up into the river, just as it had carried them out in the early morning. When they had passed the shipyards and drifted under the low span and into the shallows of the marsh, the going was harder and the oars grew heavier and longer with every pull against the dead weight of their fare of fish and the strengthening outflow of the freshwater stream from Chebacco.

It was twilight, and the river was approaching its second flood of the day when the boys bumped back to their landing. They hove the oars up and made fast. The first firefly twinkled in the high grass. Stilted solemnly against the last light of dusk, a night heron *qwawked* on the bank, stark and wise as a parson.

They were tired to the marrow, too tired to slap at the knowing swarms of skeeters and midges. But the fish couldn't lie in the dory all night, and they wouldn't head and gut themselves; the halibut had to be lugged up to Ma, and they'd have to clean up for supper, and Pa would have chores for them ... all before body could flop on bed.

Then a boy could dream of how it had been that day out on the easy, undulating back of the bay, watching the wind clouds gather behind a sail out of Gloucester that was standing off to the eastward, soon hull down in the dancing heat waves of the horizon.

That was how the sea pulled and pushed Joe Foster some time around the year 1741, when he was eleven and ripping timber into planks for the neighbors in his father's mill at the Falls.

Jeremiah Foster's dam and sawmill were at the rapids on the stream a mile below Chebacco Pond. It was the first millsite granted by Ipswich, a score of years after his great-grandfather Reginald Foster settled from England in 1638. The mill had long been in the Story family when Jeremiah bought it, with homestead, barn and nine acres, from his second cousin, John Story, for 320 pounds in 1724. [1]

The new owner is described in his deed as a mariner. He was thirty-three and had been married to Dorothy Rust since he was twenty-six and she seventeen. It may be that he had quit the sea for sawyering; during the forty-five years he had the mill he added twenty-four acres of timber, meadow, pasture and salt marsh to his holdings, so that between sawing wood and farming he must have had his hands full, even with the large family he and Dorothy had to pitch in around the place. Jeremiah, Jr., was born in 1718, then Moses, John, Joanna, Ephraim, Joseph, Martha, Dorothy, Benjamin, Mary, Elizabeth, Joshua and Miriam, the last, in 1741.[2]

Joseph, the sixth, the sea dreamer, was born on July 19, 1730. Judging from a description of him later in life, he was a wiry little devil, nursed on hard work and weaned on responsibility. His father's account book shows entries against customers for millwork done by the boy as early as 1741, when he was eleven, maybe only ten years old. Fifteen acres of timber wasn't much, and Foster relied on the business of his neighbors, charging them a toll for sawing.

There was still plenty of woodland two miles inland from the coast, not yet so thoroughly cut over that the mills must look elsewhere for their supply. It was a good mixture of soft and hard woods. The keels, floors, frames, knees, stems and other skeletal bones of the vessels built locally were hand-hewn of oak, mostly, while pine, hemlock and spruce were used for the planking, decking, finish and spars, and of course for building construction and furniture. The wilderness around rang with the crack of the broad ax, the warning shouts of *timber!* and the crash of the giants into the underbrush. Limbs were lopped, and yokes of oxen dragged the chainhitched logs to the mill, one or two at a time, or if they were small enough, stacked and lashed on a sled.

The Foster mill was in a partly open shed down beside the rushing falls. The machinery was simple and country-made. Typically, a gate which was remote-controlled from inside the shed near the saw carriage by a lever or a pulley opened and shut the sluiceway, monitoring the flow under the massive wooden waterwheel. This primitive and slow, but powerful, turbine drove the heavy pitwheel directly beneath the saw, either by a straight axle or through gears which multiplied its speed. A connecting rod called a pitman (from the old times when two men ripped logs by hand with a pit saw, one above, the other below in the pit) was fastened from the lower end of the saw above it to a point near the rim of the pitwheel; hence the diameter of the circle described by one revolution of the wheel equaled the vertical traverse of the saw.

The blade cut on the downstroke and was suspended in a square wooden frame large enough for the heaviest logs to pass through. Side blocks kept the cut straight, and the top of the blade was bolted to a springy pole that held it taut. Foster's rig probably had a gang of at least two such sash, or up-and-down, saws working in tandem, perhaps more. [3]

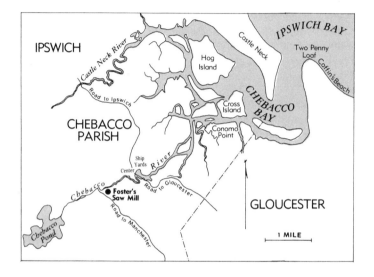

In making ready for the first cut, the log was rassled onto the carriage which traveled on tracks clear through the saw, pretty nearly the length of the mill; it was jammed firmly into position on blocks at either end by iron dogs hinged to the block facing, pounded into the timber and wedged. [4]

Open the gate and let 'er rip! The sluice hits in a rush, and with a torrential splashing the waterwheel groans into action. The pit-wheel turns, all squeaks and thumps, the pitman clanks, the saws rise, descend, back up again, and down, up and down in a gathering cadence while the carriage noisily inches forward along its track, drawn by a weight hung over a pulley, or nudged by a cogwheel from underneath giving it a shove with each downstroke. The teeth bite into the giant butt with a rasp, the shed quivers with each new revolution, the works bang and grunt and screech and sigh with satisfying regularity, the great wheel turns in a shower and whish of spray, and the air is exciting with the forest smell of fresh pitch and sawdust.

Father Foster and a son could rip a thousand board feet of pine a day, rather an improvement over two men with a pit saw, who were regarded as prodigious if they produced two hundred running feet of plank between sunup and sundown. [5]

Life in Chebacco was not all toil for a boy, but there was not much chance for loafing either, except when a couple of Foster brothers could slip away on an ebbing tide for a few hours on the bay ... and even then they were expected to bring back a fare of fish to show for it. The frontier was more than a memory to the Fosters and their neighbors. Every waking hour in the New England country family was under mandate to account for itself. Still, to the children of a sawyer, the midsummer drought or the ice of winter stilled the waterwheel and brought respite from the hard and hazardous drudgery of the mill.

When the freeze was deepest there was fishing through holes in the salt ice below the causeway, for smelt, and sometimes for eels spiked in the mud with the barbs of the eel spear. There was the spring run of the alewives, finding their mysterious way back from the sea into the salt river they had descended as fingerlings, leaping up the falls and the sluiceways and on to Chebacco Pond, the fresh water of their birth, to spawn ... and just lazing back with the current in the autumn, lazing into a Foster dip net, or trapped, flashing and frantic, in the weir of stones and branches granted as a right to Joe's Great-Grandfather Nathaniel Rust in 1674.

There were deer hunts on November nights when the men and boys with dogs and sleds and melancholy horns picked up the trail and tracked the buck through the woods and across the fields, all white and soft in the moonlight with the first snow of the winter underfoot.

And there were pigeon kills. The bane of the colonial farmer was the passenger pigeon. These voracious birds would darken the sky by the hundreds of thousands in their passage, fell great branches in the forest by the weight of their roosting and simply harvest without his permission the crop of the unlucky husbandman whose field happened to look inviting. The Fosters would bait a patch of ground, or decoy it too, and when the plague lit, rush from concealment in the brush and throw their pigeon net over as many as it could cover. The pests that there was no room for in Dorothy Foster's pot wound up back in the fields fertilizing more pigeon bait. [6]

The mother of this large family was the daughter of Chebacco's first schoolmaster, Nathaniel Rust, Jr. Her father died before Dorothy's marriage, and although she may have shared his love of learning, her opportunities for passing it on to her own children did not promise much. [7] Her rough-hewn husband's literary estate at his death amounted to his "Great and Small Bibles." The local school term was four months in the year. Probably none of the young Fosters had any formal education beyond the age of twelve. To read and write after a fashion, and to do sums under the threat of the rod were sufficient.

What Chebacco lacked in letters it more than made up for in spirit. The Reverend John Wise was minister of the parish for almost half a century until his death only five years before Joseph Foster was born. He catechized the boy's father and mother when they were children, and when they fell in love he married them. He was a poor country preacher, but what he stood up for and what he stood out against deeply affected the people of his parish for generations and influenced the course of American history. John Wise was in fact the first voice to put into ringing words the principles of self-government which his countrymen felt in their bones but had never heard so expressed before...as *democracy*.

When giant John Wise rose up in a king's star chamber and thundered against the tyranny of his colonial governor, Joe Foster's Great-Grandfather Robert Kinsman rose with him, and together they went to jail.

That was family lore, and the sort of education that made an impression on a boy.

John Wise was an impressive man. When the people in the south of Ipswich organized the Second, or Chebacco, Parish in 1680 they had engaged this young son of an indentured servant in Roxbury, recently graduated from Harvard College, as their first pastor. England had a nervous eye on France at the time, which was not unusual, and James II got the idea that his New England colonies could defend themselves better against the old enemy, should they be attacked, if he made a single province of them -- a plan he started on by nullifying the charter of Massachusetts in 1684 and making Sir Edmund Andros governor of the new dominion. Andros was able but arrogant, and one of his first acts in 1687 was arbitrarily to impose a tax of a penny a pound of valuation on the estates of New England freeholders, who were supposed to have a vote but whose customary say in such matters had been nullified along with the charter that guaranteed it. When Ipswich, with the other towns, was ordered to appoint someone to collect this deeply resented tax, six of the town fathers, including John Wise and Grandfather Kinsman, decided to resist. [8]

"We have a good God, and a good King," Pastor Wise told the town meeting, "and we shall do well to stand for our rights." The town voted as one man to choose no collector and to pay no tax. The six ringleaders were brought before a summary court in Boston presided over by Judge Joseph Dudley.

The minister from the remote shipbuilding hamlet of Chebacco, population insignificant, argued for their privileges as Englishmen: no taxation without representation, without the consent of the taxed.

The bench was dumbfounded. "Do you think" demanded one judge, "the laws of England follow you to the ends of the earth?" "Do you believe," inquired Governor Andros, "Joe and Tom may tell the King what money he may have?" And from Justice Dudley: "You shall have no more privileges left you than not to be sold as slaves."

The Ipswich six were sentenced to jail for twenty-one days, fined, ordered to post bond for a year's good behavior and suspended from holding civil office ... and Wise was suspended from his pulpit, a punishment which Andros shortly rescinded. [9]

But such inspired disobedience was catching among Englishmen who had transplanted their affection for their liberties to a wilderness, and spread to Gloucester, whose citizens likewise declined to pay the governor's tax; all five selectmen and the constable were summoned to Salem court and fined. And then it infected Boston and swelled into an armed uprising which unseated Governor Andros in 1689 after the news arrived that William of

Orange had unseated King James. A new royal charter was issued to Massachusetts, a degree of representative government was restored, and John Wise the instigator was elected from Ipswich to the General Court to help make it work.

The years passed while from the isolation of his Essex County parish Wise followed the careers of the two principal deposers of Edmund Andros, the famous divines, Increase and Cotton Mather of Boston. The more he pondered their actions and their words the more convinced he became that this self-appointed father-and-son team of watchdogs over public morality had upset a political tyranny only to set up a religious tyranny of their own. Highly intelligent, formidably self-righteous, ambitious, elitist and arrogant as any two royal governors, the Mathers had been craftily trying to persuade the independent Congregational parishes of New England that it was to their advantage to relinquish some of their most cherished prerogatives of religious self-government to an association of clergy ... dominated by the Mathers.

These were times, it should be added, when parish and town governments were virtually the same, for church and state had not yet been constitutionally separated in America.

Wise bided his time, and in 1710 published an exposé of the Mather scheme, *The Churches Quarrel Espoused,* which he followed in seven more years with *A Vindication of the Government of New-England Churches*, a tract of such logic and power that it stopped his targets in their tracks. Where could he find an antidote for "the poison of Wise's cursed Libel?" muttered Cotton Mather.

John Wise's cursed libel was the opening reveille of American democracy. "Brethren," he addressed his countrymen in language they understood, "ye have been called unto liberty, therefore hold your hold brethren!...Pull up well upon the oars, you have a rich cargo, and I hope we shall escape shipwreck...Daylight and good piloting will secure all." And what was that rich cargo?

Democracy is the form of government which the light of nature does highly value, and often directs to as most agreeable to the just and natural prerogatives of human beings...The natural equality of men amongst men must be duly favoured, in that government was never established by God or nature, to give one man a prerogative to insult over another...Honor all men. The end of all good government is to

—16—

cultivate humanity, and promote the happiness of all, and the good of every man in his rights, his life, liberty, estate, honor, etc., without injury or abuse to any. [10]

A furious man, Cotton Mather branded Wise, and so he was: "The very name of an arbitrary government is ready to put an Englishman's blood into a fermentation; but when it comes and shakes its whip over their ears, and tells them it is their master, it makes them stark mad!" [11]

A muscular man, head and shoulders above his flock, burly, strong as a plowman, yet stately and graceful of bearing whether perorating from his pulpit in the cloth of his profession, or sleeves rolled up, sweat pouring down his face, tilling his fields. For generations after, his neighbors handed down the story of one Chandler, the county champion, who, having heard that Pastor Wise could wrestle with man as well as Devil, rode over one day from Andover to give him a try. On the first fall the man of God set his visitor on his back. On the second he flipped him over the fence. The ex-champion struggled to his feet, dusted himself off, and allowed that if the reverend would pass over his horse too, he'd be on his way home.

A muscular Christian. When Metacomet, dubbed facetiously by the colonists King Philip, Sachem of the Wampanoags, organized the five tribes and sacked the white settlements in 1675, young Wise was chaplain to the New Englanders who stormed and burned the Narragansett fort at South Kingston, Rhode Island, and massacred three hundred Indian women and children. One wonders what part he took, and how he reacted. Fifteen years after this exercise in the "cultivation of humanity" by his brethren he was appointed chaplain to the expedition which Massachusetts sent to the eastward under Sir William Phipps to wrest Quebec from the French. With Grandfather Rust, he marched off from Chebacco for Boston and boarded ship. The fleet dawdled so long en route that the alerted defenders had time to set up a clever show of force they didn't actually have. The ruse worked. Sir William panicked and turned tail, and his armada straggled back to Boston in shame and disarray.

By the Treaty of Utrecht in 1713 the French retained Cape Breton, commanding the strategic St. Lawrence River, and built a strong fort there at Louisburg in 1720 from which they harassed Massachusetts fishing vessels and merchantmen with stinging effect. By the time England and France resumed their war in 1744, the Bay Colony men had been brought to a pitch of frustration and anger. Governor William Shirley had no trouble persuading the General Court to outfit an expedition to storm the French bastion. Other colonies sent men or money, and by the end of March 1745 an army of four thousand had been assembled and was preparing to embark from Boston under the command of William Pepperell.

Jeremiah Foster was captain of the Chebacco company of militia. The emotions of Dorothy and her children can be imagined as they watched the father of the family, Jeremiah, Jr., nephew Aaron Foster and many other relatives and neighbors march off around the bend of the Boston road and out of sight. Joe Foster was fourteen. Did he burn to be off with them?

Emotions ran high. The campaign had the fervid aspect of a holy war and the blessings of the Protestant ministry. Over in Gloucester pastor John White exhorted the Almighty to protect his fishermen-soldiers and to lean His weight on their side:

> Some have not unfitly called Cape Breton a hornet's nest. 'Tis not safe, in a time of war, to go near them. We have already, ever since the war commenced, been great sufferers by them. They harbor our enemies that come to lay waste our infant eastern settlements; they molest and break in upon our fisheries, and break them to pieces; they lie near the roadway of our European merchandise, and they can sally out and take our corn-vessels: and therefore our oppressions from thence, so long as it remains in the hands of the enemy, are like to be intolerable. We must remove these our enemies, or they will destroy us. There is a plain necessity for it; and woe to us if it not be reduced! [12]

If Captain Foster and his Chebacco company did not literally wear breastplates with crosses upon them, they had certainly enlisted under the banner of John Wise's muscular Christianity. The self-interest of their Gloucester friends (and their own, for they built fishing boats) in cleaning out the nest of French Catholic hornets was advanced under the cloak of an anti-papist crusade. To the New England Protestant, France and Rome were in unholy alliance to conquer and catholicize the New World. *Nil desperandum Christo duce* -- "nothing is to be despaired of with Christ for the leader" -- was the motto of a New Hampshire regiment suggested by the English evangelist George Whitefield, who was on his third hellfire tour of the colonies; one of his followers, a chaplain with the fleet of fifty vessels that sailed from Boston March 24, took along a hatchet to wield against the graven images in the French churches of Canada.

Whitefield was a powerful speaker. He could make himself heard clearly before an open-air crowd of twenty thousand, as he had one day in an English coalmining district; he remarked proudly afterwards that his "first discovery of their being affected was by seeing the white gutters made by their tears, which fell plentifully down their black cheeks."

The spellbinder spelled trouble. On a previous visit to America, when Joe Foster was ten, he had preached in Ipswich in the morning, then swung through Chebacco parish. The boy could not have helped seeing and hearing the famous man. Mild and moderate Theophilus Pickering had succeeded John Wise in the pulpit, and while he had no particular doctrinal quarrel with George Whitefield, he made no effort to conceal his distaste for the man's demagoguery. Hardly had the Calvinist fireeater departed town when the usual outpouring of hysteria that followed his appearances engulfed poor Pickering. Overnight, the general satisfaction with his ministry gave way to complaint, and it was whispered that he was too cool in the pulpit and too warm in welcoming new members to the church who were tinged with the liberalism excoriated by the revivalist. By the spring of 1745, when the men of Chebacco were mustering for the Louisburg crusade, it was neighbor against neighbor on the issue of Pastor Pickering's continued tenure in his job. Where the Fosters stood is not revealed, but Daniel Giddings, Captain Jeremiah's close friend and lieutenant, was vocally anti-Pickering and a leader in the movement to replace him.

The expedition sailed, with Whitefield's fervent blessing. The siege was laid on April 30. English men-of-war arrived off Cape Breton and commenced a bombardment of Louisburg. This time under the combined auspices of George Whitefield and God, the

New Englanders won the day, and on June 17, 1745, the French surrendered their fortress. [13]

That summer Captain Jeremiah Foster and his eldest son arrived home, flushed with victory, to be greeted with the news that Dorothy had died on May 14, two months short of her forty-fifth birthday.

Soon after his mother's death and his father's return from the war, probably before the year was up, Joseph Foster left home and went to sea. He was fifteen.

2

OUT OF GLOUCESTER

Their mother's death at Chebacco while their father and oldest brother were off smoking the French from the hornet's nest at Louisburg left Joseph Foster and his other brothers and sisters temporarily orphaned. He turned fifteen that July, and family tradition sends him to sea soon after. Not a doubt of it, for he dropped from sight, a boy, as if ocean or earth had swallowed him up, and reappeared a man, master of a vessel in the West Indies trade at twenty-five.

During those years of growing into manhood Joe Foster would have had to have gone fishing and coasting, as one must crawl before he walks, in preparation for the requisite climb out of the forecastle as mate before he had his own command.

North Shore vessels in the British colonial coastal and foreign trade were required to clear and enter through the Salem customs to and from their home ports. In March of 1756 the snow *Joanna,* eighty-four tons, Captain Joseph Foster, was so entered from a voyage to St. Martin in the West Indies.[1] The records do not identify *Joanna's* home port, but Gloucester is a good guess.

For one thing, the prime outward cargo to the West Indies was salt fish, the production of which was largely shared by Cape Ann and Marblehead. For another, Joseph Foster's first known business partner was Edward Payne, later to be a leading Boston merchant, who had a fishing business, flake yard and store at Gloucester as early as about 1755 and for

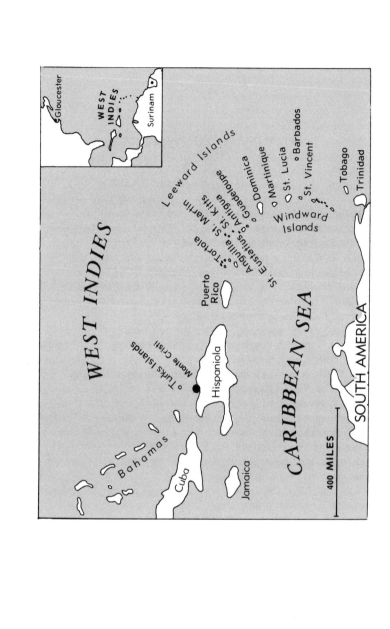

several years following. For a third, it is a known fact that Foster was sailing out of Gloucester from 1760 on. Finally, Gloucester was the nearest port to Chebacco, where there is ample reason to suppose that he hustled immediately upon stepping ashore from *Joanna* in order to make a proposal and a promise to a certain young lady, Miss Lydia Giddings by name, twenty-four years of age, in her full bloom as one of the six daughters of Daniel Giddings, the same who had served as lieutenant in Captain Jeremiah Foster's Chebacco company at the siege of Louisburg. And then he was back, probably to Gloucester, for a voyage to Lisbon, Portugal, in command of the sixty-ton schooner *Neptune*.

Neptune left the coast early in May of 1756, and it was not until they made Lisbon (unless they had spoken a vessel from Europe with the news) that they learned that England had resumed her interminable colonial war with France while they were at sea. Any pretext would do for the old enemies to have at each other wherever their imperial designs clashed, and this time it was the continental ambitions of Frederick the Great of Prussia. France, Austria, Russia, Sweden and Saxony had coalesced to clip the wings of his ambition, and since anything France was for, Britain was against, the mother country had allied herself with Frederick. Thus broke out the Seven Years' War.

Captain Foster made his voyage and cleared *Neptune* through Salem customs on September 28. On October 17 he and Lydia Giddings were married. Five weeks passed, and he was off again in *Neptune,* this time for Cadiz, Spain, not to return until early August of the next year, 1757, about in time for the birth of their first child, Mary. Having to contend with her husband's long absences at sea, Lydia perhaps remained with her parents in Chebacco, and it is a curious fact that Mary was not baptized for three more years. An unusual lapse, and one questions whether it had to do with the religious schism in Chebacco which finally did split the parish apart in 1746 when the extreme Calvinists who were so disenchanted with Theophilus Pickering broke away and organized the Fourth Church of Ipswich under a thunderation preacher more to their taste,

John Cleaveland. Joseph Foster's religious sentiments a few years later, anyway, were not with Cleaveland, and his inclination probably was to stick with the Second Parish and Pickering's successor, Nehemiah Porter; Lydia's father, Daniel Giddings, conversely was a leading elder in Cleaveland's church. This possibility of an intraparish stand-off in the family may account for the fact that little Mary was baptized in neither.

His venture to Spain was Foster's last in the European trade for three years. Beginning with his departure for the Caribbean in late September of 1757, he confined his voyaging to the West Indies. He made seven voyages in all: one in *Neptune;* three in the schooner *Speedwell* of thirty-eight tons,[2] putting in among numerous other islands at St. Martin, which was owned jointly by the French and the Dutch, and the Turks Islands in the British Bahamas; two in 1759 in a schooner *Neptune* of thirty-six tons, rather smaller than the earlier *Neptune* and probably not the same; and one in the large schooner *Wolfe,* seventy-five tons, clearing Salem on December 21, 1759.

Captain Foster's surviving accounts, commencing in 1760, indicate that he owned all or part of both the second *Neptune* and *Wolfe,* which he may have built and certainly named, since Major General James Wolfe, hero of Quebec, had fallen in the midst of victory on the Plains of Abraham on September 13, only fourteen weeks previous to the schooner's departure.

Midway in the Seven Years' War, Joe Foster was not only unperturbed and undeterred by it, but he revelled in it. He was making money hand over fist, and if he was not openly trading with the enemy, he was doing it secretly.

Why else, if he had nothing to hide, did he put in to St. Eustatius, a Dutch pinpoint in the Leeward Islands, in the middle of February, 1760--seven weeks out in *Wolfe*--and buy a brace of three-pounder deck guns? Two months later his account book locates him at "Mount Christo," loading sugar and rum; this was Monte Cristi, on the north coast of St. Dominique, close to the Haitian border, and it was a possession of France, with which American vessels were forbidden by England to have any commerce. Since Foster and *Wolfe* were in company with *Neptune* (which he owned outright or with her captain, George Bartlet), during most of this voyage, he may have given Bartlet the second deck gun. The Caribbean was a pitfall of English privateers on the lookout for Yankee adventurers carrying contraband sugar, rum and molasses from the French West Indies in exchange for fish, lumber and the like, while the warships of Louis XV lay in wait for Americans carrying English goods. Who knows but that a compact three-pounder might hold off a boarding party long enough to catch a leading wind and escape?

By early summer both *Wolfe* and *Neptune* had crossed the Atlantic and were at Gibraltar, where Captain Foster sold their cargoes (*Neptune's* was mainly sugar and barrel staves) and bid in for the hundred-ton brig *Sanders* at auction; she seems to have been a prize condemned by the British Admiralty Court at The Rock. Then he purchased brandy, wine, sweet oil, marble soap, Russian duck, Barcelona handkerchiefs, raisins and lemons, and divided this choice cargo amongst his fleet of three, giving *Sanders* to Captain Bartlet to sail back, and *Neptune* to John Rust, his mate, and sent them home in August. Foster himself sailed in *Wolfe* from Gibraltar in October and touched at Cadiz, maybe to top off his cargo. He arrived at Gloucester November 3, 1760, whence he coasted wines, lemons, and raisins to Boston and Portsmouth, New Hampshire, and raisins to Newburyport, before laying up *Wolfe* for a winter refit.

The voyage was typical of the triangular trade between New England, the West Indies and Europe,[3] and of the resourcefulness of a Yankee captain-trader, taking advantage of the war to acquire contraband from one contestant and a prize ship from the other, arriving home safe and sound with part of his profits in goods and part in the form of a fifty per cent increase in his vessel holdings.

Richard Derby, Salem's leading merchant, tried to pull off the same kind of deal, but not so luckily, when he bought a French prize ship of three hundred tons at Gibraltar with the proceeds of a cargo to Spain, renamed her *Ranger* and sent her to the West Indies with wine, only to have her captured on her return voyage to Europe. In the course of trying to regain her, Derby revealed in a letter that in three years of the war at least two hundred colonial vessels had been seized by the British. Evidence of the risk Foster was running is the twenty-three vessels in the West Indies trade from Salem alone that were taken by the French between July 1, 1760 and November 1, 1761.

So Joseph Foster knew what he was about. Salem insurance rates as high as twenty-three per cent on outward voyages and fifteen on inward imply enormous profits that far outweighed the risks. The fount of these profits was the trade with the French West Indies, which was illegal to the point of treason as far as the English crown was concerned, but in the eyes of their countrymen made demiheroes of the New England merchants who engaged in it. Smuggling was the foundation of the Derby fortune, and, pretty obviously, of Joseph Foster's. It was a matter of the simplest tariff economics: Parliament had passed the Molasses Act in 1733 placing almost prohibitive duties on all foreign molasses, sugar and rum imported into the American colonies, in an effort to siphon off this long-standing colonial trade with the French and Dutch West Indies and the Spanish Main, so long a sore point with the London merchants and planters of the British West Indies. But between the corruption and laxity of the British customs, and the *penchant endiablé* of the French for pegging the tariff on exports from *their* islands lower than the English on *theirs*...well, to the Fosters and Pearces and Plummers and Sargents of Gloucester, the Derbys of Salem and the Hancocks of Boston, such a sporting proposition was not to be resisted.

Buy cheap--sell dear. The rule of trade, not the rhyme of name and hail, attracted Foster to Gloucester. And fish was cheap at Cape Ann, where the fishery, never prosperous, was having a harder time than ever. "Indeed," declared John J. Babson in his *History of Gloucester,* "it is a matter of wonder that the discouragements of that period did not cause a total abandonment of the business. But notwithstanding the wars between France and England, and the consequent annoyance and occasional capture of our vessels by the cruisers of the enemy, and the demand for men for the provincial armies and for the naval service, the fishery was still pursued. The truth is, it had now become the basis of a profitable foreign trade, for the maintenance of which the merchants of the town would willingly encounter great risks, and could even afford to bear considerable losses." [4]

It might be added that the historian observed of Joseph Foster that "he was brought up in humble circumstances, and was indebted solely to his own energy and shrewdness for his advancement in life." [5]

If the man had been sailing out of Gloucester since 1755 or so, he had certainly settled in the town by 1760, when Lydia gave birth to her second daughter. They named her for her mother, and she and Mary were baptized together in the church of the First Parish above the harbor (everybody called the thickest settled part of town here "the Harbor") on September 7 of the same year while their father was still in Europe in *Wolfe.* He didn't get home from Spain until November, when he laid up *Wolfe* for the winter.

"We were alarmed this week by the small-pox in the Harbour," Samuel Chandler jotted in his Journal on January 9, 1761. He was the minister of the First, or Harbor, Parish. "A child of Pool's was supposed to have it; the family moved up to Boston Pest House."

Twice before, the smallpox is recorded as threatening Gloucester. In 1730 Captain John Prince was paid two pounds by a grateful town for having stopped it from entering, probably by setting up a guard against suspected cases, and for helping to bury a man who evidently died of it aboard a vessel which was ordered out of the harbor. Twenty-two years later, when an epidemic swept Boston in 1752, Captain Prince again moved into the breech and guarded the gate at the Cut to keep suspects on the other side of Squam River.

But now the worst had come to pass. The pox had appeared out of nowhere in the most heavily settled part of town. What to do? There was no cure and no treatment (unless bleeding, purging and puking be considered treatment), and no prevention but isolation or flight. Inoculation was feared almost as much as taking the disease "in the natural way" and was embarked upon only as a last resort, and then only by a majority vote of town meeting. People were understandably anxious about having someone who passed himself off as a doctor making a shallow incision in the arm and laying a thread in it that had been drawn through the foul matter from a broken pustule on the skin of a mildly ill patient...then praying to God that the dreaded disease, taken this way, wouldn't flare up and kill them. The fact is that under reasonably well controlled conditions, with reasonably skillful and scrupulous "specialists" managing the procedure, mortality from inoculation was incomparably lower than from the natural disease; but there was a risk, an outside one to be sure, and the nonimmune population was scared of it.

Because Gloucester had never had an epidemic of smallpox, thanks to the vigilance of its John Princes and a lot of luck, there was very little residue of immunity in the community. Only the chance mariner who had taken it somewhere in his travels was safe, and to these the town looked for initiative in the crisis; the immune could be the only deliberate contacts between the well on the one side, and the sick and those already exposed to the sick on the other.

One who wore this armorial badge of the pock mark, souvenir of a wracking hard time somewhere, was Joseph Foster, and though he held no town office and dubious authority, if any, for what he now proceeded to do, he did it and evicted Samuel Pool and his family from Gloucester. Pool was accused of trying to conceal the sickness of his child from his neighbors. The Gloucester selectmen paid Joseph Littlehale twenty shillings for carting the Pool family effects to the wharf, and Captain Ebenezer Collins three pounds for taking them to Boston in his vessel, all arranged for by Captain Foster.

"Widow Ellery has the small-pox," Parson Chandler wrote in his Journal January 24, and three days later, "We moved upon account of the small-pox at widow Ellery's to Capt. Parsons' over the Cut." Fortunately, perhaps because of Foster's timely action, that was about the end of the scare, and a fortnight afterwards the Harbor was considered safe enough for the minister to move his family back from the woods country the other side of Annisquam River.

It was not quite the end, however. On the last day of the year the question was raised in town meeting of prosecuting Samuel Pool "for misbehaviour in the affair of the smallpox last winter," and the following March of 1762 Thomas Sanders, Jr., was instructed by the meeting "to enquire into the state of Samuel Pool's case who is supposed to have concealed the small pox in his house and report to the town." In May his townsmen voted to consider "what may be thought proper thereon" with respect to Captain Foster's relief from a prosecution which Pool apparently had counterinitiated. They decided not to move against Pool, and then the question was put "whether the town will pay and satisfy the execution against Captain Foster for what he did in removing Samuel Pool and family when his child had the small pox in the Harbour in the year 1761 to Boston, and it past in the affirmative. Voted that the Town Treasurer hire the money to satisfy the execution aforsd if he can not procure it otherwise in season."[6]

There is an implication in the outcome that Captain Foster acted with quarterdeck command for the good of the town. Pool perhaps was oversensitive to being kicked around.

Through the winter and into the spring of 1761 Foster had been refitting the prize brig *Sanders* he bought at Gibraltar, and on May 25 he was under sail for the West Indies.[7] Before sailing, he arranged to buy his first house. The place was almost brand new. It was a trim, foursquare, gambrel-roofed, frame "mansion house," as town dwellings of solidarity were called, that stood on a small lot as central as could be, on the south side of Middle Street in the Harbor. Directly on the west of the house a narrow lane ran down to Fore Street, later to be Front, and still later, Main Street, above the waterfront. Middle Street was a shaded dirt road, formerly known as Cornhill Street. It paralleled Fore Street and the wharves on the south, and Back Street, later Prospect Street, upland a block to the north.

Already several leading merchants of Gloucester were living in similar gambreled homes on both sides of Middle Street. It was the town's Quality Row, running from Pleasant Street on the east even more pleasantly the whole way above the harbor to the long sandy beach which curved around to the old Cut. This canal, first excavated by Pastor Richard Blynman in 1642, sometimes made Squam River navigable to the harbor and sometimes not, depending on whether storms had blocked it with sand, whether it had been dredged, or whether the bridge at various stages in its long history happened to be fixed or draw.

Before coming out at what was later Pavilion Beach, where small boats were frequently built and repaired, and the wooden frames called flakes were set up for drying salt codfish, Middle Street crossed the main thoroughfare, now Washington Street, which communicated the heart of the port up in Harbor Cove with the first permanent settlement of 1642 at Meetinghouse Green. The original First Parish was "up in town" at the Green, and its church too, but in Foster's day "Up-town Parish" had been largely forsaken in the inevitable shift of activity over to the Harbor. The Green was on the edge of Squam River and its marshes, near the ferry landing over to Rust Island and West Parish, and was the hub of the various roads to the Harbor, across the Cape to Sandy Bay, skirting the salt inlet of Mill River and Goose Cove to Riverdale, Annisquam, Dogtown and the Back of the Cape, and along the spine of the Neck of House Lots to Wheeler's Point, then known as Gee's Point.

The ambitious young sea captain couldn't have picked a location closer to the heartbeat of the town to settle down with Lydia and bring up their growing family. All around him for neighbors were the merchants and captains of Gloucester, with their houses like his, their gorgeous gardens of flowers brightened by the salt air and their splendid views over the stunning harbor and out to the glinting sea beyond Eastern Point where they could watch for their vessels rounding in from distant voyages, heavy--they hoped--with profits. A step below Captain Foster's were the small warehouses and shops betwixt other neat mansions along Fore Street. Below them were the wharves, rattling, clanking, thumping, squealing, smoking, smelling, echoing to the fleet's work...and all in and out, dories, wherries, skiffs, woodboats, sloops, shallops, and the vessels of the fleet, many fore and aft, a few square-rigged, none very large, even in the foreign trade.

The main entrance to the Foster house was from the lane leading down from Middle Street, and the walk curved through a spacious garden to the front door which was on the south side, overlooking the harbor. On the Middle Street side, the tavern a hundred yards to the east of them was counterbalanced by the meetinghouse with its landmark steeple, a hundred yards to the west and across the road.

For some reason Joseph Foster was in the West Indies the day the papers were passed for his house. It was June 22, 1761, and his partner Edward Payne acted on his behalf in paying John Balch of Topsfield and William Goldsmith of Ipswich, yeomen, £ 333 for the property. They had bought it only six weeks earlier themselves, on May 8, before Foster sailed in *Sanders*, paying Thomas Hodgdon, a Gloucester cordwainer, £ 246. There is no evidence that Balch and Goldsmith got the house by foreclosure, leading one to wonder whether they may have been men of straw advanced by an absent buyer to cozen an unfriendly seller. Hodgdon had purchased the lot in his turn from John Wheeler in 1757 for only fifty-three pounds and obviously built the house soon after. Before that it was Elwell land, back probably to the initial grant of it in settlement days. It is possible that Foster rented the place before he decided to buy it.

Soon after his partner secured his mansion house for him, Joseph Foster ran into some kind of trouble in the West Indies. Whether *Sanders* was stopped on the high seas by a French or English armed vessel and suffered the seizure of part or all of her cargo, or whether cargo or vessel was damaged during a storm, either event would have been grounds for the protest intended to absolve himself, his crew and his vessel from liability which he formally lodged with the British authorities at St. Kitts in the Leewards. No more is known of the matter.

By the end of summer Captain Foster was back in Gloucester in *Sanders,* and he must have made a profitable voyage in spite of the necessity for a protest because he at once bought a half interest with Nathaniel Allen in the schooner *Joseph,* ninety tons, rather larger than the average Cape Ann trading vessel. In October and November he took his newly-acquired schooner down east for lumber, and on December 7 embarked again for the West Indies with this cargo and mayhap a few quintals of salt fish. They were in the Caribbean all winter, not returning until April 2, 1762, when he handed *Joseph* over to his cousin, Aaron Foster, the Louisburg veteran, who made at least three more West Indian voyages in the schooner over the next five years.

That West Indies voyage was Joseph Foster's last, as far as is known, for another eighteen years. At thirty-one he appears to have swallowed the anchor, as they say, to run his trading business from ashore. The denouement of the Seven Years' War may have affected his decision. England had been unremittingly wearing down French sea power, which meant France's colonial foothold in the western hemisphere. The fortress of Louisburg had been captured by exultant New Englanders in 1745 only to be handed back to the French by the Treaty of Aix-la-Chapelle in 1748. Ten years later it was retaken and destroyed by Admiral Boscawen's expeditionary force of Yankees; that blow cracked the Gallic grip on Canada and its offshore fishing grounds, which fell to England the following year.

In the West Indies the French lost first Guadeloupe and then Martinique, their last major colonial holdings except St. Dominique, and by the spring of 1762, when Captain Foster brought *Joseph* home from the Caribbean, the western Atlantic from South America to Newfoundland had been all but cleared of the warships and privateers of France. The roar of the British lion was heard halfway around the world, and the Prussian foundations of Germany had been cemented in place.

This is not to imply that the Atlantic was now an English lake. Before a year passed, a schooner from Martinique for Cape Ann was captured by a Spanish privateer, "but the men soon after rose upon the Spaniards and carried the vessel into St. Kitts," and at length she arrived home. And three years after the British had cleared the seas of French power, Gloucester schooners would be returning from the Grand Bank with the news that "great numbers of French ships were fishing on the banks, who were very insulting, and did considerable damage to many of our fishermen by running foul of their vessels, etc."[8] It was a big ocean.

All the same, by the spring of 1762 there was reason for optimism, and money enough he had made, for Joseph Foster to set about acquiring vessels and entrusting the command of them and the conduct of his business overseas to other Gloucester captains. It is not clear when he became associated with Edward Payne or when Payne moved up to Boston, but Foster's account book with him covers the period from July 8, 1762 to April 8, 1767; it shows Payne as half-owner of most of his outward and inward cargoes for the five years, and Payne's account with him at one time was £ 5026.

Another merchant with whom he had extensive dealings was Isaac Smith, ten years his senior. Smith ran a fishing business in Gloucester for several years before moving to Boston, probably during the Revolution. John Hancock is said to have called him the most reliable man in Boston and to have entrusted the bulk of his own estate to his management. Isaac's brother, the Reverend William Smith of Weymouth, was the father of Abigail Smith Adams, wife of the second president of the United States.

By the autumn of 1763, the first year of an uneasy international peace, Foster had dispatched *Sanders* on a voyage to Gibraltar; he had *Wolfe* and *Joseph* (under Cousin Aaron) in commission, probably in the West Indies trade; he had an interest in the schooner *Industry;* he had built the fifty-ton schooner *Swan* in June at Annisquam on halves with Samuel Sayward, filled her with salt and bait clams and sent her fishing.

And he had even found time for some sport, as Pastor Chandler noted in his Journal of July 2: "I took a sail with Elder Warner, Hubbard Haskell, Capt. Foster, etc., about the harbor; went on to Ten Pound Island and fried some fish."

On the second of January, 1764, the selectmen of Boston announced in the *Boston Gazette* that one Joseph Bulkley had died that morning of smallpox; there were no other known cases in the town. Thirteen days later Pastor Chandler "rose at break of day; about 9 o'clock news was brought in that the small-pox was in the neighborhood; Charles Glover has it; several families moved today."

Gloucester was in a panic. The Glover home was upwind of the Middle Street meetinghouse (it was blowing southerly at the time), and the parish committee and the selectmen decided it was too risky to call an emergency session of townspeople there because of their belief that the infection might be carried into the building by the breeze.

Joseph Foster had been elected a constable the previous spring, and his immunity, and his rough-and-tumble view of quarantine, brought him to the fore in pulling together the town's defenses against an unseen and insidious foe. He was later reimbursed £ 26.10.10 by the town for "hiring men & horse & sundry supplys for the small pox." Isaac Parsons was hired to put up a fence and gate at the Cut and Thomas Tippen to guard it, "to prevent the small pox being brought into the town." On January 21 Martha Glover died. Three days later a heavy snowstorm blanketed Cape Ann. The cold was bitter and the traveling terrible.

On the fifth of February Pastor Chandler noted nervously that the disease was spreading; five were sick and others suspected. Two more days and "almost all the Harbour are moving on account of the smallpox; nothing but carting; all in motion, there are four sick of the smallpox at old Mr. Dolliver's, himself, John Warner, James Tyler and Zebulon Witham, Jr.; very bad; and two at Tarbox's." Next day: "I carried my wife over the Cut, she is uneasy on account of the small-pox." Three more days, February 12: "There was a meeting in the Harbour on account of the small-pox; Mr. Dolliver's house is the hospital; I was at home with my two daughters; in the evening visited and prayed at Elder Warner's; his son supposed to be dying--small-pox."

Eighteen citizens elected to take the disease by inoculation, and in all probability they traveled up to Boston, where the epidemic was now raging, to have it done in one of the special hospitals there. One of them died, Nathaniel Allen, Jr., the son of Foster's friend and business associate.

Eight died in Gloucester, including old Mr. Peter Dolliver. The public health regulations required flags to be put outside houses where the sick lay; everything had to be fumigated--sickrooms, beds, bedding and clothing; the dead must be buried in a tarred sheet and the coffin carried off in the middle of the night, preceded by someone with a lantern, crying out a warning.

By March 7 the epidemic had abated, and people were moving back from the interior to the Harbor. Gloucester had been well guarded, and favored by fortune. The smallpox was not fully checked in Boston until June, when the toll was toted up: of 699 who took it in the natural way, 124 died; 4977 were inoculated, with forty-six casualties.

Captain Foster would have been justified in moving his wife and three daughters across the moat of Squam River into the isolation of West Parish; none of the girls had been previously exposed, since Mary was seven, Lydia four, and Sarah, the baby born in 1762, only two. Furthermore, their mother was five months with child at the worst of the pox, when no one could guess which way it would go. If he did evacuate his family, he had them all back in the house on Middle Street by early spring, because on May 23, faithful Parson Chandler, always at the call of his flock, returned home a few doors to the west of them and recorded in his Journal: "I was sent for about 8 o'clock to Capt. Foster's; she was in travail, dangerous." But Lydia came through it, and a son was born, their first. They named him Joseph after his father.

Her victory over France had laid a staggering debt on England while her American colonies prospered by the war. The colonies and the empire had been secured under William Pitt, and now there began the series of taxes aimed by George Grenville at restoring solvency and tipping over onto the Americans, who had been the beneficiaries of home sacrifices, the burden of paying for their own defense. Now was raised the threat in the colonies of their worst fear, a standing army of British regulars, symbol of absentee government.

Grenville was a pennypincher and budget-balancer, in reaction to Pitt's war-winning profligacy, and he was bound he would put a stop to New England's smuggling. First he pushed the Sugar Act of 1764 through Parliament. This measure halved the sixpence-per-gallon duty under the unenforced Molasses Act of 1733 but at the same time set about determinedly to collect it by reforming the customs service, enlisting the navy for enforcement and enlarging the punitive jurisdiction of the admiralty courts at the expense of the rights of accused smugglers to trial by jury.

Many thought the welfare of the colonies was being sacrificed to test the ability of England to raise a revenue in America and to line the pockets of the planters in the British West Indies. New England merchants argued that they had to import foreign molasses because more than half of the fish of inferior quality exported by Massachusetts was acceptable only in the French West Indies...and *that* in exchange for molasses and sugar only, as required by the French. In 1763 only five hundred of the fifteen thousand hogsheads of molasses imported into Massachusetts were produced in the British West Indies; yet the whole West Indies trade took some sixty-four per cent of the total production of the New England fisheries.

This latest in the succession of Navigation Acts, so-called, threatened to be in sharp and shocking contrast with the impotence to which the Molasses Act of 1733 had been reduced by the collusion of customs inspectors, French planters and Yankee merchant-smugglers like Joseph Foster. The Americans screamed bloody murder and predicted a quick and dismal end to their fisheries. The first result was indeed to upset the balance of trade by jacking up the price the northern colonies had to pay for molasses and sugar, and depressing the West Indian market for their fish, lumber and livestock. And then the inevitable reaction set in. Buyers would find sellers, and sellers buyers. Notwithstanding a few clashes and seizures, enforcement of the Sugar Act took a milder turn, and it is said that customs officers after a while seldom exacted more than half of legal duty.

Captain Foster owned a half-interest in the schooner *Swan*, and it may be conjectured from which of the West Indies Captain John Rust brought back 60,652 pounds of sugar in her sometime in 1764, and whether it was before the Sugar Act took effect, and whether a duty was paid. Also subjects of speculation are the origin and nature of Foster cargoes which cleared Anguilla in the Leeward Islands on two occasions of record and perhaps others intentionally unspecified...in the first instance, April of 1762 when Captain Foster had command of the schooner *Joseph*, and again, when Captain William Wyer cleared the island in the sloop *Benjamin* in early 1769. There would be nothing suspicious about these visits except that for several years before and after the passage of the Sugar Act the governor of this thirty-five-square-mile swatch of green in the blue of the British Caribbean, who doubled as customs inspector, was selling fake clearances to New England vessels which touched there for that express purpose on their passage home with contraband French molasses and sugar. "This island was so small," relates Sabine, "as not to afford a cargo for a single vessel, as was well known to the collectors of the customs in New England; yet they permitted vessels furnished with the 'Anguilla clearances' to enter with their cargoes without inquiry, for a considerable time."

The real significance of the Sugar Act was in the fact that it turned out to be the parliamentary nose under the American tent. Forewarned by it, the New England merchants were ready to yell, and did, at Grenville's next rather mild measure --just a touch of tyranny to it--a modest stamp duty on legal documents, newspapers and that sort of thing. Here in the Stamp Act clearly was an effort by Parliament to raise a revenue in the colonies, to tax British subjects abroad by rank discrimination, without their having any representatives in the taxing body, and without their consent.

John Wise...ah yes, there were those around who remembered hearing about the famous case in Chebacco, and reading his pamphlets.

The Stamp Act was to take effect on November 1, 1765 on a rising tide of economic grievance, and the complaints found political voice which was nowhere more clarion than in that den of contrabandage, Gloucester. The freeholders assembled on October 7 in "a very full meeting" in the Middle Street meetinghouse and voted *"nemine contradicente* and most unanimously that the Stamp Act, the Minutes whereof were read, is disagreeable." They instructed their representatives to the General Court to oppose it by every lawful means as a measure that "would greatly obstruct, if not (in time) totally ruin, the trade and business of the Province, and lay an insupportable burden upon all, more especially upon the middle and poorer sort of the people...and take from us (though always allowed to have all the liberties of natural Englishmen)...the general privilege of taxing ourselves, which appear to be the original rights of all mankind that are not slaves, the unalienable rights of Englishmen, and the rights of the inhabitants of this Province by their particular charter."

Much protest, much poor-mouthing, but there is no sign that Grenville's colonial tax bills greatly obstructed the trade and business of Joseph Foster, for one. In fact, he was adding to his fleet. Besides *Wolfe* and *Joseph* and *Swan,* he had half ownership with his father-in-law, Daniel Giddings, of the schooner *Swallow,* which he gave for a voyage early in the year to his friend and neighbor, Captain Isaac Somes. Then he owned or held an interest in the sloop *Benjamin,* which cousins Aaron Foster and John Rust took successively in the West Indian trade; the schooner *Molly and Betsy* ⁹ which Nehemiah Somes, a cousin of Isaac, sailed to Cadiz and Malaga; the schooner *Badger* of fifty-eight tons, Captain George Denning, which sailed to the Caribbean twice with fish and rice, bringing home sugar, wine, raisins and lemons; and the schooner *Victory,* Captain Samuel Elwell.

The most remunerative revenue of the Stamp Act never found its way into the Exchequer; it remained on American soil, feeding the spreading roots of an underground of agitators who called themselves the Sons of Liberty. It provided them with fiery speeches and midnight riots, congresses, conventions, blizzards of pamphlets and whirlwinds of resolutions. Public opinion against Grenville's measures was brought to a pitch which coincided with his fall from the grace of George III, who never liked him anyway, and the rise of Rockingham, who thought a swing of the pendulum in the other direction might be called for. Rockingham was helped along to that conclusion by the tremendous push the pendulum had already received from hundreds of American merchants who signed agreements refusing to import British goods, and American courts which closed their doors in preference to permitting the hated stamps to officialize their proceedings.

Business was business. The London merchants felt the pinch and howled. Parliament repealed the Stamp Act.

Even the loss of seven vessels and forty men or more in a wild storm that scattered the banks fleet in March was for a moment forgotten in the rejoicing which swept through Cape Ann with the news of Repeal. On May 19, 1766 the selectmen happily adopted an order to deliver to Captain Epes Sargent "a cask of powder to be used toward expressing our joy for the repeal of the Stamp Act by the Parliament. News arrived on Fryday last."

More than one cask of rum, taxed or untaxed, helped to lift the spirits of the day, and at last it seemed to everyone that all Englishmen were reconciled, and the colonies might go their way in peace.

3

DOWSE VS. THIRTY-THREE
HOGSHEADS OF MOLASSES

Out of a fleet of some eighty sail caught in the great gale which swept across the fishing banks in March of 1766, seven vessels from Gloucester and forty men were lost. Two more schooners were wrecked, and others were so badly damaged they had to be taken out of service for the season. At the end of the year the selectmen went to the General Court for an abatement of the Province tax, pleading that "the fishery in said town has this year been very unsuccessful and their trading stock is considerably diminished." The sympathetic legislature reduced it by fifty pounds.

The diminished supply of salt fish failed to bring Joseph Foster up short, however. His business on the sea continued as brisk as ever. He sent his vessels to the banks fishing, then coasting to the eastward for lumber and staves and to South Carolina for rice, and then off to the West Indies, Gibraltar and Spain. Fairly typical were the voyages of *Badger* and *Dolphin*.

Captain Andrew Giddings, a cousin of Lydia, sailed *Badger* early in 1767 with a mixed cargo, mainly fish and lumber, to St. Kitts, Guadeloupe, Turks Islands, St. Eustatius and St. Martin and was back in July with molasses, on which Parliament had reduced the threepenny duty to a penny a gallon of all foreign production (nonBritish) entering the colonies. Next month he was right back for the Indies with lumber, flour, candles and 105 sheep, and was home again in November. Foster and his father-in-law, Daniel Giddings, bought or built *Dolphin*, sixty tons, in 1766 and sped her off to Gibraltar under Captain James Garcelon with rum, candles and staves. From there she sailed along the sunny southern Spanish coast to Malaga, loaded raisins and lemons and was no sooner back at Gloucester when Foster turned her around fishing for a month in June ... and then off again in July for Gibraltar with rum and rice ... and once home, fishing again in the fall. At this time a dispute arose over her proceeds, and John Emerson of Ipswich, who may have been the husband of Captain Foster's younger sister, Dorothy, sued the co-owners in the Circuit Court of Common Pleas for money due him from the voyage. He recovered twenty-seven pounds and thirteen shillings.

In addition to Giddings and Garcelon in *Badger* and *Dolphin*, Joseph Foster had Aaron Foster, Isaac Somes, George Denning, John Rust, William Wyer, Benjamin Colman and David Bruce fishing and trading in *Joseph, Swan, Benjamin, Victory, Gloriosa* and *William,* ranging the Gulf of Maine, the broad Atlantic, the Caribbean and up the Straits into the Mediterranean in the months that followed repeal of the Stamp Act when it seemed as if her colonies had taught England that they were not to be treated as naughty children, that they had the muscle to achieve equal status in the British family, and to keep it.

The lull was not to last. Parliament had tipped its hand when on the same day it repealed the Stamp Act it adopted the generally overlooked Declaratory Act affirming its authority to make laws binding on the American colonies "in all cases whatsoever." The eye of the storm moved on, and on June 29, 1767 the Townshend Acts for raising a colonial revenue were passed. They imposed a new set of duties on certain imports which were in themselves not particularly onerous; it was the answerable-to-the-crown-alone machinery for collection and enforcement, chiefly the new American Board of Customs Commissioners at Boston, by which the lion bared his teeth again, and caused Yankee teeth to grind. This renewed show of imperial authority was to take effect on November 20.

The Sons of Liberty came to life. The nonimportation agreements which had unstuck the Stamp Act were dusted off. In October the radical hotbed of Boston posted an index of

British imports (mostly nonessential). Providence merchants did the same on December 2, Newport two days later, and Gloucester voted not to import the boycotted products in town meeting December 14. The Customs Commissioners added nothing to the palatability of the new Townshend duties by hiring an army and navy of hangers-on, petty bureaucrats, sons of nepotism and informers as searchers, tide waiters, collectors, surveyors, clerks, land waiters and comptrollers to enforce them ... "so many BLOODSUCKERS upon our TRADE," Salem's *Essex Gazette* called them.

Overblown with bravado, the Commissioners in June of 1768 seized John Hancock's sloop *Liberty* while she was offloading smuggled wine at Boston. The Sons of Liberty reacted with such effective terror that the crown officials, in fear for their lives, fled to the protection of Castle William island in the harbor.

All these signs of rising British petulance and pique by now had the coast in an uproar. Fuses were no shorter anywhere than at Gloucester, haven of smugglers, when into the powder-house blundered Sam Fellows with a tinder box. The *Essex Gazette* gave its version of how it started:

One Samuel Fellows who lately commanded a vessel belonging to a merchant in Cape-Ann, having behaved in such a manner in the West Indies, as to make it difficult for him to render a fair and just account of his transactions, chose an easier way of settlement, by informing the Custom-House Officers upon oath, that more molasses had been landed, than was reported; for which the vessel, etc. was seized, to the almost ruin of his owners. So flagrant an instance of baseness and perfidy could not but intitle him to the favour of such a set of men as [Governor] G[eorge] B[ernard] and the B[oar]d of C[om]m[issione]rs, in consequence of which, he had a command given him in one of our little Guarda Coastas, and was also furnished, as other such infamous and inconsiderate Marine Officers have lately been, with a commission, constituting him an Officer of the Customs, with the power of making seizures.

Thus commissioned and empowered, he soon commenced hostilities against the merchants, by stopping such vessels as he met with in cruises, rummaging and searching them for pretences for a seizure, impressing men, etc. etc.[1]

The vessel Fellows informed against was the schooner *Earl of Gloucester,* owned by David Plummer. She had arrived home at Gloucester in August from St. Eustatius, and her former master passed the word to Joseph Dowse, surveyor and searcher of customs for Salem and Marblehead, that she landed undutied molasses. On September 6 Dowse showed up in Gloucester and seized thirty-three hogsheads and four tierces (forty-two gallon casks) of molasses allegedly smuggled ashore from Plummer's schooner.

Two days later an army of around seventy Gloucestermen marched on the home of Jesse Saville, a tanner who lived up on the ridge beyond the head of Goose Cove, not far off the Squam road.[2] He identified the following: David Plummer, merchant; Benjamin Somes, cooper; Joseph Foster, merchant; Elichander Smith, blockmaker; Lebeday Day, mason; Samuel Rogers, physician; William Lowther, tinman; David Day, shoemaker; and Philemon Haskell and Daniel Warner, blacksmiths. Plummer, Somes, Haskell and probably others were close neighbors of Joseph Foster, whom Saville placed among the ringleaders. Declared the tanner in a statement to the Customs Commissioners, themselves embattled:

> They asked leave to go into the house to search for Capt. Fellows, which they did, not then offering any abuse only in talk. My wife sent my servant of an errand. David Plummer seized him by the collar refusing to let him go. His mistress called him back. They would not let him come out but said if he was sent he should not go unless they knew his business. But Doctor Rogers took out his instruments, the which he hauls teeth with, threatened to haul all his teeth out unless he told where Capt. Fellows was, threatening to split his head open with a club, holding it over his head. Then they left the house about an hour, in which time Capt. Fellows rode up to our house. Thomas Griffin, shore man, seeing him ride up

that way ran after the mob, told them he was gone up there.

In about one hour's time they returned, which my wife seeing them told Capt. Fellows of. He immediately ran out of doors as fast as possible. No person was in the house except my wife and my mother, Dorcas Haskell, Mary Savell, with two of my small children. They came up to the doors and surrounded the house with clubs and axes. The women seeing them run in such a manner affrighted, fastening the doors and windows. They cries with shouting, we got him. They cried, open the doors.

They refused, declaring to the mob there was no man body in the house except a child of 5 months old they could give oath. Mr. Plummer told them, Gentlemen why dont you walk in. Mr. Plummer did not go into the house himself. My mother told them they come in upon the peril of their lives if they offered to break down the doors.

They immediately stove down one door and entered a great number of the above persons and William Stevens, bricklayer, likewise and a great many strangers which they did not know. They likewise beat off a latch and buttons of another door, struck the pole of the ax into the door and causing very much damaging. The same broke a celler window to pieces, a chain, throwed over barrels, chests, tables and tubs, ransacked the house, all parts of it, broke a bundle of dried fish to pieces, destroyed a good deal of the same, took a gun and broke it by throwing it out of the garret window.

Benjamin Somes, the cooper, pointed it, a loaded gun, toward my wife, ordered her out of doors. A little girl of about two or three of ours so terrified, cried to my wife fainting away. They called my mother, my wife all the whores and all the damned bitches and every evil name that they could think of, striking down their clubs on the floor each side of them. My mother begged they would spare her life for it was not possible she could live one hour. They would not listen to her intreaties. They searched the house over and over several times, hauling all the beds onto the floors.

—44—

After a while they left the house, then went down to the meetinghouse. There Joseph York, shoemaker, gave them vittles and drink ... Our folks sent for some of the neighbors to come, for they expected to be killed if they came again. Some said they were glad. Some was afraid to come, so a bitter afternoon they had. I was not at home but was about two miles off by water, neither could I get home by reason of the tide.

I came home about ten o'clock at night, very dark and rainy. Had occasion to go out of doors, so took my gun for I was afraid without her. A few minutes after I was gone out adoors they surrounded our house, attempting to come in. My father was then in bed. He told them they should not come in such a manner, but they might three or four of them come in and search the house. A great number flocked in headed by Dudley Sargent, merchant...[3]

I stood a little way of them, heard them swear they would tear down the house but what they would have him. I made a pass to go into the door. They surrounded me. I asked them who was there, was answered by Dudley Sargent, half a dozen of us. I asked what half a dozen of such black guard did there. They answered me, Damn you we will tell you. They said where is Sam Fellows. I answered none of your business. They immediately scared me. About eight or thereaway told me to let go the gun I possessed. Desired a pass into the house. My mother cried out Jesse is dead. My wife fainting away. They knocked me down, took away my gun, fired it off, broke it in pieces over a rock. My father hauled me into the house by my feet as I lay on the ground. It was terrible to see the womens countenances and the cries of the children, for part of the children was at school in the day time.

So they left the house after I threatening them in the law ... We were afraid to go to sleep ever since safely, for word has been threatened to tear down the house several times and if ever they catched me in the Harbor they would serve me as bad as they would Capt. Fellows, or if they ever could find out I concealed him or by any means aided him or gave him any sustenance they would tear down the house and mob me, which since I dare not appear to prosecute my business but shall be obliged to leave the town. If I want to go out of town I am obliged to go and come in the night or on the Sabbath day.

About a fortnight ago I was at Mr. Plummer's shop. I told him he must make good the damage I had sustained. His answer was I would prosecute him. I said he must expect to make me satisfaction. He challenged me to do it, for he said, they wanted another frolic, they did not desire no better sport. Wherefor my interest and body is in danger every day. [4]

Three days later, at midnight on September 11, another seizure of contraband Dowse had made at about the same time as his impoundment of the thirty-three hogsheads of molasses was rescued at Squam by unidentified culprits for whose capture the crown offered a vain fifty-pound reward. On October 14, emboldened perhaps by the landing of the two regiments of regulars at Boston a fortnight previously, Saville submitted his complaint to the Commissioners. Eight more days, and *Earl of Gloucester* was seized for smuggling.

Early in November the grand jury of the Essex Superior Court, sitting in Ipswich, handed down indictments against eight citizens of Gloucester "and others unknown" charging them with unlawful assembly on the night of September 8 at the house of Jesse Saville, breach of the peace, riot, breaking and entering, and assault. All pleaded innocent and were released on their own recognizance for trial the following June. They were Samuel Rogers, physician; Benjamin Somes, cooper; Joseph Foster, merchant; Parker Knights, cordwainer; William Stevens, bricklayer; William Tarbox, yeoman; William Lowther, tinman; and Paul Dudley Sargent, merchant. Apparently the king's attorney concluded he had a better case against Knights and Tarbox than against some of those named by Saville in his complaint who escaped indictment, notably David Plummer.

The crown in the meanwhile had filed informations against Plummer, six other defendants and *Earl of Gloucester* as well, since vessel and cargo both were subject to forfeiture for evasion of duties. Plummer engaged John Adams as his attorney. The case came to trial in December of 1768, but the Gloucester merchant had been caught pretty much with the goods, and for all his skill and acumen, Adams failed to convince. Officer Dowse was victorious over the thirty-three hogsheads and four tierces. They were ordered sold for the crown in March of 1769, and *Earl of Gloucester* went on the block in April.

Sam Fellows had fingered David Plummer, eluded a vengeful mob, observed with satisfaction the punitive results of his revelations and reaped their reward, a coast guard commission to bring as many of his former associates before admiralty court as he could search and seize. Whether he was a self-seeker or an avid advocate of law and order may be further judged by his next caper, on May 15; this was reported through the colonies as an example of the "treatment we are to expect, so long as we are held under a Military Government," in a weekly syndicated compilation of horrors allegedly perpetrated by British soldiers and crown officials called "Journal of the Times," which originated in Boston and was featured by the Whig newspapers:

> The inhabitants of Cape-Ann had spirit and strength enough to have immediately taken, punished or secured a wretch who had shewn as little regard to their lives, as to laws of the community; but prudence got the better of their resentment, and we have this affair fully related in a memorial which Mr. Jacob Parsons, the deputy sheriff, by their desire, presented to the Governor and Council of this Province:

> Representing, that on the 25th instant [it was the 15th], he had in his custody, having duly taken by a process of law, one Josiah Merril, as a prisoner; that while he was in the due execution of his office, one Samuel Fellows, a commander of one of his Majesty's armed cutters, then in the harbour of Cape-Ann, with four of his men with fire-arms, cutlasses, etc. came on shore in a boat, and said Fellows immediately accosted the said Merril, by asking him, "What did he there?" Upon which, said Merril replied, that "an officer had taken him, and had him in custody for debt." That in consequence

of this reply, said Fellows commanded said Merril to come away with him, and that he would protect said Merril.

That on this encouragement, said Merril broke away from the deputy sheriff, and ran towards said Fellows; whereupon the deputy sheriff commanded, in his Majesty's name, several persons to assist in seizing and stopping his prisoner; whom they obeyed and seized, and held said prisoner; while this passed, said Fellows, who was within four rods from the deputy sheriff, and his assistants, ordered his four men to fire; whereupon two of Fellows's men leaped upon the beach, and ran towards them, until they had got within two rods, when they presented their arms directly to the deputy sheriff and his assistants, and then fired; the shot and ball scarcely missing them, and entered a store within a few inches of where they stood. The prisoner taking advantage of the consternation they were in, broke away and ran towards said Fellows's boat.

That during the whole of this time, said Fellows, and his men, although they were repeatedly told that the deputy sheriff was a King's Officer, kept a constant round of oaths and imprecations upon the deputy sheriff and his assistants; damning the King's Officer, and all who belonged to him; swearing he would blow the brains out of the first man who offered to touch said Merril, or come towards the boat; that they would take better sight the next time, and the like; that as said Merril came nearer to the boat, said Fellows and his men kept firing at the deputy sheriff, till said Fellows commanded his men not to fire any more yet; but to keep a reserve for any who should attempt a retaking of said Merril.

And that after said Fellows and his men fired six or seven times, by which the deputy sheriff and his assistants were in the most imminent hazard of their lives, the said Fellows and his men yet defending said Merril, retired on board the boat, and still kept firing as they left the shore; and the sheriff has not since been able to retake the prisoner, or bring said Fellows to justice.[5]

Word of his friend's impetuous conduct toward the Gloucester deputy sheriff, swift as sails could arry it, manifestly sought out and discovered Jesse Saville in Providence, Rhode Island, where he too had found employment as a crown customs officer, figuring apparently that if he was going to be damned and knocked in the head for a Tory he might as well make the best of it. The *Essex Gazette* reported on June 20 that the Commissioners of Customs had posted a fifty-pound reward for the discovery and conviction of any of a mob in Providence which on the evening of May 18 (three days after Fellows again aroused the wrath of Gloucester, although it may have been only a coincidence, of course) seized Jesse Saville, a tidesman of the customs house there, gagged him, dumped him in a wheelbarrow and trundled him to a wharf from which they offered to throw him into Narragansett Bay. Then they tied a handkerchief around his face, cut his clothes to pieces, stripped him naked, daubed him with turpentine and feathers, bound him, threw dirt in his face, beat him with their fists and sticks, knocked him to the pavement and left him there.

The opening of the June sitting of Essex Superior Court was signaled by a flutter of subpoenas in Gloucester and a noisy clatter of hoofbeats on the Chebacco road as plaintiffs, defendants, witnesses, lawyers, families, friends and foes hastened to Ipswich for the trials of Saville's complaint against Joseph Foster and his crowd, and Sheriff Parsons's against Fellows, who had been brought to justice after all.

As for the first, the entire affair was too blatant, and witnessed by too many of Jesse's family with the courage to testify. The jury found Captain Foster and all his co-defendants save Paul Dudley Sargent guilty on all counts of riotous misconduct, breaking and entering, and assault. The court fined Foster and Benjamin Somes fifteen pounds each, Dr. Rogers ten, and required all three to post bonds of fifty pounds for keeping the peace and good behavior for two years. Knights, Stevens, Tarbox and Lowther, men of lesser means, were fined five pounds and ordered to provide bonds of twenty pounds for the same probationary period.

As for Captain Fellows, charged with interfering with justice, he was permitted to change his plea from innocent to *nolo contendere* and was dismissed with a fine of ten pounds — "a favour not usually granted in cases of importance, and to such high handed offenders," commented the "Journal of the Times," which thought it strange that at this same court session a mob which tarred and feathered "an infamous creature" at Newbury but hadn't fired on anybody should draw fines of twenty to forty pounds, but not a word did it include on the indictments and fines in the case of Jesse Saville of Gloucester.[6]

Having tasted justice and found it to his satisfaction (the Essex County brand, not Providence), Saville entered a suit for damages of two hundred pounds against the seven guilty ones, "with other evil minded persons unknown," placing Joseph Foster at their head and adding the name of Thomas Griffin, yeoman. Among their travesties that night of terror, he alleged, they had beaten him so severely that his life was despaired of, and so frightened his wife "that by reason thereof she has been ever since sick and the said Jesse hath in a great measure thereby lost her benefit and comfort." His suit was tried in the Circuit Court at Newburyport in September, 1769. The defendants pleaded innocent. And so the jury pronounced them ... not liable for damages. The court ordered Jesse to pay the costs.

The Annisquam tanner was not a man to give up easily. He appealed, and a hearing was docketed for the term of March 1770. But the fates would not have it so.

On the fifth of March, provoked beyond endurance and frightened by a baiting mob of Sam Adams's Boston bully boys, a detachment of the British Twenty-ninth Regiment fired into them and killed five. The tensions which had been building between citizens and soldiery since the regulars were first quartered in Boston in October of 1768 exploded. Lieutenant Governor Thomas Hutchinson was running the colony in the absence of Governor George Bernard, who had gone to England to report on the situation, never to return, and Sam Adams, in a tense confrontation, demanded that he withdraw the troops. Fearful of further bloodshed, he did, to the harbor islands. The victorious patriots sent their laundered version of "the Horrid Massacre" to every corner of settled America and abroad, and everywhere the fired-up colonists cast about for scapegoats on whom to vent their emotions.

Jesse Saville's appeal from the adverse verdict in his damage suit against Joseph Foster and friends was at that moment on the current docket of the Circuit Court, awaiting a hearing as soon as he should appear.

But he did not appear, nor did any of the defendants, and the case was dropped. The reason for the intrepid tanner's failure to show up in court to press his case perhaps appears in an item from the *Essex Gazette* of March 27, 1770:

> We hear from Cape-Ann, that on Friday night last [March 23], a number of people there, who knew that town had sustained great damage by the misdoings of one Jesse Savil an informer, and that he deserved chastisement therefor, went in a body to his house for that purpose, about 10 o'clock, and finding him in bed, took him from thence, and walk'd him barefoot about 4 miles to the Harbour, then placed him in a cart they had provided for that purpose, and putting a lanthorn with a lighted candle in his hand, that every one might see him, they carted him through all their streets, and stopping at every house they roused the inhabitants, and obliged him to declare and publish unto them that he was Jesse Savil the informer; and having gone round in this manner, they then bestowed a handsome coat of tar upon him, and placed him upon the town-pump, caused him to swear that he would never more inform against any person in that or any other town, and then dismissed him, after having received his thanks for the gentle discipline they had administered to him.

This approving account of Gloucester's special brand of gentle discipline neglected to detail, as did the single indictment to emerge from the investigation which ensued, that nine men broke into Saville's Annisquam house, pulled him outside by his hair, beat him and did then "drag the said Jesse by his heels and by the hair of his head, thro' snow and over hills, dales and rocks" the four miles to the Harbor, where they stripped him almost naked prior to putting him in the cart for a ride of four hours through the streets "exposed to cold, scorn and derision" before tarring him, pummelling him again and leaving him. The widely reprinted newspaper story also failed to mention that the Gloucester Sons of Liberty were disguised on this mission of chastisement as Indians and black men, a reminder that Captain Foster and his six associates were on strict probation pursuant to their conviction for the first attack on Saville, and were they to have been discovered in a further breach of the same man's peace so soon, the angry judges would no doubt have thrown the book at them, and them in jail.

While Jesse Saville lay gasping on his bed of pain, the freeholders of Gloucester (including some whose countenances may still have betrayed traces of paint) gathered in town meeting on March 27 to shout forth their unanimous indictment of man's inhumanity to man:

> That the first settlers of this country left their native land and came into this when a wild uncultivated wilderness inhabited by no human creatures except savages, and suffered extreme hardship, risqued their lives, and spent their fortunes, to obtain and secure their civil and ecclesiastical liberties and privileges, invaded and wrested from them by violence.

> That their posterity enjoyed those liberties and privileges (except in the tyrannical and arbitrary government of King James the Second) with very little molestation or interruption for almost one hundred and fifty years, until the late execrable Stamp Act since repealed.

> That these liberties and privileges are greatly invaded and infringed, and all the English inhabitants of America reduced to a state little better than slavery by the late Acts of Parliament imposing duties for the sole purpose of raising a revenue, the collection of which is enforced by a lawless and licentious soldiery, and a crew of petty officers who have in some measure awed and resisted the civil magistrates in the execution of their office; and some time since a sheriff of this town was attacked by a petty officer and several under his command, and several times fired upon and a prisoner lawfully taken rescued. And when said officer was prosecuted, he was only punished by a fine of ten pounds which has so emboldened them, that they have committed

many hostilities, and at last the horrid Massacre the fifth instant at Boston, wherein they have wantonly spilt the blood of many of our brethren which called for our highest resentment...

The style in which Gloucester vented its resentment on Jesse Saville was relayed to Lieutenant Governor Hutchinson on April 7 by Justice of the Peace James Davis, who had tried to no avail to interpose himself between the royal customs officer and his disciplinarians. Hutchinson was still smarting from having been forced to withdraw the regulars from Boston as the result of the bloody encounter in King Street, and furthermore, the House of Representatives had refused to renew a weapon he wished he had, the recently expired provincial riot act. So the same day he received Squire Davis's agitated report from Gloucester, the acting governor addressed a message to the General Court: [7]

Gentlemen of the Council, and House of Representatives, The Secretary will lay before you several papers which I have received from one of his Majesty's Justices of the Peace, and divers other persons, inhabitants of the Town of Glocester, and which relate to a very disorderly riotous transaction in the said town. A person appears to have been most inhumanly treated, for seeking redress in the course of the law, for former injuries received. As this information comes to me while the General Court is sitting, I have thought it proper to communicate it to the House of Representatives, as well as to his Majesty's Council, that if any Act or Order of the whole Legislature shall be judged necessary for strengthening or encouraging the executive Powers of Government, there may be an opportunity for it. I must observe to you that a number of persons of the same Town were prosecuted and fined at the Superior Court for the County of Essex in June last, for injuring the person and property of the present complainant in a barbarous manner; and if it be truly represented, that the same persons have been concerned in this second offence, it is a great aggravation of their crime, and a defiance of the Laws and Authority of Government.

Council-Chamber
April 7, 1770   T. Hutchinson [8]

A committee unhurriedly drafted a coolly evasive answer which in due course was adopted by the hostile majority of the House, and John Hancock was named chairman of a delegation to wait on the lieutenant governor with it. It was a sparring match whereby the radical leaders chose to box with the harassed chief executive, or with his shadow, as suited their purposes.

The House in its answer thought laws enough were on the books, if duly executed, to preserve order, but "it cannot be expected that a people accustomed to the freedom of the English Constitution will be patient, while they are under the hand of tyranny and arbitrary power. They will discover their resentment in a manner which will naturally displease their oppressors; and in such a case, the severest laws and the most rigorous execution will be to little or no purpose. The most effectual method to restore tranquility would be to remove their burthens, and to punish all those who have been the procurers of their oppression."

His Excellency had hardly produced enough evidence of a riotous transaction in a town "hitherto unimpeached in point of good order" for the House to form a judgment on the matter, and the members found themselves at a loss to understand why he should have brought this instance to their attention when he had as yet failed to take any notice of the "enormities which have been notoriously committed by the Soldiery of late" and which could scarcely be any less threatening to the government than what had occurred at Gloucester.

The House then proceeded angrily to harangue Hutchinson that the presence of the standing army which had given rise to the "most horrid Slaughter of a number of inhabitants, but a few days before the sitting of this Assembly ... threatens the total subversion of a free Constitution; much more, is designed to execute a system of corrupt and arbitrary power and even to exterminate the liberties of the country ... is an unlawful assembly of all others the most dangerous and alarming," unconsented to by the populace, and sanctioned by neither Parliament nor the General Court of Massachusetts.

Military violence, "added to the most rigorous and oppressive prosecutions carried on by the officers of the Crown against the subjects, grounded upon unconstitutional Acts, and in the Court of Admiralty, uncontroul'd by the Courts of Common Law, have been justly alarming to the people. The Disorder which your Honor so earnestly recommends to the consideration of the Assembly, very probably took its rise from such provocations. The use therefore which we shall make of the information in your Message, shall be to enquire into the grounds of the peoples uneasiness, and to seek a radical redress of their grievances."[9]

It was a masterful explication of the radical technique, a revelation of the unfolding strategy by which every misstep of every servant of the crown from royal governor to tidesman was to be turned to patriotic account. And what wonderful political alchemy ... to make popular heroes, indeed martyrs, of a mob of tarrers and featherers!

The acting governor was shocked that the House should treat the matter as a "trifling affair." He was a brilliant and dedicated public servant and man of letters (though slightly venal in the way he passed out high offices to his family), and Thomas Hutchinson was hopelessly trapped between loyalty to his king and his respect for the English institutions of government and law, and his passionate love for his native Massachusetts.

Some years later, when he had followed Bernard to England forever, he wrote a learned history of Massachusetts and reflected on the Gloucester affair. In his view it was "a triumph over the laws of the province, as well as the acts of parliament for the regulation of trade," and he was "not more astonished than grieved" at the answer of the House "which had so direct a tendency to encourage the people in acts of tumult and riot, and to incense the authority of government in England against the colony. The friends to America, in England, had always urged in its favour, that the people acknowledged the authority of parliament in all cases except that of taxes. Its authority to establish courts of admiralty for trying and determining offences against the acts of trade, is now denied, unless their decrees are to be controlled by the courts of common law."[10]

The closing scene of one of the dirtiest episodes in the deterioration of the bonds of fraternity between England and her American colonies was so ironic, so cruel, as to stagger belief.

George was a mulatto slave owned by Dr. Samuel Plummer of Gloucester, brother of the David Plummer whose thirty-three hogsheads of molasses had set the affair in motion. Jesse Saville must have recognized him, or thought he did, as the only genuine black man among the painted gang which dragged him out of bed that horrifying night of March 23.

How Dr. Plummer's "molatto man-slave" came to be in such company is a mystery, but he alone was apprehended, taken up to Salem and indicted for the assault with eight others "unknown." He pleaded innocent. The jury found him guilty.[11] On November 6, 1770, the judges of the Essex Superior Court passed sentence:

> That the said George be set upon the gallows with a rope about his neck, and the other end cast over the gallows, for the space of one hour, that he be whipped thirty-nine stripes under the gallows upon his naked back, that he suffer two years imprisonment, that he give security for his good behaviour for the term of seven years, from and after the expiration of his said imprisonment, in the sum of one hundred pounds.

Dr. Plummer's slave remained stolid and silent, and so far as is known he never revealed to a living soul the identity of the white masters who were disguised that night of infamy as Indians and blacks.

4

STORM CLOUDS TO THE EASTWARD

Joseph Foster had been looking for a wharf of his own since 1766, when he, Samuel Whittemore and John Low, two of the selectmen, were turned down by town meeting in their request for permission to build one on the Harbor Cove shore of Watch House Point under the shadow of the decayed earthworks of French and Indian War days. Finally he found what he wanted, in May of 1770, which happens to be the last year any of his vessels are recorded in the European trade for two more decades.

It was a first-class location, midway on the south side of Front Street between Sea Street, which was the extension of the lane west of his house that came to be called Hancock Street, and the alley to the harbor subsequently known as Parsons Street. He bought it for 173 pounds from Philemon Haskell, who had been accused with him by Saville as one of his attackers on that first invasion, but escaped indictment. The lot was two hundred feet deep from Front Street to high water, and fifty feet wide between Nathaniel Kinsman's (who probably was one of his) on the east and James Porter's on the west. Foster and Porter had been partners in *Badger* a few voyages, which suggests that hitherto he had made do with his accumulating vessel interests at Porter's and the wharves of other associates such as Isaac Smith and Edward Payne.

A combination small house and shop, possibly a cooperage, stood at the head of the wharf, and up at the Front Street end of the property was a cellar hole which after a few years he covered over with a second mansion house for himself.

In the ten years Captain Foster had been a freeholder in his adopted town he had come to the front, at forty, as a leader of men, whatever one may think of his part in the first and perhaps the second of the visitations upon Jesse Saville. These were brutal times, when shipmasters ruled with strength of will backed up by fist, lash and pistol if need be, and the spirit of the times was on his side. Smuggling Gloucester admired men who stood up to the hated customs officers, defended themselves in court and walked the streets wearing their probation for keeping the peace like a badge of honor. He rose steadily in the esteem of his townsmen.

Since his first election as constable in 1763, Foster had moved from one to another of the humble town offices whose titles and duties were quaint holdovers from the English country shire, brought to America by the settlers. He had been a clerk of the market, with responsibility for the honesty of weights and measures; a fire warden for his neighborhood; a hogreeve to enforce the town's annual vote that "the swine may go at large under the restrictions of the law;" a culler of hoops and staves, measurer of wood and surveyor of lumber. And so it went.

Beyond the town limits politics was at an ebb. The crisis of the spring of 1770 had cooled with the withdrawal of the troops from Boston, and a sufficiently united nonimportation front had been instrumental in deciding Parliament that it would be a wise move to roll back all of the Townshend duties, leaving only the impost on tea as a token of its right to impose a colonial tax. This was followed by a welcome flood of British merchandise which had the desired effect of subverting the Puritan conscience and worse still, from Sam Adams's point of view, sense of political outrage. Men were beginning to wonder if perhaps Britain hadn't come round after all, and they could tend their affairs and plan for their futures.

Joseph Foster was no exception. His *honoured father*, Captain Jeremiah Foster, had died on March 25, 1769 in Chebacco at the good age of seventy-eight, and as the oldest surviving son, he was appointed administrator of his estate. The probate court decided that the real property was indivisible for all practical purposes and directed him to dispose of it and divide the proceeds among the heirs. On April 30, 1771 he sold the sawmill and homestead at Chebacco Falls to Jonathan Story for 375 pounds, thus returning them after forty-seven years with the Fosters to the Storys.

Two weeks later he bought Captain Robert Elwell's house and barn next door to the east of his own, claimed to be the oldest on Middle Street, for 160 pounds. It was a well-kept gambreled home matching his, set back a few feet farther from the road. He may have taken possession by foreclosure, because Captain Elwell six years earlier had mortgaged the place to Foster and the merchant Daniel Rogers.

Toward the end of the year Captain Foster rented his latest acquisition as a "publick house of entertainment and a tavern" to James Broome, an elderly Englishman who converted a corner room into a tonsorial parlor; after teaching his daughter Rebecca how to clip, shave, powder and pin a perfect curl, he established her therein as the reigning barberess. Unfortunately, Broome and his landlord didn't hit it off, because in July of 1773 Foster took him to Salem court to collect £19.3.5 back rent owed for seventeen months. Under these trying circumstances, it is not likely that father and daughter held sway here for more than three or four years; some time later, around the end of the Revolution, the house was occupied by Captain Jeremiah Foster, who was probably the son of Joseph Foster's late brother John. But the name stuck, and ever after it was known as the old Broome Tavern. Becca Broome married Andrew Ingersol and taught *their* daughter Rebecca how to cultivate the male vanity, and harvest from it, and for some years before and during the coming war mother and daughter ruled the southeast room of the one-story house at the south corner of Middle and Pleasant streets. "By professional skill, and lively and intelligent conversation," says Babson, "they made it a noted place of resort for the merchants, ship-masters, sailors, and soldiers of those times...for all the wits and genteel idlers of the town." [1]

Judith, the Fosters' fifth daughter, was born in 1772; Elizabeth and Benjamin had arrived in 1766 and 1769. Mrs. Mary

Booshell, Mrs. Mary Davis and Barnett Harkin taught one or another of the children at various times during these years. In his accounts for schooling, their father called Mary *Polly*, spelled Lydia sometimes *Liddia*, and Sarah *Sall* or *Sary*. Their parents saw to it that all the girls as they came along had drummed into them a practical education in cooking and housekeeping. Middle Street laid tables which were not lacking in fine linen and the best of settings, nor unprovided with the products of the Malagan hillsides and the plantations of the West Indies, and Middle Street husbands were to be desired.

The head of this growing, dominantly girlish household is said to have been "rather short and stout." A family silhouette outlines a figure of handsome profile, even-featured, firm chin, in fringed shirt front, seemingly scornful of a wig. If *short and stout* applied with any accuracy to his later years, *stocky* would better suit his youth and middle age. He was assuredly a man of extraordinary strength and hardihood, well knit, tough physically and mentally, early accustomed to fend for himself, to take responsibility, to make up his mind instantly, to set a course, to lead others and bend them to his will, by push or by pull.

All had been so tranquil between England and her colonies since the conciliatory rollback of the Townshend duties that the Sons of Liberty despaired their cause would again get moving. Governor Hutchinson observed this frustration and the squabbling in the popular ranks with satisfaction and decided that "the union in the colonies is pretty well broke." If the administration and Parliament continue to maintain their authority with an even hand, he predicted, "all this new doctrine of independence would be disavowed, and the first inventors or broachers of it would be sacrificed to the rage of the people who had been deluded by them." [2]

Early in June of 1772 the royal revenue schooner *Gaspee* ran aground chasing a Rhode Island smuggler, and on the night of the ninth, some people from Providence in their rage rowed out and burned *Gaspee* to the water's edge. The patriotic arson created no great stir in America, but when the news reached

England the furious ministry in one stroke undid all the careful conciliation of the past two years. It swore that if the perpetrators of this outrage were ever caught they would be tried, not in an American court and by a jury of their peers, but in England. This blow at colonial justice was alarming enough when word of it reached America at the end of the summer. But what really revived the flagging spirits of the radicals was Lord Dartmouth's decree that henceforth the salaries of the judges of Massachusetts would be taken out of the jurisdiction of the General Court and paid directly by the king. When Governor Hutchinson's pay had been placed under the royal pursestrings in June it had caused hardly a stir, for he was appointed by the king anyway. But the judges were different; their appointment was subject to legislative approval. These were barefisted attempts to make American justice beholden to the crown.

"The last vessels from England," reported the *Boston Gazette* of September 28, "tell us the judges and the subalterns have got salaries from Great Britain! Is it possible this last movement should not move us, and drive us, not to desperation, but to our duty? The blind may see, the callous must feel, the spirited will act!" So wrote the flaming patriot Josiah Quincy, Jr., and the very next day Gloucester acted. [3]

Casting about for the nearest convenient representative of the crown to vent their spirits upon, the selectmen met on September 29 and summarily ordered Richard Silvester, the resident district customs officer, to gather together his family and get out of town. It was a pretext, an obscure technicality which has not survived its own rationale.

Silvester replied with a card in the *Boston News Letter* on October 15 thanking them for their "kind remonstrance" in sending the constable after him, but "he thinks they have been asleep for some considerable time, or otherwise the motion for the compliment must have been in debate upwards of twenty months, the said Silvester having resided there that time, without receiving any such ceremonial message. He prays leave to acquaint those worthies, that he cannot nor will not comply with their request, so long as his duty requires his stay in Cape Ann." [4]

His personal discretion, however, seems to have prevailed over his official valor.

Sam Adams and his Boston town meeting reacted to the welcome resumption of royal displeasure less viscerally than Gloucester, and with better effect. They created a standing committee of correspondence, as they called it, for the purpose of getting the radical message across to other towns in the colony, and to the other colonies, with the suggestion that they set up similar committees of their own so that all might have a network of communication for the exchange of grievances and intelligence, and to plan united action.

This was the thin framework of union!

Excitement was in the air as Gloucester assembled in special town meeting in the Fourth Parish meetinghouse at the Green on Christmas Day, 1772. Statements of colonial rights and the particulars of their infringements by the ministry, just received from Boston, were read, and a committee was elected to study them, and to consider what to do. Joseph Foster was chosen chairman. With him were four of the five selectmen: Samuel Whittemore, the merchant; Farmer Peter Coffin from West Parish; John Low, farmer and merchant from Up-town Parish; Dr. Daniel Witham, Harvard graduate, respected town clerk for thirty-eight years. And then Daniel Rogers, the rising merchant-shipowner and Foster's Middle Street neighbor; Sheriff Jacob Parsons; Jacob Allen, captain of militia; and Solomon Parsons.

There was a feeling of anxiety, of foreboding at this Christmas meeting, a sense that the town was caught up in large events beyond the control of anyone. After choosing this committee to recommend a course of action, the town turned again to a problem which had been in the back of people's minds all year, its defenses in case of war. Already men with a long view at the annual March meeting had persuaded the selectmen to fit up the old Battery House for the town's stock of powder and ammunition. It was located at the earthworks on Watch House Point which had been erected and armed with eight twelve-pounder guns during the 1746 war scare when everybody was afraid the French fleet might show up one day and bombard the harbor. Now, what about access to the old fort? To secure it and be sure, the town voted to buy from the estate of Nathaniel Allen the neck, nothing much more than a long sand bar, which led out to the point dominated by the crumbling works.

The meeting adjourned for three days. On December 28 the voters came together again, this time in the Middle Street meetinghouse, and endorsed the Foster committee's recommendation that Gloucester establish a committee of correspondence to join with Boston "and all others in exerting ourselves in every legal way to oppose tyranny in all its forms." The town elected Foster, Whittemore, Jacob and Solomon Parsons, Allen, Coffin and Dr. Witham, chairman.

But as it had before, following each new crisis, the political pot refused to boil for long. England refrained from further provocations, and by March of 1773 the colonies had relaxed again. Gloucester left off worrying about its defenses and decided to find a tenant for the Battery House, reserving the right to reoccupy it if the time ever came.

And something pulled Joseph Foster back to the land.

It may have been the selling of the old family place in Chebacco where he grew up, where the falls chattered below the house on their run through to the sea, and the clanking of the sawmill still in his ears made him wistful for the back country of his boyhood. And if the storm clouds of war were piling up to the eastward, however remote they looked over the horizon, a prudent man might do well to have a place to retreat to with his family, back from the most likely object of attack, the Harbor.

After a run of hard luck, Nathaniel Allen, a respected Gloucester merchant, had gone bankrupt, and his estate was put up for sale to satisfy his creditors in the summer of '72. The trustees were friends of Foster...Isaac Smith, his partner, and Dan Sargent and Sam Whittemore...and they sold him Allen's seven acres of salt marsh at Dunfudgin, where the tides meet on Squam River, and his forty-five acres of woodland lying between the Sandy Bay road and Cape Pond on the southeast slope of Great Hill.

Now it was the summer of '73. He'd had his eye on a fair piece of bottomland adjoining his new woodlot, twenty acres of it across the road to the west, and on July 13 he bought it, from the estate of James Witham. It was mostly meadow, some fresh marsh, and Alewife Brook ran through it out of the Cape Pond on its way to Mill River and the sea. The Withams were old settlers up here past the section known as The Farms, above Little Good Harbor Beach and Joppa ("down Joppy"), populated by Parsonses. The heart of the Beaver Dam Farm he had now acquired was described in his deed thus:

> Beginning at a little run of water crossing the highway that goes from the meeting house in the fourth parish in Gloucester aforesd to Sandy Bay and thence northerly or westerly across the meadow to a great split rock at the head of a cove of the meadow, thence northeasterly to a red oak tree upon a rock by the meadow, thence northeasterly along the marsh to an hemlock tree, thence south easterly eight rods to the northern side of the said Beaver Dam bridge, thence southerly & westerly along the highway to the brook or run the first mentioned bound, together with all the privileges & appurtenances to the same anyway belonging.

The highway first referred to was the woods lane known since as the Old Rockport Road which cut across Cape Ann from the Green, parallel to Alewife Brook. The "little run of water" was where the brook flowed from Cape Pond underneath the road and hooked west behind the cooperage built there in the middle of the seventeenth century, right next to the beaver dam, by James Babson, the pioneer owner of the tract. There is no record of a farmhouse there until Captain Foster bought the land from the Withams, who came into it through marriage with the Babsons. [5]

The presence of an abandoned sawmill dam and millpond three quarters of a mile down the brook did not detract from the evocative atmosphere of the Beaver Dam Farm. Just as the millsite the new owner had known as a boy was the first granted in Ipswich, so this ghostly location was the first on Cape Ann in 1642. It had long since been put out of operation by the tidal mills at Riverdale, but the earth dam remained. [6]

Late that summer Gloucester suffered a scare, and the way out of it led to a famous story about Captain Foster. It started in Marblehead, in June of '73, when the wife of a fisherman came down sick and was treated for "poison" on the theory that she had been harmed by washing his clothes with some soap he'd obtained from a French vessel on the Grand Bank. Nothing was thought of it until July, when others in the family, and then neighbors who had come over to take care of them, were "poisoned." Only then was it diagnosed as smallpox. The alarm of the townspeople, few of whom had had the disease, was not allayed by the news that a beloved old lady, visited by some hundred and fifty of them, had died of it.

By August more than thirty Marblehead people were dead, and the town voted with many misgivings to sanction the construction of an inoculation hospital on Cat Island. (Hardly had the last nail been driven when an hysterical mob burned it to the ground.)

The nearby coast, of course, shrank from Marblehead in horror. Gloucester rushed Adam Huffin and John Avery over to Watch House Point to ward off contaminated strangers by sea, and hied husky John McKean off to the Cut to watch the gate and hustle all out-of-towners and suspects into his smoke house for a fumigation, which was thought to be the most effective preventative. There was talk that fall of buying or leasing the farmhouse at Eastern Point between the harbor and the pond for a pesthouse, but nothing came of it. Marblehead's "poison" was warded off. Still fearful, the town next spring designated Joseph Foster and Jacob Allen special constables "in case the smallpox should come, they having had it," but it didn't.

It was undoubtedly during this scare that the services of John McKean at the Cut were enlisted by Captain Foster against a two-legged plague far more detested than the pox by the patriotic freetraders of Gloucester. A schooner of Foster's had come in during the night, no doubt from the West Indies...

> According to custom, the hatches were immediately opened, and the landing of the cargo was commenced, the owner himself assisting. A considerable part was landed and stored before daybreak; but more than half was still

on board, and, early in the morning, a tide-waiter was expected from Salem. The fertile mind of Foster hit at once upon an expedient. On the Cut was a watch-house, where John McKean, a stout Irishman, had been employed, in a time of alarm about the smallpox, to stop all strangers entering the town, and subject them to a fumigating process. It is sufficient to say, that his Majesty's officer of the customs was on that morning ushered into the watchhouse by John McKean; that he was kept there all day, and released after dark, purified from all infectious diseases, so far as a thorough smoking could do it. [7]

Was there a chest or two of Dutch tea for the ladies of Gloucester in the clandestine cargo Captain Foster assisted his men getting ashore in those early morning hours...Dutch tea to slake the thirst of tea-addicted Americans while the tea of the East India Company, on which they refused to pay the hated tax, piled up in its London warehouses?

Boycotted by the colonists, milked by its own corrupt officials, the East India Company teetered on the edge of bankruptcy. It was without any deliberate intention of stirring up the pot again that Lord North moved in to recoup the government's heavy tax equity in the revenues of the giant monopoly and to protect its stake in India which was daily more jeopardized by the company's precarious position. The Tea Act was passed by Parliament. By cancelling the home duty on tea, and advancing the East India Company an enormous loan -- at the same time permitting it to sell directly to American consignees instead of through English middlemen -- North believed he would undercut the contraband Dutch tea in America, while retaining the Townshend import duty as a continuing symbol of Parliament's right to tax the colonies as it pleased. The cynical ministry guessed the Americans, for all their great talk, would wink at the tax for the sake of a cheaper cup of tea.

It was a disastrous miscalculation of American opinion. Colonial merchants saw the Tea Act as the opening move in a campaign to root the East India monopoly in America, then to extend it to other goods and eventually to strangle them. The radicals regarded it as one more sinister ploy in a strategy aimed at forcing the colonies to acknowledge Parliament's claimed right of unilateral taxation.

The simple act of loading the tea aboard ships and sending it on its way across the Atlantic joined the issue. Of the tea consignees in the various ports of destination, only those in Boston (and they included two sons and a nephew of Governor Hutchinson) refused to resign under pressure from the radical party. Hutchinson was determined to make a strong show of royal sovereignty in this most troublesome town, which he yet loved dearly; he had consignees he controlled, the strongest customs enforcement on the coast, and a fleet of naval vessels in the harbor.

Dartmouth was the first of the three tea ships to arrive at Boston on November 27, 1773. The regulations stated that the tea must be unloaded, and the duty paid, within twenty days or be subject to seizure in lieu of the tax. Once impounded under the guns of the warships and bayonets of the regulars, Sam Adams and the other leaders were afraid, the tea would be sold secretly; the duty would be withheld by the customs from the proceeds, and the patriotic cause would have missed the boat. They called mass meetings which demanded that *Dartmouth* leave port with her cargo. Hutchinson refused. The consignees stood firm. The deadline for seizure, December 17, approached. Boston sped messengers to the nearby seaports, exhorting the people there to hold fast in case attempts should be made to slip tea past them.

At the last minute, on December 15, Gloucester held an emergency town meeting. All felt the drama of the crisis that day. England had thrown down the gauntlet at Boston. The moment had arrived for Cape Ann people to stand up for the counting. What would they do if one of the tea ships tried to land and unload at Gloucester? The committee of correspondence brought in its report and recommendations. Joseph Foster and the others watched their townsmen as Dr. Witham read:

> When every effort is exerted, every outrage commit-
> ted, and every refinement of despotism practised, by a
> wicked and corrupt administration, to involve a free and

loyal people in the ignominious gulf of slavery and servile subjection, this town, animated by that ardor which is ever the companion of virtuous freedom, cannot with tame composure observe this last political manoeuvre of the British ministry, in permitting the East-India Company to import their tea into America for the purpose of extorting a revenue from us.

We, with the greatest satisfaction, see the town of Boston, and other towns in this province, gloriously opposing this pernicious innovation, notwithstanding the numerous obstacles thrown in their way by the great enemies to the liberties of mankind.

This town think it an indispensable duty we owe to ourselves, to our countrymen, and to posterity, to declare, and we do declare --

That we will use our most strenuous exertions, not only that there shall be no teas landed in this town, subject to a duty payable in America; but that we shall have no commerce with any person or persons that have, or shall have, any concern in buying or selling that detestable herb.

That we are determined to oppose every species of tyranny and usurpation, however dignified by splendid titles, or any character that bears the sacred pride of human virtue.

That, if we are compelled to make the last appeal to Heaven, we will defend our resolutions and liberties at the expense of all that is dear to us.

That we will hold ourselves in readiness to join the town of Boston, and all other towns, in all measures to extricate ourselves from tyranny and oppression; and --

That the thanks of this town be presented to the town of Boston for the vigilance and activity they have always discovered in guarding against the subtle machinations, and in combatting the open outrages, of our enemies in Great Britain and in this country; and this town shall always record them the friends of human nature, and guardians of that heavenly palladium -- the liberties of America.

If we are compelled to make the last appeal to Heaven, we will defend our resolutions and liberties at the expense of all that is dear to us.

Gloucester adopted this resolution *with great unanimity* and hastened it to Boston. The next night a tribe of patriots disguised as Indians boarded the ships from England and dumped all 342 chests of the East India Company's tea, duty unpaid, into Boston Harbor.

It was the irreversible act of independence.

5

WITH HEAVY HEARTS

When the news reached England that a mob of Americans masquerading as Mohawks had made a teapot of Boston Harbor under the very guns of the greatest navy in the world, the conservative majority in Parliament was beside itself. One after another the furious members passed and flung the Coercive Acts across the Atlantic in passionate broadsides of recrimination that spring of 1774, to the utter dismay of America's friends, the Whigs.

First the Boston Port Bill blockaded the offending town until every pennysworth of dumped tea, and the duty on it, should be made good. Then Parliament virtually nullified the sacred Massachusetts charter by suspending elections except to the House of Representatives, and decreeing the Council, prosecuttors, judges, sheriffs and even juries subject to royal appointment. Finally, in a consummate misapprehension of the temper of their American cousins, the English legislators struck at the heart of colonial self-government: reasoning that the institution of the town meeting was the prime mover of sedition, they forbad every town in Massachusetts to assemble at any time outside the regular annual session without the governor's prior approval of both the call and the agenda.

Nothing Sam Adams and his cabal could have dreamed of was more perfectly calculated to drive the loyal moderates of America into their camp.

Someone had rediscovered what John Wise of Chebacco had to say about the American democracy sixty years earlier, and thoughtful people were reading his pamphlets, reprinted and widely distributed...*The very name of an arbitrary government is ready to put an Englishman's blood into a fermentation; but when it comes and shakes its whip over their ears, and tells them it is their master it makes them stark mad.* And they were pondering the highly charged words of John Locke and John Dickinson, Samuel Adams and Dr. Joseph Warren. These Coercive Acts...was it to come to this that the fathers had fled the old country and made a new life in the wilderness, that their descendants should be tyrannized across three thousand miles of sea?

The seacoast was put in special fear by the blockade of the port of Boston, and the closer to Nantasket Roads, where the British squadron lay placidly at anchor, the more nervously aware were the nearby ports that their fates were intertwined ...nowhere more so than at Cape Ann, where a great harbor was tucked safe inside a headland which commanded the eastern approach to Boston Bay.

One town was brother to the other, a bond which Gloucester men, in the words of their tea resolution, were prepared to seal with their blood. They were brethren towns, and when Boston was spanked, Gloucester yelped. Pigeon Hill, rising out of the haze above Sandy Bay, was the first landfall from the eastward for Boston by day, and by night the twin beams of the lighthouses on Thacher's Island, which had been built at the instigation of the selectmen of Salem in 1771, guided the mariner in. Many merchants, like Joseph Foster and his partners, conducted their business and owned vessels in both ports. There was much passing back and forth, to a great extent by water. Obviously, the fleet that blockaded the one could blockade the other, only three hours' fair sail away. In the months of punishment that followed Boston's frolic with the tea, there was plenty of yelping down Cape Ann way.

One of the strongest but least visible ties between Boston and Cape Ann was the secret fraternal bond of Freemasonry. For a number of years the only lodge of Masons in Boston was St.

John's, conservative, nonpolitical, mercantile, and chartered by the "modern" Grand Lodge of England. In 1760 some younger men, many of them artisans, shopkeepers and sea captains who had been denied membership in St. John's, obtained a charter from the rival "ancient" Grand Lodge of Scotland, as the Lodge of St. Andrew. Within ten years St. Andrew's, interlocking with the North End Caucus of working men, was the hotbed of radicalism in Boston.

By 1770 the leader of St. Andrew's was the handsome, fiery patriot Dr. Joseph Warren, not yet thirty; his right hand man was the silversmith and engraver, Paul Revere. The lodge met for ritual and conviviality, and intense political discussion and planning, at the Green Dragon and gave that famous tavern its reputation for infamy in Tory eyes as "a nest where rebel plots are hatched." Looking to enlarge their influence (for Masonic, social and certainly political reasons), several members of St. Andrew's in 1769 got a charter for a provincial grand lodge from the Scottish parent, with Dr. Warren their grand master, and the authority in turn to charter other local lodges.

The first of these roots of St. Andrew's to spring into bloom on other soil was the Tyrian Lodge of Gloucester, whose charter was signed by Warren and Revere on March 2, 1770, in response to a petition from eight Masons of Cape Ann. At least two, Epes Sargent, Jr., and Phillip Marrett, and possibly all eight, were already members of St. Andrew's. Sargent was a staunch Whig whose father was an equally staunch Tory, and Captain Marrett was a close relative of Paul Revere, who had a special interest in the new lodge, pushed for its charter, made its jewels and was its proxy for several years in the provincial grand lodge. The other petitioners were Captain Andrew Giddings, of Lydia Foster's family, a strong patriot; schoolmaster Barnett Harkin, Tyrian's first master, a position he and Sargent swapped back and forth for most of the first sixteen years; Captain John Fletcher; George Brown; David Parker; and Andrew Faneuil Philips, all Free and Accepted Masons residing in Gloucester.

Tyrian's roster of the first few years is a roll of revolutionary leadership on Cape Ann...Ebenezer Parsons, Philemon Stacy,

Cornelius Fellows, Isaac Somes, William Wyer, Nathaniel Warner, John Babson, William Pearson, Daniel Collins, James Prentice, Peter Coffin, William Pearce, William Coas, John Beach and others...shipmasters, merchants, soldiers, privateersmen and politicians. Many a rebel plot laid by the brethren of St. Andrew was hatched across the bay in Tyrian's nest, which from midsummer of 1770 until the end of 1779 was James Prentice's tavern, two doors east across Middle Street from Joseph Foster. They met convivially and secretly, and emerged in public infrequently but impressively, as on their annual feast day of St. John the Baptist on June 24, 1773, when the Tyrians were joined by Grand Master Joseph Webb and Grand Senior Warden Paul Revere from Boston, with officers from St. Andrew's, for a parade in all their jewels and finery the hundred yards down Middle Street from Prentice's to the meetinghouse to listen solemnly to a discourse by Pastor Chandler. The occasion was recorded in the lodge records:

> The remainder of the day and evening was spent in all the pleasures that flow from social intercourse when Felicity, Harmony and innocent Freedom preside--add to these the uncommon beauty of the season, the brilliant appearance of a numerous concourse of gentlemen and ladies from Boston and the neighboring towns, the universal satisfaction and applause marked on the countenances of persons of every rank and condition; and their emulous endeavours to make the day illustrious, rendered the commemoration as remarkable as it was happy.

Although his son Joseph and other members of his family were admitted as brethren after the Revolution, and many of his friends were Tyrians, Captain Foster was not a Mason. Candidates were not officially tapped for membership but were expected to make known their interest. He was a brusque sort, and it may be that the ceremonial amenities of the society held no charms for him, and he declined to apply.

Epes Sargent, Jr., Harvard graduate, twenty-six, was in his second term as master of the Tyrian Masons when he and Joseph Foster were elected selectmen of Gloucester in March of 1774. Epes, his younger brother, John Osborne Sargent, his uncles Winthrop, Daniel and Paul Dudley Sargent, and his cousin Winthrop Sargent, Jr., all were patriots true and blue, but his father, Epes Sargent, Esqr., who presided over the Sargent manse at the northeast corner of Front and Pleasant streets, was as true and blue a Tory and made no bones about it. ' The two joined the veteran selectmen Peter Coffin and John Low, both of whom, significantly, were also officers of the militia, just as events took a more ominous turn with the fresh arrival of every stale dispatch from England.

The Boston newspapers on May 10 printed the text of the Port Bill, which had been signed by the king on March 31. Three days later General Thomas Gage arrived, carrying his appointment to succeed Thomas Hutchinson as governor. Hutchinson was ordered to England to report on the situation, and never returned to his native land. Gage retained his commission as commander-in-chief of all British forces in North America. His orders were to execute the Port Bill, bring Boston and Massachusetts to submission and arrest the ringleaders in the affair of the tea and send them to England for trial, a warrant which he held in abeyance.

The day of General Gage's arrival, Boston had a standing-room-only meeting in Faneuil Hall and voted to recommend to the other colonies to cease all trade with Britain and the West Indies until the Port Act was repealed. The new governor's commission was officially proclaimed on May 17. Boston had a second emergency meeting on the eighteenth, and on May 19 the Gloucester selectmen called a special town meeting; Edward Payne, Foster's old partner, living now in Boston, had just arrived with a copy of the Port Bill.

Payne read the Act before this full meeting, and its implications were discussed. It was to go into effect less than two weeks hence, on June 1. Boston's proposal of a boycott was debated. The merchants of Newburyport had just joined it, and the agreement they had signed was read. The meeting then voted without dissent that Gloucester traders be desired to enter into a similar boycott. Joseph Foster was appointed to a committee of merchants to consult with the commercial interests of the other ports on the coast "on measures to relieve the colonies under the Act of Parliament blocking up the Town of Boston."

Five days after Boston was closed officially by the British fleet it was still talking up the boycott and finding that the conversion of promissory notes of support into the currency of action was not an easy matter. The town drew up and broadcast a Solemn League and Covenant against trade with Britain but pushed the effective date back to October 1 because of a certain caution which came over towns as they faced the hard facts, towns with certain dependent economic interests such as Gloucester which voted on July 19 that "the articles hemp, cordage, lead and duck be excepted in the aforsd Covenant & that the said Covenant is understood not to be binding on the signers unless the seaport towns generally come into it."

General Gage had troops back in Boston by now, and it seemed to him that it would be a prudent precautionary tactic to send a detachment out into the country to seize the provincial stores of cannon and powder in Charlestown and Cambridge, just in case. This he did on September 1, and the astounding reaction gave him pause. The "Powder Alarm" flew through the colonies with uncanny speed. Within hours, and literally for days, the word spread out like ripples in a pool, and in successive waves the militia at ever greater distances took up arms and set out for Cambridge, where several thousands arrived. Cool heads prevailed, and a premature clash was averted, but Gage now clearly saw himself surrounded by a hostile country, his back to the sea.

Lacking the strength to march forth and subdue the country-side, the general elected his only alternative and fortified Boston's only access by land to the mainland, the Roxbury Neck without which the town would be effectively an island. He turned it into that, an armed island, and Bostonians into prisoners in their streets and homes.

Likewise politically, Gage found himself faced with more fires than he had buckets to douse them with. Dr. Warren forged the red-hot Suffolk Resolves; Paul Revere galloped them to Philadelphia and the first Continental Congress adopted them with shouts as its own. They would flame into the Declaration of Independence. In Salem the House of Representatives met in equally hot defiance of Governor Gage's orders, and Peter Coffin and Dr. Witham were there, voting with other towns to defy governor, Parliament and king and to make laws and war, if necessary, as the first Provincial Congress of the Massachusetts Bay Colony.

By January of 1775 the radicals had pulled the royal carpet so far out from under the royal governor that another special and forbidden Gloucester town meeting was instructing Peter Coffin and Samuel Whittemore, its delegates to the second, forbidden Provincial Congress at Cambridge, "not to consent to the assuming the civil government of the Province without approbation of the Town having a plan of such government laid before them, nor without the consent of the Continental Congress."

Overrunning the cautions of Gloucester and some of the other towns which thought they were being swept along at rather a breakneck speed, the radicals already had assumed the civil government of Massachusetts through the machinations of the underground network of committees of correspondence which had produced out of the corpse of the royally murdered General Court the resurrection of the Provincial Congress. *Pro bono publico* now, this most palpable ghost nonchalantly resumed the legislative authority of the colony, including that vital power to gather in the fuel of government, the power of taxation. Gage found himself governor-general of Boston, cornered there with his fleet and his soldiers, facing the probability of an uprising.

First the assumption of civil government, then that next fateful move which Thomas Hutchinson had dreaded with fear and melancholy..."there cannot be a greater step toward independency than that of assuming the sole power of raising and directing all military force."

A Worcester County convention had proposed a scheme, which was taken up throughout Massachusetts, for separating General Gage from his authority as commander-in-chief of the militia. It was quite simple, and it worked: put overwhelming local pressure to resign on the thirty regimental commanders of the militia, at least half of whom were known to be Tories. The towns would then reorganize their regiments. The rank and file, overwhelmingly radical, would elect their captains, lieutenants and ensigns, who in turn would choose reliable men for field officers--colonels, lieutenant colonels and majors. Theoretically, a third of each reconstituted regiment would be enlisted as "minute men," ready to spring to arms on a minute's notice.

In Gloucester, Colonel John Stevens, who commanded the seven companies, including one from Manchester, of the Sixth Essex Regiment, was a dedicated patriot and quietly resigned in order to further the larger objective. He was a well-to-do merchant of Middle Street, owned the Eastern Point farm, and was over age at sixty-eight anyway. The Sixth was mustered, and John Lee was elected colonel, Peter Coffin and John Low lieutenant colonels, Samuel Whittemore and Dr. Samuel Rogers majors. The next order of the day for the Cape Ann militia was the imparting of an appearance of discipline among the ranks of independent fishermen and yeomen, and an inventory to find out who didn't have musket, bayonet and ammunition.

The North Shore that winter had the experience of British sword-rattling, and the British had the experience of the North Shore. A company of regulars had been encamped on Marblehead Neck in the fall of 1774 to enforce the ban against town meetings not authorized by the governor, but when their presence had no effect on the Headers except to provoke their taunts, they were withdrawn in February and replaced by HMS *Lively,* which anchored in Marblehead Harbor, sent search parties aboard vessels coming and going, and generally made the town aware of the fact that she carried twenty guns. *Lively* was joined on February 26 by a transport which disembarked a regiment of redcoats who marched through town, making it no secret that their objective was provincial artillery said to be at Salem. The alarm raced ahead of them, and when they fetched up at North Bridge, the draw was open, and militia were massing. Colonel Leslie swallowed his pride and wisely marched his regulars back to Marblehead to fife and drum, and the hoots and catcalls of the Yankee Doodles along the route, and ferried them back aboard the transport.

What effect the gathering of the storm clouds had on the fishing industry is difficult to assay, except that it kept fainter hearts in port, without doubt. In April of '74 sixteen owners or sharers in forty-seven Gloucester fishing schooners signed a mutual agreement insuring against loss or salvage of any vessel "taken, totally lost or stranded" while on a voyage to the banks from Gloucester Harbor or Annisquam River between February 24 and October 10; the majority were owned by Daniel Rogers, Isaac Smith, and Epes and Daniel Sargent. Winthrop Sargent, David Pearce and a few others whose holdings brought the fishing fleet to eighty sail did not participate. Fishing schooners at Sandy Bay (probably not more than a couple of dozen) and the thirty sail of merchant vessels at Gloucester were not insured. Neither was Joseph Foster, whose accounts for 1774 and 1775 show him owning only the schooner *Badger*.

All of the insured vessels apparently arrived home safe before the October deadline; it was their last full season with hook and line for ten years. As Babson sized it up:

> The Revolutionary crisis approached, and the commerce and fishery of the town could be no longer pursued. A great majority of the people--comprising the merchants, mechanics, fishermen, and sailors, who depended upon the maritime business of the place for their livelihood--could find no employment in their regular pursuits; and were the more eager, therefore, to prove the sincerity of their declaration, that they would defend their liberties at the expense of all that was dear to them. [2]

Gloucester's annual town meeting on March 6, 1775 was called duly and properly in the name of his Majesty, George the Third. Its most important piece of business was to vote a general muster of all men eligible to bear arms (against his Majesty, George the Third) in response to increasing pressure from the Provincial Congress on towns to provide guns and ammunition for those who owned none of their own. Joseph Foster did not stand for re-election as selectman, but did continue on the committee of correspondence.

The meeting adjourned for two weeks, when Captain Foster was chosen head of a committee to wait on Epes Sargent "and others suspected to be Tories and desire them to attend this meeting at the adjournment to give the Town satisfaction in that particular." (Towns were employing the device of continual adjournment to circumvent Parliament's ban on extraordinary meetings held without the governor's consent.)

As if to give some substance to Gloucester's suspicions of informers in her midst, HMS *Lively* scudded down from Marblehead two days after the creation of this interrogatory committee, on March 22, and seized a schooner recently arrived in the harbor from Dominica, for "breach of the Acts of Trade."

Perhaps spurred by *Lively*'s incursion, the Foster committee completed its assignment and reported to the town on March 27

> that they had waited on him [Sargent] and upon David Plumer and Zebulon Lufkin suspected to be Tories and said Epes Sargent replied that his business would detain him from coming. The other two said they would come ...appeared and after some debate they both declared they highly approved of the proceedings and resolves of the Continental Congress and will defend them.
>
> Voted that this their declaration is satisfactory.
>
> Voted that they will not have any commerce with any suspected to be Tories nor those connected with them and their abettors till they give publick satisfaction that they have quite changed their sentiments.
>
> Whereas Epes Sargent Esqr. has refused to comply with the town's advice.
>
> Voted that no person should have any commerce with him or his abettors.

The object of this proceeding was to starve the elder Sargent out of town. It succeeded, and he escaped to Boston "where even greater indignities were heaped upon him." How David

Plummer, whose quarrels with the customs had set off a succession of trauma which shook up even the governor, came under suspicion of Toryism is a mystery. Likewise with Zebulon Lufkin, of whom it is known only that he moved to Freeport, Maine, during the Revolution, about 1780, and died there in 1813 at the age of ninety-one.

Gloucester had been derelict in acting on the urgent directive of the Provincial Congress the previous autumn that all regiments speedily organize companies of minute men, and on April 10 the meeting voted "that fifty Minute Men be raised [and] be allowed eighteen pence for each half day they meet and that they meet twice a week." The selectmen were directed to spend a hundred pounds for fifty small arms, and to sort out the town's supply of musket balls and have powder cartridges prepared. Captain Nathaniel Warner was assigned to recruit the minute men, and given command of the unit.

The New England spring was coming to life when on the thirteenth of April Captain Ignatius Webber sailed out Gloucester Harbor and turned his helm for the eastward and Spain with a cargo of Indian corn. He was not happy about this voyage. The times were anxious; everyone was on edge; there was no telling what the morrow would bring. The Gloucester selectmen had been against his leaving the country with such an important commodity as corn, but when Captain Webber's Boston owners offered to cancel the voyage if the town would pay charges for storing the corn ashore, they refused. Ignatius, Jr., just eighteen, was in his father's crew, and he recalled in his *Journal* what happened:

> Consequently my father prosecuted the voyage he was engaged in, tho with much reluctance, as there was likely to be a rupture between Great Britain & the Colonies. However on the 13th of April 1775 we set sail leaving our native land with heavy hearts apparently one & all. On the 25th inst. spoke the *Lively* 20 gun ship direct from England the Capt. of which told my father there was great preparation making in England to compell the Colonies to subjection (my father wished himself at

home) & of course it was not a very pleasant hearing to none of us (we were all young before the mast, the eldest not more than twenty-two years of age). We one and all wished ourselves at home again but in vain.[3]

In vain for sure. Young Webber was not to set eyes on the sentinel oaks of Eastern Point again for twenty-eight months.

So, the firelocks were primed, loaded and rammed. The powder was dry. Trigger fingers itched, and nerves were stretched.

6

WAR

This day we were alarmed upon the descent of a party of
Regulars leaving Boston very early. When arrived at
Lexington they killed several persens and did other
mischief.

Only hours before Pastor Daniel Fuller of West Parish
committed the bloody news of the nineteenth of April, 1775, to
his diary, the alarm set in motion by Dr. Warren and Paul
Revere had been relayed through Gloucester's western wilderness, clattered across the Cut on the back of a lathered horse
and was shouted out to a hoof-beat cadence along the dusty
road past Captain Foster's Beaver Dam farm to Sandy Bay.

The men were out fishing, keeping cautiously within sight of
shore. The alarm passed from rider to boatman. Boatman
raised sail, took the wind, and from one craft to another called
out that the British had crossed over to Charlestown and were
striking after the military stores at Concord. The fishermen
made for shore, ran to their homes, grabbed their guns and
were in Gloucester before nightfall, forced-marching for Concord, when another rider galloped up with word that it was all
over: the redcoats were on their way back to Boston, under fire
from the militia all along the route.

This was Wednesday. The full impact of what had happened,
that war had begun, could not have been felt on Cape Ann until
a more complete account arrived from the provincial army
headquarters in Cambridge the next day. On Friday the

Gloucester selectmen called an emergency town meeting. Captain Nathaniel Warner was dispatched "express to Cambridge for advice & see if any fire arms could be purchased" for his minute men. Gloucester was in dire fear of an attack from the sea at any hour. Joseph Foster and Epes Sargent, Jr., were assigned "to joyn with committees of the other seaport towns to consult on measures to be pursued in the present state of affairs."

On Sunday Mr. Fuller sat down in the parsonage study and got out his diary again. It had been a hard day:

> People in this Parish chiefly employed in removing house hold furniture and provision of all kinds from the harbours to this place. Preached, but very few people attended, the flight was on the Sabbath. The Horrid Massacre committed by the fore mentioned Regulars under the command of Col. Smith greatly alarmed us. Never saw such a Sabbath before. The ever to be dreaded Sword of Civil War is drawn. The Lord grant that it may be speedily sheathed again.

On Monday the anxious townspeople streamed into the Middle Street meetinghouse for the second time. While war, be it civil or punitive, had not been officially proclaimed, who could suppose that swords once drawn would be speedily sheathed, or fail to wonder where the next blood would flow? The whole of the coast lay at the mercy of the mightiest navy in the world. None of the colonies possessed a single armed vessel. American merchantmen and fishing schooners were as chickens before the fox. The supply of arms and ammunition was the butt of wry jokes. And Boston swelled at the Neck with ruddy redcoats bursting to have back at the rebels who had given them such a cowardly stinging on the nineteenth, from behind trees and stone walls.

And Gloucester...one man-o'-war no doubt could make a shambles of the Harbor. What if Gage sent in a transport and landed a regiment, with orders to burn the town and subdue Cape Ann?

Inside the meeting house, defense was the first order of concern. The Provincial Congress had urged every town in the colony to elect a committee of safety with extraordinary powers to take measures for its defense. Gloucester chose a thirty-one-member committee with Colonel John Stevens, late of the Sixth Essex, as chairman. Captain Foster was the fourth elected. The meeting directed the committee of safety to join with the selectmen in setting up a close watch all around the Cape Ann shore, day and night. Foster was elected captain of the alarm list, which was the reserve home guard, and the town voted to repair the gun of any man who couldn't afford to have it done himself.

Captain Warner of the minute men evidently had returned from Cambridge in time to report to this meeting that firearms were not to be had there, and furthermore, the Provincial Congress had just agreed that the British must be driven from Boston, and that the raising of an army of 13,600 men would have to take precedence over all local defense considerations. So Warner was ordered by the town to disband and pay off his minute men, whom he had hardly started to organize; instead, all local recruitment must be directed toward enlistments for the Provincial Army at Cambridge.

The provincial call to patriotism only tightened the squeeze on Gloucester. A hundred and ten sail of vessels -- the town's bread and butter -- were bottled up in the inner harbor, and it was the reckless, or desperate, crew that would venture outside. The strategic importance of the harbor, and its vulnerability to attack, and its defenselessness, were obvious. The effect of the British blockade on commerce had already caused some food shortage, and this anxious meeting urged the town to buy pork and flour when and where and if they could be found. Captain Webber's regret at the selectmen's failure to prevent his sailing with his cargo of Indian corn eleven days earlier was now surpassed only by theirs.

This was Monday, April 24. On Tuesday Gloucester Harbor was the setting for a tragic twist of fate.

The brilliant and magnetic Boston patriot leader, Josiah Quincy, Jr., not yet thirty-one, burning with idealism, and with tuberculosis, had sailed on a secret mission to England in September to present the case of the colonies in quarters where it might do some good. On March 15 he left London for home, deathly ill, with information of such significance that he dared not put it in writing. Prostrate in his bunk within sight of Gloucester Harbor, Quincy whispered to a sailor that his last wish was to live long enough to breathe what he had learned in England to Dr. Warren, now president of the Provincial Congress, or Sam Adams, his closest friends. But...

> Last Tuesday arrived here [at Gloucester] the ship *Boston Packet*, Capt. Lyde, from London, in whom came as passenger our good friend and worthy patriot, Josiah Quincy, Jr., Esq., far gone in consumption, who was immediately visited by one of the physicians of this place and other respectable persons; but as he appeared to be actually expiring no assistance could be afforded him, and a few hours put an end to his valuable life. Great care was taken by the selectmen to forward to his friends the account of his death, but as through the perplexity of the times no returns could be obtained from them, his remains were yesterday with great respect interred in the public burying ground of this place.[1]

While General Gage bided his time in Boston, awaiting the reinforcements he continually sought so that he could take the offensive, the Americans under the aging and cautious General Artemus Ward were scrounging supplies, powder, arms and cannon and trying to enlist new men faster than the militia were drifting home to get the crops planted.

All through May at Gloucester the selectmen bought guns and blankets from the people for the recruits, most pressingly for the company which Captain Nathaniel Warner had enlisted in only four days and marched to the Cambridge camp before the month's end. The town met on May 22 and reassigned Joseph Foster from the command of the alarm list to the more important captaincy of the militia company of the west ward; this was the thickest-settled area of the Harbor, and he knew it thoroughly from his years as fire warden. More jealous than ever of the civilian prerogative, the meeting ordered militia captains to muster their units weekly for instructions from the town. All patriotic citizens were directed to inform on anyone who acted suspiciously as if he were getting ready to leave Cape Ann for British Nova Scotia, or anywhere else.

Three days after this meeting, on May 25, Generals William Howe, John Burgoyne and Henry Clinton landed at Boston with the reinforcements Gage had been waiting for -- not as many as he had wanted, but the time had arrived, and he must make his move. The generals began drawing up a battle plan to burst out of Boston. To throw the moral burden on the other side, Gage proclaimed martial law on June 12, pronounced the Americans in open rebellion and offered amnesty to all who would lay down their arms immediately and go home, excepting Sam Adams and John Hancock. The British general addressed his ultimatum to "the infatuated multitudes." It drew a counter-proclamation from the Provincial Congress offering a pardon to all who surrendered to the Massachusetts army, excepting General Thomas Gage and Admiral Samuel Graves.

American headquarters at Cambridge learned on June 15 that Gage was preparing to move out of Boston in three days and occupy Dorchester Heights. It was decided to check him by fortifying the opposing high ground that overlooked Boston from the north, the height of Charlestown peninsula called Bunker Hill. Dr. Warren, who had been voted a major general by the Provincial Congress he presided over but had not yet received his commission, had his misgivings about the wisdom of the tactic, especially in view of the short supplies of ammunition, but the majority of the council of war persuaded him to go along.

After nightfall on June 16, twelve hundred Americans led by Colonel William Prescott moved out from Cambridge and silently crossed Charlestown Neck. But instead of halting them on Bunker Hill, their officers in the confusion of the dark ordered the men on to Breed's Hill, lower by forty feet and looking straight down into the gun barrels of the enemy's fleet and shore batteries in Boston. All night the main force dug and piled up a redoubt on the crown of the wrong hill, while a smaller detachment built a rail fence as a barricade behind which they were expected to protect the flank down the slope to the Mystic River.

Among the diggers was Captain John Rowe's company of sixty-six Cape Ann men and boys (seventeen under twenty-one, the youngest fourteen) from Sandy Bay and The Farms. They had marched from Gloucester four days before, swung at a leisurely clip along the Wenham road toward Cambridge and happened to reach the Mystic at dusk as the main body of Prescott's force was approaching Charlestown. They fell in with Colonel Ebenezer Bridge's Middlesex regiment and soon had picks and spades in hand, pitching up the earthworks under the stars.

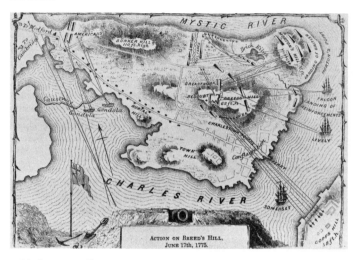

ACTION ON BREED'S HILL,
JUNE 17th, 1775.

At dawn on the seventeenth of June the unsuspecting British were dumbfounded to discover that a fort had sprung up before them during the night. They recovered themselves quickly. General Howe massed twenty-four hundred infantry, marines and grenadiers on the double for a crossing of the Charles River under the guns of Admiral Graves's flotilla. *Lively, Somerset, Falcon, Spitfire, Glasgow* and *Symmetry* were already bombarding the American earthworks and Charlestown Neck, the lifeline to Cambridge whence some four hundred reinforcements were on the march for Breed's Hill.

Among this fresh contingent was Captain Warner's company of Gloucestermen in Colonel Moses Little's Essex regiment.

Some of Warner's men had fallen behind during this forced march, and others broke ranks dodging *Glasgow*'s screaming cannonballs as they sprinted across the exposed Neck in their baptism of fire. When Warner and those who kept with him made the hill on the run, the first British assault wave had landed. He left Ensign Daniel Collins to regroup his stragglers and headed for the redoubt where he had been sent by General Israel Putnam. In the confusion, a third segment of Warner's Gloucester company took a stand under Lieutenant John Burnham outside the southwest corner of the earthwork, on the British left flank, where the enemy marines were attacking.

At daybreak Captain Rowe had been ordered with part of his company to carry the digging tools to the rear. On their return they were told to help finish the rail fence and a small breastwork on the American left, and thus were separated from the rest of their unit, which was in the redoubt under Ensign Ebenezer Cleaveland when the first line of redcoats advanced up the slope.

The fighting was desperate. The sun burned brown behind clouds of dust and acrid powder smoke. The cannonballs from the British artillery and warships hissed up the hill and overhead...or not overhead, ploughing into the ground, rebounding, bouncing with shattering effect. All was a crackle of musketry, against the background of the booming guns, pierced by shouts, curses, unintelligible orders and the awful screams and groans of the wounded and dying. The first wave of British infantry was repulsed. Then the second. On came the third line of foot soldiers to fife and drum, step, step, step by step, up the slope, over the bodies of their comrades.

The defenders were down to the end of their ammunition. Up and over the redoubt this time staggered the third wave of English soldiers, bayonets fixed. For a few moments they fought hand to hand.

Then, overwhelmed, the Americans fell back through the thunder and the smoke and the rain of musket fire.

Roaring to his Gloucestermen to follow him for one more stand at the rail fence, Captain Warner fired at a redcoat. His gun blew up. He grabbed another; the stock flew apart in his hand, split by an enemy ball. He picked up a third gun and felt the rip of a bullet through his britches pocket; it destroyed his pen knife and never scratched him.

From the captured redoubt the British were pouring lead down on the Americans, who stumbled for their lives off the god-forsaken hill. At the rail fence Captain Rowe lost Francis Pool. Josiah Brooks, badly wounded, was killed on the back of William Jumper, trying to carry him away.

Lieutenant Burnham lost two men, both of them indentured servants. Benjamin Smith, bound to Captain William Ellery of Gloucester, took a cannonball and was knocked dead across the feet of Benjamin Webber. Daniel Callahan, indentured to Stephen Low, fell mortally wounded.[2] Webber himself was shot in the arm as he raised his gun to fire the last round he had left. Sergeant Alexander Parran was hit by a ball which shattered his right collar bone and lodged against his shoulder blade; three months later it was removed by a surgeon from the opposite side of his back. Corporal Nymphas Stacy was struck in the leg by a spent ball during the retreat from the right flank with Lieutenant Burnham when they were overrun by the marines. Burnham picked him up and carried him on his shoulders, and when he paused to rest, Stacy thought he felt recovered enough to take a turn, and trudged along carrying his exhausted lieutenant for a spell. Burnham had enlisted in spite of a severe case of supposed tuberculosis; he served through the end of the war and died in New Hampshire at the age of ninety-four. Besides their dead, Rowe's men left behind them on the hill fourteen blankets supplied by the town, as was carefully noted by the selectmen a week later…"lost in the ingagement."

The most lamented casualty in the misplaced and misnamed Battle of Bunker Hill was the strongest critic of the tactic from the outset, Dr. Joseph Warren, the dynamic president of the Provincial Congress who fought as a private though he had been elected a general. In the retreat, while urging one last fusilade, he fell with a ball in his skull.

American casualties were 140 dead, 271 wounded and thirty captured. The British lost 226 professional soldiers killed and 828 wounded. "Damn the rebels, they would not flinch!" cursed an enemy officer.

Two days before the battle, the Congress in Philadelphia had without a dissenting vote elected George Washington commander-in-chief. All six-feet-two of the Virginian arrived in Cambridge on the third of July, and from that moment the fourteen thousand Yankee Doodles camped and quartered there were the Continental Army. From that moment it was no longer a rustic fray, but a war. The British must force the colonies to their knees. The Americans must defend their resolutions and their liberties, as Gloucester town meeting had so bravely voiced it, at the expense of all that was dear to them, and join in measures to extricate themselves from tyranny and oppression. The bargain had been sealed in blood on the soil of Breed's Hill.

General Washington was still sizing up the ragtag ranks of his grandly named army when the Provincial Congress, sitting in Watertown and looking seaward, asked Gloucester, Chelsea and Plymouth to douse the lighthouses in their jurisdictions. Someone had pointed out that the beams of Thacher's, Boston Light and the Gurnet shone impartially on friend and foe and were guiding enemy warships and transports in and out of Boston Bay. In four days Captain Sam Rogers, that fierce doctor with the tooth-pullers, led his militiamen on an amphibious invasion. The results were reported to British headquarters:

> This day (July 6) two or three companies went from Cape Ann to Thatcher's Island, broke the light house glasses and lamps all to pieces, brought away all the oyl together with Captain Kirkwood's family and all he had on the island and put them on the main to shift for themselves.[3]

It was not until Hingham patriots preempted the initiative from Chelsea and went off in a whaleboat from Nantasket and burned Boston Lighthouse to its foundations on July 20 that Admiral Graves, who was not strong on initiative himself, reacted with a circular to mariners:

> This is to give notice, that the light house on Thatcher's island (commonly called Cape Ann Lights) and the light

house at the entrance of Boston harbour, are burnt and destroyed by the rebels. And further notice is given, that all seafaring people be careful that they are not deceived by false lights, which the rebels threaten to hang out, in order to decoy vessels into destruction.

By command of the Admiral   G. Gefferina [4]
Preston, at Boston, July 20, 1775

A month to the day after the battle, on July 17, Gloucester held another town meeting and was relieved to hear that the Provincial Congress had voted to send five hundred men to the defense of the seaports.

His townsmen then voted to send Captain Joseph Foster as the Cape Ann delegate to the Provincial Congress. The session would open in Watertown two days hence, on his forty-fifth birthday. Whether Gloucester had turned to the right man in the moment of its greatest crisis, time would have to tell.

7

PEREGRINE,
SWOOPING FROM ON HIGH

It was late in the first watch, close to midnight, before Captain John Linzee was able to retire to his cabin and account for the day's events in the journal of his Majesty's Sloop of War *Falcon*:

> June 1775   At single anchor in Boston Harbour
> Saturday 17   AM Recd   20 men from the *Sommersett*. Weigh'd and shifted to the entrance of Charlestown River and by springs on our cable got our broad side to bear on the rebells and began to fire with round, grape & small arms. Continued to fire on the rebells till 4 PM at which time Charles Town took fire. Our boats empd carrying wounded men over to Boston.[1]

Springing his cable was getting to be a bit of a bore for the young British naval officer. The purpose of the procedure was to keep his guns as nearly as possible on a land target against an adverse wind or tide or both. It involved running a springline from *Falcon*'s quarter to well ahead on her anchor cable, then heaving in this spring on the capstan to bring her stern around until her guns were broadside to the objective. John Linzee had engaged in the same maneuver on his first arrival at Boston in command of *Beaver*. Then he was in the squadron which brought the Fourteenth and Twenty-ninth regiments and a train of artillery from Halifax on September 30, 1768, that quartering of troops after the *Liberty* affair which so upset the people of Boston. The soldiers landed under the protection of *Beaver*'s guns.

Linzee was only twenty-six then. It was his first visit to America in his own ship. Needing nothing much more than naval glamour and his good looks, he was soon a young lion in the household of John Rowe, a wealthy merchant of Boston who wished politics wouldn't keep interfering with business and his night's sleep. More than money, almost, the childless Mr. Rowe and his dame were attached to Susanna Inman, an orphaned niece of Mrs. Rowe whom they had adopted. Sucky was then fifteen. The dashing English naval officer bided his time; on September 1, 1772, he married her and three days later embarked with her for England in *Beaver*.

If John Rowe was not precisely overjoyed at the return of his son-in-law in his new command, the splendid *Falcon*, which dropped anchor in the harbor on April 16, 1775, he was all smiles as he pressed Sucky to his breast once again and bounced her first-born, Samuel Hood Linzee, on his knee. The infant responded to this salute with a burp, the first genteel sign that he was destined to be a British admiral. His father had made port just in time to be ordered by his new chief, Vice Admiral Samuel Graves, to stand by in *Falcon* to ferry back across the Charles River to Boston the exhausted regulars who had fought a bloody retreat from Lexington to Charlestown.

Falcon and HM Sloop *Nautilus* had arrived from England, as Admiral Graves noted, "in want of many men and stores, and very leaky, having had blowing weather in their passage." *Falcon* was designated a sloop, or sloop of war, and sometimes a corvette; the term as used in the Royal Navy meant not a small vessel with a single spar, but a three-master, usually ship-rigged as *Falcon* was, carrying one deck of guns. She had been built at the navy yard at Portsmouth, England, in 1769, ninety-five feet long overall, twenty-seven feet in beam, 302 tons burthen, and she drew thirteen feet of water. She carried twelve swivel half-pounders and fourteen six- pounder carriage guns which weighed a ton apiece. Seasick and short-rationed, all aboard the leaking warship --not the least the pump gang-- were unspeakably relieved when *Falcon* fetched Thacher's lights.

Graves was a cautious man and bothered by his dwindling stores of meat, a fresh supply from the countryside having been shut off by the gathering provincial army. On April 30th he ordered Captain Linzee to sail *Falcon* to Tarpaulin Cove on the Vineyard Sound shore of Naushon, one of the Elizabeth Islands which are strung out between Buzzard's Bay and Martha's Vineyard. There he was to hinder the islanders from evacuating their large herds to the mainland and to find out if they were disposed to sell some off "for his Majesty's use." As an afterthought, Graves instructed Linzee to proceed first to the Vineyard and capture the ship *Champion*, which was reported to be there or en route there with a cargo of wheat and flour.

Apparently Linzee found that his quarry had not yet arrived at Martha's Vineyard, for on May 5 he anchored at Tarpaulin Cove, where he went on shore with an armed crew and banged on the door of innkeeper Elisha Nye. "You need not be scared," he glowered at mine host, who retorted that "it was enough to scare anybody to see so many men come on shore armed; and the women are fled and to where he knew not." Linzee looked around and told Nye not to sell any of his stock to anyone but him and was rowed back to *Falcon*.

The warship's log locates her in Rhode Island Harbor, or Narragansett Bay, next day, and on the eleventh, at seven in the morning, he hove to off Holmes Hole (Vineyard Haven) and "spoke a ship from Maryland to Cork laden with flower and corn which we detain." It was *Champion*. Captain Linzee put seven men aboard and sent his prize on her way to Boston. First assignment completed.

Early that evening Captain Thomas Wing was sailing by Holmes Hole in his sloop, returning from Nantucket on his regular passage carrying wood from Sandwich, up at the head of Buzzards Bay, when Captain Linzee sent out his barge and seized him. An Indian crew member told the British commander that Captain Jesse Barlow's sloop laden with provisions from the West Indies had arrived in the Bay. Next morning Linzee put fourteen more of his men aboard the captured woodboat; they sailed across Vineyard Sound and the Bay, found the West Indiaman in Dartmouth Harbor (New

Bedford), where she had already unloaded, and took her. The lieutenant in charge of the *Falcon* party divided his crew between his prizes, recrossed the Bay and the Sound and came to anchor off the Vineyard shore.

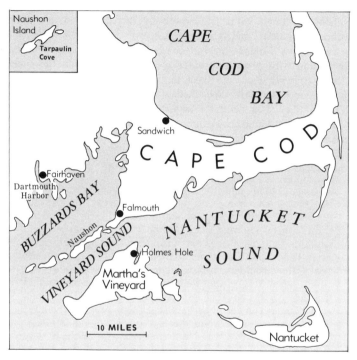

The loss of his vessel did not sit well with Captain Barlow. He rounded up thirty armed men at Dartmouth and another sloop, mounted two swivel guns and made sail in search of the enemy. They came up on the first of *Falcon*'s prizes at anchor, recaptured her without a shot fired and put men aboard. Then these two sloops went after the second of the prizes, which was trying to get sail up as they approached. In a brief fire fight the lieutenant lost his arm, and a gunner and the doctor's mate were wounded. The woodboat, the West Indiaman and fourteen prisoners from *Falcon*'s crew were convoyed triumphantly into Fairhaven.

Meanwhile, after dispatching his about-to-be-bungled expedition in the prize woodboat, Captain Linzee had sailed from Holmes Hole for Tarpaulin Cove. On the way he spoke two schooners laden with fish, which he brought to with a few rounds of gunfire and sent to Boston with prize crews. For two more weeks *Falcon* hovered in the Cove. Once she prowled forth and with a warning salvo of six-pounders took the sloop *Three Friends*, from the West Indies with a cargo of wine and fruit. A few days later four shots stopped a brig from Dominica, and on May 25 a brace of sixes bagged a schooner from St. Vincent. It is doubtful that any of these victims knew there was a war on.

On May 26 Elisha Nye, the innkeeper at Tarpaulin Cove, and the *Falcon* commander met for the second time:

> A sloop came into the Cove, with about twenty passengers, men, women, & children in great distress for provisions, and made application to me for supplyes. Capt. Linzey knowing that, (his boat having boarded her) sent his boat on shore, and forbid my letting them have any. Then I advised them to apply to Capt. Linzey, and see if they could not prevail upon him to let them have some; accordingly they went; afterwards the captain of the sloop told me, that he absolutely refused them, and said "Damn the dog that would let them have any; and if they were not gone immediately, he would sink them." Upon which, they set sail immediately without any supplyes. [2]

A schooner was sent from Boston to take on two hundred sheep from the west end of Naushon. Linzee directed an armed crew in herding them aboard, assuring the shepherds he would pay for them. They shrugged their shoulders and replied that "they should not molest him as most of the owners of the sheep were of the people called Quakers and that they would not be concerned in defending themselves or their interest by force of arms but would treat him with civility."

That evening the ship's surgeon came ashore at Tarpaulin Cove to pick out a leg of mutton from Elisha Nye's flock. He had introduced himself the day before by having his men stove in three of the island's boats. He was beside himself when he found out that Nye had let his sheep out of the pen and they were out there somewhere in the dark. The doctor cursed him roundly and threatened to carry him aboard *Falcon* as a prisoner. At last Nye agreed to go into the night and try to round up a lamb or two. "Well, damn you! Make haste!" shouted the doctor (he was very put out at losing his surgeon's mate to the Dartmouth people) and "swang his sword" over the innkeeper's head.

Elisha made haste, all right. He slipped away in the murk, found an unstove boat and sailed to Falmouth. There he aroused the people with his tale of royal rustling on the islands, which at the time pastured a rich reserve of some ten thousand head of sheep, cattle and horses.

When the Falmouth minute men slipped ashore at Tarpaulin Cove in the pre-dawn, "they placed themselves in the bushes & lay undiscovered," in the words of Stephen Nye. "In the morning the boat came on shore with the doctor, boatswain, &c; whom they might have taken had they not expected the capn ashore soon; however the boat soon went back without going to the house & both vessels immediately weighed anchor & went down to Homes' Hole where they lay last night at anchor."

On the second of June *Falcon* and the sheep schooner were back in Boston harbor with their spoils, topped off with six of Elisha Nye's calves, four of his sheep, four quarters of his veal, and his gun, "taken out of my house by the doctor of the ship, of great value."

Two weeks passed, and John Rowe's son-in-law was pitching round and grape at John Rowe's countrymen up on the crest of Breed's Hill. The day after the battle Captain Linzee bullied through the streets and alleys of Boston with four press gangs and orders from Admiral Graves to seize carpenters, caulkers, and seamen and hold them prisoners until the shipwrights, who had that morning refused to work on a brig being built for the crown, returned to the yard.

One who got in the way of Linzee's press was the boy Peter Edes, son of Benjamin Edes, who published the radical *Boston*

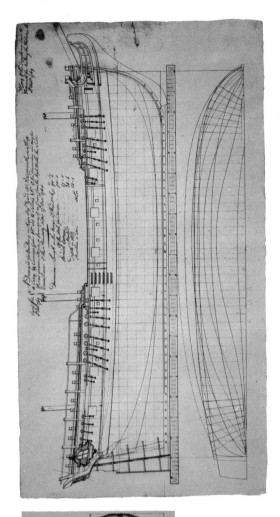

Admiralty lines of HM Sloop of War *Falcon*, built at Portsmouth, England, in 1769.

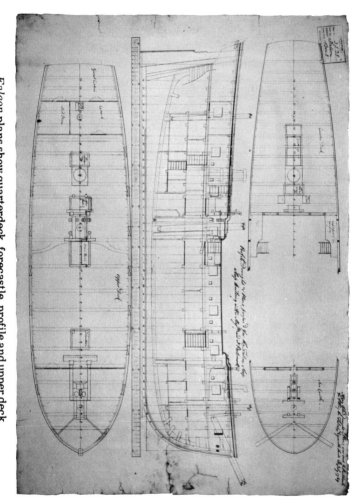

Falcon plans show quarterdeck, forecastle, profile and upper deck.

Gazette with John Gill. His father had fled Boston and set up in Watertown, leaving Peter behind to watch the shop, where he was collared. *Falcon*'s commander damned him and offered to knock him down and Peter later lamented to his diary, "to fall into the hands of a more worthless, infamous fellow, I don't wish my enemies." The impressed workmen were released after a few days when construction of the brig resumed. The sailors, however, landed in the Royal Navy working ship against their own country.

To the eastward the New Hampshire patriots had been making life so difficult for John Wentworth, their royal governor, that he deemed it prudent finally to retreat from Portsmouth to the security of HMS *Scarborough* in the Piscataqua River. Graves ordered Linzee on June 20 to sail in company with the transport *Resolution* and secure the cannon and artillery stores from Fort William and Mary in the river. The two vessels returned to Boston in ten days with fifty-seven big guns, and round and grape shot to keep them red-hot for a week, but no powder. That had been quietly borrowed on the night of the previous December 13 after Paul Revere galloped through the snow from Boston to Durham and warned John Sullivan that the British were on the point of reinforcing the fort with two regiments. The burly future general and his plough-boys floated down the river in their gundalows in the dark of night, waded ashore, overpowered the slim garrison and carried ninety-seven kegs of gunpowder and a hundred small arms back to Durham, where they stashed them in a pit under the church pulpit.

For several days *Falcon* lay at anchor in Nantasket Gut of Boston Harbor, between Hull and Peddocks Island, under instructions from the admiral to seize all suspicious-looking rebel craft passing between Nantasket Roads and Hingham Bay.

Then arrived new orders more to John Linzee's combattive taste. They were from the business end of Lord North's displeasure with the American boycott of English goods which had so provoked the crown that in February the prime minister sent to Parliament a bill declaring Massachusetts to be in rebellion, forbidding the New England colonies from trading with any nation but Britain and the British West Indies after July 1, and barring them completely from the North Atlantic fisheries after July 20. The penalty for infractions was forfeiture of vessel and cargo. North knew where to tighten the screws; the codfishery alone was responsible for nearly half of the remittances of the northern colonies for British manufactures. The royal bill was desperately opposed by the Whigs, but in vain. On March 21 the New England Restraining Act was passed by the House of Lords and signed by George the Third. The twenty-one peers who voted in the minority were horrified at its implica tions:

> We dissent because the attempt to coerce, by famine, the whole body of the inhabitants of great and populous provinces, is without example in the history of this or, perhaps, of any civilized nation, and is one of those unhappy inventions to which Parliament is driven by the difficulties which daily multiply upon us from an obstinate adherence to an unwise plan of government. We do not know exactly the extent of the combination against our commerce in New England and the other colonies; but we do know the extent of the punishment we inflict upon it, which is universal, and includes all the inhabitants: among these, many are admitted to be innocent, and several are alleged by ministers to be, in their sense, even meritorious. That government which attempts to preserve its authority by destroying the trade of its subjects, and by involving the innocent and guilty in a common ruin, if it acts from a choice of such means, confesses itself unworthy; if from inability to find any other, admits itself wholly incompetent to the ends of its institution.[3]

Three days in anticipation of the effective date of coercion by famine, on July 17, Admiral Graves ordered Captain Linzee to put to sea in *Falcon* as soon as possible

> and cruize between Cape Cod and Cape Anne in order to carry into execution the late Acts for restraining the trade of the Colonies and to seize and send to Boston all vessels with arms, ammunition, flour, grain, salt, me-

lasses, wood, &c. &c. And you are hereby required and directed to look into the Harbour within the Bay of Boston, and to anchor therein and sail again at such uncertain times as you think are most likely to deceive and intercept the trade of the Rebels. And whereas there are many reports of armed vessels being fitted out to annoy the trade of his Majesty's loyal subjects: In case of your meeting any such rebel pyrates either in harbour or at sea, you are hereby required and directed to use every means in your power to take or destroy them.[4]

Falcon cruised off Race Point for several days without encountering a prize until July 25, when she stopped the schooner *Industry*, from West Indies for Salem with rum and sugar, and sent her into Boston, where Captain John Fisk was permitted to sell his cargo for the pleasure of his captors and then to proceed home in his vessel. *Falcon* returned to Nantasket Roads and was ordered back to sea on July 30 to convoy the transport *Russia Merchant* twenty leagues to the eastward of Cape Cod on her voyage to England, then to go on station between Cape Ann and the Isles of Shoals in Ipswich Bay to intercept ammunition and provisions that might be destined for the Americans.

It was the bad luck of Captain John Fletcher to come within sight of Gloucester from a West Indian voyage in the schooner *Byfield* just as he came within *Falcon*'s sight, returning from her convoy of *Russia Merchant*. It was his worse luck to have aboard, besides rum and sugar, a swivel gun (he was one of those ardently patriotic Masons who founded Tyrian Lodge). Linzee seized him and took him in tow. This was August 1. At six the next morning, cruising nine or ten miles southeast of Cape Ann, *Falcon* stopped the wood-coasting schooner *Deborah* with a round across her bow, and set both of her prizes on a course for Boston.

Three days passed without event while *Falcon* hovered offshore in Ipswich Bay. On the morning of August 5 Linzee bore in for shore and came to anchor at the edge of Squam Bar off Peter Coffin's beach, sounding as he approached, for *Falcon* drew a deep two fathoms and the sands are ever restless with the current sweeping in and out of Squam River.

Captain Linzee could all but smell the sizzling leg of mutton which since time forgotten has titillated English nostrils. He had spied the raw material browsing in the thin grass along the dazzling dunes that rimmed the beach, in company with a few cattle which had wandered off Coffin's pasture through the strip of woods that held back the sand hills from suffocating the rich forage. He had also inspected a schooner at anchor in the tidal stream at the entrance to Lobster Cove; she appeared a West Indiaman worth the taking.

A captain from Newburyport who had been pressed into service aboard *Falcon* advised Linzee that Peter Coffin was not the man to stand around with his hands in his pockets while the British navy helped itself to his stock; his slaves and farm hands were crack shots from practising on the foxes which preyed on his lambs and chickens, besides which, a couple of companies of militia were said to be guarding on this side of the cape. [5]

Linzee ignored this unwelcome advice and directed his lieutenant to take a couple of dozen men in to the beach and cut out a few of the best sheep. [6]

Peter Coffin had been watching *Falcon* closely since she first appeared in Ipswich Bay, and when the warship approached and prepared to anchor he sent word through West Parish and across the river to Annisquam for help. Then he deployed his half a dozen slaves and hired hands behind his dunes, and waited. Smart salt marsh duckhunter that he was, he may have shooed a few enticing samples of his herd out on the beach in plain view from asea as decoys.

The pinnace was lowered from *Falcon* and moved away. The rowers bent to the oars, blades flashing in the sun. Their officer stood above them. The steersman braced himself against his sweep in the stern. On they came, surging forward with each swinging stroke, into the light surf. The boat had not fully grounded in the sand when a shout from behind the dunes reached their ears, "WHEEL BY BATTALIONS! FIRE BY GENERATIONS!" ... followed instantly by a rattle of musketry. Balls zinged by their heads and spit with white *thunks* into the knee-deep water. One only found a mark, and that ricocheted harmlessly off the astonished lieutenant's sword belt plate.

Visualizing a company of rebels behind the dunes, the officer barked at his rowers to back water, which they did without further urging, and quicker than they came. They sprinted for *Falcon* ahead of the next volley, mute and muttonless. [1]

John Linzee had been regarding this turnabout through his glass, not without annoyance; but since he had no notion how many lay hidden in the enfilade of the dunes and the woods in back of them, and could see reinforcements running up from either end of the beach, he decided he must forego his mutton. He directed the pinnace, when it came within hail, to row up into Squam River and cut out the deep-laden West Indiaman anchored there. He would have something if he could not have lamb.

Upon inspection, the schooner was found to be deep-laden with sand from the beach the boarding party had recently evacuated, the fine white kind favored by thrifty housewives for scrubbing their kitchen floors. The pinnace returned and was hoisted aboard, and *Falcon* weighed anchor, made sail and resumed patrol.

Captain Linzee, to put it mildly, was in a bad frame of mind. Twice since the war broke out he had been outsmarted by rebel bumpkins. This time his nose had been tweaked before an audience of a hundred of his crew. A proud officer of his Majesty's Royal Navy in such pique could be an unpredictable adversary, and a dangerous one when he was armed with fourteen six-pounder carriage guns, twelve swivels and an ingrained sense of vengeance.

8

THE *FALCON* FIGHT

On Tuesday last
A falcon, towering in her pride of place,
Was by a mousing owl hawk'd at and kill'd.
Macbeth II, iv

The coming of the grey dawn was the signal to get under way, and at 5 a.m. sharp, Tuesday, the eighth of August, 1775, his Majesty's Sloop of War *Falcon* weighed anchor and made sail. That night she had lain a cable's length off the dark ledges of Norman's Woe at the entrance to Gloucester Harbor, riding out a stiff breeze which was unusual for midsummer on this coast. It was a new day now, and Captain John Linzee had his orders to stop everything American afloat in enforcement of the restraining acts of Parliament.

At eight, as the forenoon watch was piped, a fresh pair of eyes was at the masthead and the shout came down: two sail to the eastward! Give chase, Linzee ordered his sailing master, Robert Arnold.

The late night gale had moderated to a light variable wind, most probably from the southwest as it is liable to be on an August morning along the North Shore above Boston, and it was noon before it freshened sufficiently to bring *Falcon* up with the slower of the two, which came to heel without a shot fired. She was a schooner bound for Salem from Hispaniola, or French Haiti. Linzee sent Master Arnold and a prize crew on board in the tender, with orders to keep company with *Falcon*.

Then he came about and went after the larger, which besides being the faster, had taken advantage of the several minutes it had required to bring *Falcon* aback and put master and men over the side, borne off her course (which was likewise for Salem from the West Indies), and was running with a fair breeze on her quarter into Gloucester Harbor.

The wily skipper of this second fugitive was familiar with the inner recesses of Gloucester and knew what he was about. Whether it occurred to him that he might be bait for a trap, or whether he was merely following the course of native instinct, he boiled in with the air at his back, along inside the protecting length of Eastern Point, scudded past Ten Pound Island and through the narrows between the old grassed-over fort of the French Wars and Rocky Neck's sheep pasture, slid by the wharves where the fishing schooners and the merchantmen lay idle, just missed the rocks of Duncan's Point, skirted the end of Epes Sargent's wharf on the west of the channel that opened into Vincent's Cove, and brought his West Indies voyage to a jolting end hard aground in the shoal water betwixt the cove and little Five Pound Island. [1]

The extraordinary flight of the West Indiaman into Gloucester Harbor had naturally directed the attention of all who witnessed it to the pursuer, which soon was recognized with some dismay to be a British sloop of war, hove to with her main and mizzen yards aback, broad off Norman's Woe. To the seaward of her could be made out a Yankee schooner, also hove to, obviously her prize.

It was about half past noon. An alert citizen ran into the vestibule of the Middle Street meetinghouse and leaped for the bell rope. The southerly air carried the wild clamorous clanging across the Cape. Men had been alerted by reports of *Falcon*'s rebuff at Coffin's beach three days before, and had watched her offshore. Something was up. They dropped whatever they were doing, went for their guns and took off for the Harbor.

Joseph Foster was home from the July session of the Provincial Congress in Watertown, and he was captain of the west ward militia. He studied the enemy warship lying just outside the harbor with one prize, and the vessel she had been chasing, aground deep in the pocket of the inner harbor, sized up the ugly prospects, and took charge.

Falcon's log describes the early afternoon weather as hazy, and the breeze as fresh. The wind may have backed to southeast, off the Atlantic, and in any case it was blowing downharbor. To poke the bow of a three hundred-ton square-rigged ship into this potential *cul-de-sac* lacking any knowledge of the freak winds, calms and currents of a nearly landlocked bay, of hidden shoals, ledges and underwater wrecks, of forts, guns and rebels, would be madness. All the same, frustration and ill temper got the better of John Linzee. He would follow the rabbit down the hole and catch it by the tail. But first he must have someone who knew the hole.

In his recent cruising off the coast, Linzee had impressed no less than ten Americans as seamen, including that Newburyport captain, but none, it seems, would acknowledge a thorough enough acquaintance with Cape Ann Harbor to be relied upon. Just as he was wavering in his resolve, *Falcon*'s commander noticed two fishermen in their dory, near his ship, plying their lines unconcernedly off Dog Bar. The thought was father to the deed, and the likeliest of the pair, Babson by name, was brought before him. His descendant, the historian, related their conversation:

> William Babson, a man between fifty and sixty years old, of infirm health, was required to act as pilot. Thoroughly imbued with the patriotic sentiment of his townsmen, he tried to avoid the hateful task, pleading poor eyesight. "Who lives there?" asked Linzee, pointing to the house of Solomon Parsons, which stood on rising ground on the west side of the harbor, and was used for one of the marks for running in. The poor fisherman faltered out the name of the owner. "Now," said Linzee, "I find you can see well enough, and if you let this ship strike bottom, I will shoot you on the spot." Under such compulsion the ship was brought to safe anchorage; but the unhappy pilot was brought to the grave, for he died shortly, in consequence, it is thought, of the shock of his nervous system, occasioned by sorrow that he should have been made an

instrument, however unwittingly, in the cruel work of Linzee on that day.[2]

The safe anchorage to which the unfortunate William Babson brought his enemy was squarely before the town between Stage Head and Ten Pound Island. Master Arnold followed with the prize schooner and anchored outside *Falcon*. It was one in the afternoon. There had been no visible reaction from Gloucester, not a shot, not a sound but the incessant tolling of the bell from the meetinghouse, whose steeple spiked high and solitary above the plain clapboard houses which crowded in tiers back up the rising ground behind the wharves.[3]

From the warship the shrill of the bos'n's pipe, the shouted orders with all their h's dropped, the squeak of blocks were wafted by the breeze across the water. People could see the tars aloft in the yards, clewing up sail even as the wind set *Falcon* back on her cable, stern to the town. The deck gang had bent halyards from the main and fore masts to the bow and stern beckets of the smallest of the boats nested amidships, by appearances the jolly boat, and was hauling away before taking up the slack of the yard tackles which would swing it out and over the rail. Then on to the next one, as Captain Linzee had ordered all three put over -- jolly boat, long boat and pinnace. The spring line had been run out a stern port, carried forward and bent to the anchor cable, more cable let go and stopped, and the capstan crew was walking the line in, backs to it, slowly winching her stern around, slowly, slowly swinging *Falcon* and seven of her fourteen six-pounders broadside to Gloucester.

The *rat-a-tat-tat* of drum beat snapped across the water, a snarl of malice, calling to quarters. Gun crews took stations. Ports swung open. Lashings were cast off smartly, carriages run in, tampions yanked from muzzles, powder cartridges hustled up on the double from the magazine. The deck now was crowded with armed men, bayonets glinting in the sun, waiting to drop into the boats which ranged alongside, each set up with a swivel gun in the bow. *Falcon*'s first officer, Lieutenant Thornborough, consulted briefly with Captain Linzee and then swung over the side himself.

Ashore, Captain Foster had voiced in language that all could understand the determination of all not to give up the grounded schooner, and had by the consent of all taken command. The town had not a solitary cannon in service, and only two ancient swivel guns, which he told those who knew how to serve them to mount on anything that would pass for carriages, and be quick about it. His own militia company wheeled their gun on the run down to Duncan's Point, not far below his house, where they emplaced it behind such available cover as afforded in the vicinity of Sargent's Wharf. As others came running up, he deployed them along the wharves on the Point, behind sheds and hogsheads and in the mud of the docks behind the hulls of grounded schooners. This would be the first ambush.

In the hope of catching the enemy landing party in a cross fire, Foster directed Captain Bradbury Sanders and his company to haul the second swivel up on the high ground to the east of Vincent's Cove, not a stone's throw above the Sanders house at Rose Bank.[4] They found cover along the shore to the northwest of Five Pound Island where they could get a clear view of the grounded schooner, which lay deserted by her crew about a hundred yards out in the harbor, her masts at an angle where she had heeled on one bilge, her lower sails in a heap on deck.

The urgent tolling of the First Parish meetinghouse bell must by now have been taken up by the other churches, and it clanged one clear message round Cape Ann: we have visitors who mean us no good. The alarm brought on the run every ablebodied man who was not in Cambridge with the army. One of these was Peter Lurvey, huckleberrying with his wife and a neighbor child, little Mary Millett, on Pearce's Island in Squam River when he heard the distant alarm bell. He kissed his missus, jumped in his skiff, rowed across the river, sprinted the two miles to his house up on the wild heath of Dogtown, seized his flintlock and was off down the road to the Harbor.[5]

Gloucester watched, and waited.

The last man in Captain Linzee's assault party climbed over the side and dropped into his assigned boat. They pushed away from *Falcon,* into the stream. The rowers dug in, making neat swirls of water, and bent to it. A few strokes brought them up to the others. Lieutenant Thornborough gave the signal, and his flotilla moved away from the mother ship, strung out in line, oars flashing in an easy beat, into the mid-channel.

Thornborough was in the lead, probably in the jolly boat, with six marines at the oars. In his wake were the pinnace and the long boat, fifteen men in each. This was the count of a watcher on shore. The lieutenant had recruited a mixed force, as he had to, for it took nearly half of *Falcon*'s complement to make up the expedition. He had seven of the marines who served the permanent triple duty on every British naval vessel of soldier-ing, sailoring and keeping discipline among a rough crew. And he had ten pressed Americans, including four from Gloucester -- hardly a reliable contingent on such a mission. The balance of his party consisted of a brace of quartermasters, a sailmaker, several ordinary seamen, the steward, the captain of the forecastle, the servant of the always disgruntled doctor, two young midshipmen and *Falcon*'s master gunner, Justin Budd. This Budd was a veteran of the first naval engagement of the war; he had been taken prisoner when the patriots at Machias, Maine, sailed forth in two small craft on June 11 and captured the diminutive British armed schooner *Margaretta* during a brief but brisk action in which twenty-five men were killed or wounded. Gunner Budd had been jailed in Worcester but was so clever as to escape, along with several Tories, and had made his way to Boston and aboard *Falcon,* where he was more than welcomed.

The ship's boats surged on, almost soundless save for the click-clacking rhythm of the sweeps in the oarlocks, the audible gurgle of their hulls, the swish of dripping blades on the backswing. A pageantry in red and blue. A royal bristle of bayonets. A parliamentary proclamation of brass in buckles and buttons. A ministerial menace of cold English steel, glinting in a hot New England sun.

Onward and inward rowed *Falcon*'s boats, into the narrows between Rocky Neck's stone-studded pasture, fluffed with placid sheep, and Gloucester's old grassgrown fort, relic of

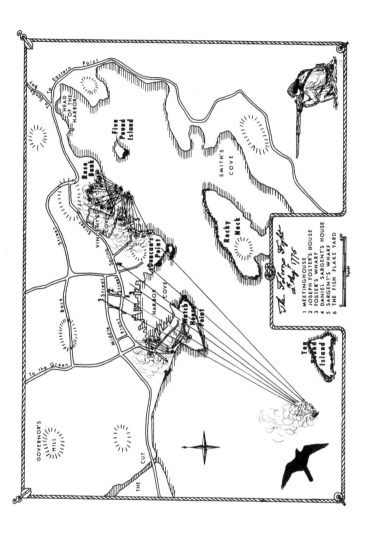

The Harbor Fight
at Aug. 1775

1 MEETINGHOUSE
2 JOSEPH FOSTER'S HOUSE
3 FOSTER'S WHARF
4 DANIEL SARGENT'S HOUSE
5 SARGENT'S WHARF
6 THE FISH FLAKE YARD

To Eastern Point
To Sandy Bay
HEAD OF THE HARBOR
Five Pound Island
SMITH'S COVE
Rose Bank
VINE Street
Duncan's Point
Rocky Neck
Squam Street
Pleasant Street
Front Street
Middle Street
Back Street
HARBOR COVE
Watch House Point
To the Green
To Ten Pound Island
GOVERNOR'S HILL
THE CUT

happier days when every loyal yeoman loved his liege. Now they were in the calm water of the lee, coursing easily through the tide, past the mouth of Harbor Cove where the crude vessels of the colonists crowded in the docks. The wharves looked to be deserted. Ahead, a few strokes on, the fleeing schooner had fetched up flying on the Five Pound Island flats and bilged. Her sails were in a heap on deck. No sign of her crew. Up in the town the bell in the white, spiking steeple of the church pealed insistently, incessantly.

Onward rowed the Royal Navy, into the deepest pocket of the second deepest harbor in Massachuetts Bay, three thousand miles from home, to administer a small lesson in large obedience. Not a bloody Yank in sight. A covey of cowards. A quail shoot.

Now the three boatloads were abreast of stony Duncan's Point. Just ahead, almost under their plowing bows, the loot lay helpless on her keel.

At that exact moment the stocky figure of Joseph Foster, sea captain, smuggler, politician and patriot, rose up in silhouette against the August sky. He slashed the air and bellowed to his fishermen and his farmers, and from behind those silent rocks and wharves the flintlocks and fowling pieces and the one rusty old swivel gun of his first ambush barked and roared.

Solomon Parsons, owner of Will Babson's landmark, drew a bead on a figure standing prominently in the bow of one of the boats and was squeezing his trigger when it shouted: "Don't shoot! I'm Duncan Piper, Duncan Piper!" In that split second Parsons recognized his friend who had been impressed a few days earlier at sea, and lowered his gun with trembling hands.

This first volley from shore was not devastating. It was returned sharply from the boats, which plunged on as the oarsmen discovered strength in fear. Within perhaps a minute or less they were alongside the grounded schooner, and Lieutenant Thornborough led his men scramblng aboard through the stern-gallery windows. They took cover below decks amidst the spoils they had come for, and wondered how they would get away themselves, for whenever a jack poked his head out of a hatch some Gloucester sharpshooter took a shot at it.

Back on his quarterdeck facing the town, Captain Linzee had the evidence of his ears that his plan to intimidate these simple fishermen into handing over his prize had gone awry. He had supposed that one boatload of armed men could board the schooner and run their hawser round her windlass. The others would then merely carry the two anchors they came with into the deeper water, and the crew on board would kedge her out the harbor, first with one, and after that was fetched in, the other, while the marines and the swivels held the rebels at their distance and the population looked quaveringly down the throats of *Falcon*'s guns.

But not so, plainly not so. Well, he still held his ace, the broadside. Let us give them a taste of cast iron in the round, and they will run like partridges. Firing orders were barked. Seven cartridges were rammed in seven breeches. Seven solid balls were dropped down seven muzzles, and rammed, and then the wads. Touchholes were primed. Seven carriages were run out.

FIRE!

Seven spurts of flame seen even in the bright sun, a broken roar rebounding, crashing between the shores, seven pouncing puffs of smoke. Her deck and bulwarks all but obscured, *Falcon* rolled back on her cable, as seven six-pound cannonballs wobbled and hissed into Gloucester.

Foster and Sanders exhorted their townsmen, whose shooting, with practice, was sharpening. Hot lead ripped through Thornborough's thigh, and three of his men were hit. His entire force was pinned down by a semicircle of fire from shore. They were prisoners aboard their prize. The trap Joseph Foster had built so quickly around the bait had sprung.

One broadside after another *Falcon* flung into the town, syncopated by the snap and crack of her swivel guns scattering an indiscriminate hail of half-pound shot. The almost encircling hills, which had been settled by Englishmen a century and a half before, echoed to the salvoes of Englishmen bent on destroying their cousins' descendants. A pungent ground fog of gunsmoke crept over the water and enveloped the wharves, insinuated through the alleys and into the open windows of summer, and the waterfront reeked and sneezed with the sharpness of it.

All that hazy hot August afternoon the six-pounders and swivel shot whistled across the harbor. They crashed into the wood buildings, rolled up the lanes and ploughed new furrows in the vegetable gardens, but the only living target any of them connected up with (partly because so many citizens had evacuated their homes) was William Kinsman's hog, which suffered as neatly as if by the butcher's blade the removal of its backbone while grubbing beside the Deacon's house, midway on Front Street.

One cannonball invaded Daniel Sargent's house, second east from Duncan Street on the water side of Spring Street. It was retrieved and enshrined.[6] Another soared across Middle Street and struck the First Parish meetinghouse. It buried itself in the girt of the front gallery, not to be discovered for another seventeen years by workmen undoing the damage of "the waste of time, and the wanton spoilations of Captain Lynzey." It, too, was preserved,[7] along with a high-colored contemporary interpretation of his deviltry:

> Linzee stood himself, with diabolical pleasure to see what havock his cannon might make. "Now," said he, "my boys, we will aim at the damn'd presbyterian church -- Well, my brave fellows, one shot more and the house of God will fall before you." While he was thus venting his hellish rage, and setting himself as it were against heaven, the Almighty was on our side; not a ball struck or wounded an individual person, although they went through our houses in almost every direction when filled with women and children.[8]

Among those women and children of Gloucester were Captain Foster's wife and their infant son, William, one week old. Lydia was still recovering from childbirth, nursing her baby -- so says family tradition -- when a *Falcon* six-pounder smashed through the wall of the Middle Street house and came to rest near the head of her bed.[9]

By his own account, John Linzee was less consumed with hellish rage than he was with a desire to rescue his landing party:

I very soon observed the rebels paid very little attention to the firing from the ship, and seeing their fire continued very heavy in the schooner the Lieutt. had boarded, I made an attempt to set fire to the Town of Cape Anne and had I succeeded I flatter myself would have given the Lieutt. an opportunity of bringing the schooner off, or have left her by the boats, as the rebels attention must have been to the fire.[10]

The wind favored a good brisk conflagration, and to that end Linzee sent a party of six in one of his remaining small boats to land on the beach on the south shore of Watch House Neck and touch off the wooden flakes where the fishermen spread their codfish to dry. The breeze ought to carry the flames up from the waterfront into the town, he figured. But he was betrayed -- or so he thought:

But an American, part of my complement, who had always been very active in our cause, set fire to the powder before it was properly placed; our attempt to fire the town therefore not only failed but one of the men was blown up, and the American deserted. A second attempt was made to set fire to the town, but did not succeed. The rebels coming to the Fort obliged the four men to leave it.[11]

While his incendiaries were ashore, Captain Linzee had suspended his cannonading. Now he paced his quarterdeck, stared at the fools flailing the ocean with their oars as they pulled away from the beach in a rain of lead, and listened morosely to the intermittent cracks of musketry from the direction of his trapped expeditionary force.

I then began a second time to fire on the town, but the houses being built of wood, could do no great damage.

At about four o'clock, after nearly three hours under fire, the wounded Lieutenant Thornborough was rowed back to *Falcon* in a small skiff which fortunately had been towed in behind one of his landing boats. One or two of his men had been able to get him out of the embattled schooner and into this craft and away, under the cover of a heavy fire from Master Arnold's crew, who remained trapped with the rest of their party in the grounded vessel. The groaning lieutenant reported to Linzee the plight of his sailing master and the others, adding, with a grimace, that the three good boats they went off in -- abandoned as they were on the exposed side of the schooner -- were shot so full of holes by the rebels that they must be useless.

On my being acquainted with the situation of the master I sent the prize schooner to anchor ahead of the schooner the master was in, and veer alongside to take him and people away, who were much exposed to the rebels fire; but for want of an officer to send in her it was not performed, the vessel not anchored properly; And as, I apprehend, the master could not see any prospect of being assisted, and a heavy fire from the rebels, and numbers coming to their assistance, delivered himself up about 7 in the evening with the gunner, fifteen seamen, seven marines, one boy and ten prest Americans. The schooner I sent in to assist the master, on his going ashore ran in and was retaken by the rebels. I am inclined to think the company of the schooner had been hid and took that opportunity of retaking the vessel that was sent to assist the master. After the master was landed I found I could not do him any good, or distress the rebels by firing. I therefore left off.

The falconer's bold strategy that day had cost him thirty-five men taken prisoner, including seven crack marines, his sailing master, his master gunner, several of his best non-commissioned officers, among them two of his quartermasters wounded, and one John Molloy, said to be formerly from Salem, killed. [12] He got his lieutenant back on board, rather seriously wounded, but he left behind, besides nearly half his ship's complement, the three best boats he had, [13] three first-rate swivel guns, a quantity of small arms, ammunition, powder, six-pound round shot totalling in Parson Fuller's estimation almost three hundred, and all the precious powder it took to fire them off, the richly laden West Indiaman he captured and had safely under *Falcon*'s wing, and the one he sent her in to rescue.

Pride of place had lost a towering falcon the day, and as Admiral Graves unhappily reported to Philip Stevens, Secretary of the Admiralty in London: "It is so difficult to procure British seamen that the loss becomes considerable. At present they cannot be replaced with Europeans and experience shews Americans are not to be trusted." [14]

Gloucester lost two sons by British musket balls. Benjamin Rowe was killed instantly, and Peter Lurvey, the patriotic berrypicker, died soon after he was struck. A third man was hurt slightly. Various houses and the church proudly displayed their wounds. It is not known that any caught fire, though the rumors flew so fast and far that the next day Second Lieutenant Benjamin Craft of Manchester, with the army at Cambridge, wrote in his journal: "Just now I hear that a man-of-war has burnt twenty-five houses at Cape Ann and that eight of the British were killed and wounded and twenty-six of the man-of-war's men taken prisoner." [15]

The sun was setting through a halo of battle smoke over Stage Head and Fishermen's Field when Captain Linzee called it quits. Soon *Falcon*'s lanterns were shining, but not upon deck scenes of victory where she lay, still at anchor off the west ledges of Ten Pound Island. The victory was Gloucester's, with her alarm list, and her two rusty swivels.

That night, while *Falcon*'s lights glimmered glumly out in the harbor through a downpour of rain, the victors rejoiced in Jimmy Prentice's tavern, with supper, rum, and thirteen buckets of toddy ... on the town.

"Tradition," averred John J. Babson a hundred years later, "has handed down the name of no one in particular as the hero of the day, for the reason that all acted the part of patriotic citizens in defense of their country and their homes. It has, however, always been asserted that Captain Joseph Foster, then a man of middle age, who had been in early life a fisherman and sailor, and afterwards a sea-captain and merchant, was the leader of his townsmen on that occasion, and displayed great energy and excellent judgment from the beginning to the end." [16]

As the first light of a new dawn brought the sentinel oaks on Eastern Point into profile against the grey Atlantic sky, *Falcon* weighed anchor. John Linzee opened his log and dipped his quill:

at 5 AM began to warp out of the Harbour.

9

THEIR SPIRIT SEEMS EQUAL
TO THEIR ABILITIES

Captain Foster's victorious Gloucestermen slept on their arms if they slept at all that August night, and the sight and sounds of *Falcon* warping ingloriously out of their harbor as the rosy dawn fingered the east raised shouts of joy and hoots of derision from the shore, tempered with relief.

The relief was the eye of the hurricane. The savagery with which the commander of the enemy sloop of war had tried to burn the town, the ignominy of his defeat, the dirtying of his pride, the affront to the fleet, the undoubted rage of the admiral...what reason was there not to suppose that a flock of falcons might return one day--and soon--to inflict retribution on the upstart fishermen?

Many who had declined to be stampeded by news of the Lexington battle were now persuaded by six hours of whistling cannonballs and shot to pack up and join the inland exodus. Some fled to Chebacco and farther; others removed women and children from the range of British naval guns and hoped that Gage and Graves would not resolve upon an invasion of Cape Ann.

Among these latter was Joseph Foster. The day after they were so narrowly missed by Linzee's cannonball, he bedded Lydia and her infant in a cartload of hay, and probably most of the other children, and drove them out to the Beaver Dam farm. The next, and last, recorded event of William's brief life was his baptism eight weeks later. He died soon after.

Falcon had attacked on Tuesday, August 8. On Thursday morning Captain Foster rejoined the Provincial Congress in Watertown with an urgent motion to the House "for an additional force and supply of ammunition" for the defense of Gloucester. Speaker James Warren without delay appointed Colonel Samuel Thompson of Brunswick, Maine, Major Stephen Cross of Newburyport and Captain Josiah Batchelor, Jr., of Beverly (replaced next day by Amos Singletary of Sutton) a committee to consider the Foster motion. That afternoon they recommended that "Mr. Story and Captain [Noah] Goodman [of South Hadley], with such as the honourable Board [Council] shall join, be a committee to wait on his Excellency General Washington, and confer with him on the propriety and manner of supplying the Town of Gloucester with ammunition and men for their defense in the present exigence, and to inquire particularly with regard to a company raised by Captain John Lane, part of which are now in the Camp at Cambridge." [1]

Late that day this delegation traveled to Cambridge and conferred with General Washington, and the next morning, August 11, submitted its recommendation, which was passed by the House that afternoon and by the Council on the twelfth:

Resolved, That the Committee of Supplies be directed to deliver three hundred weight of powder, out of that which has or may be first brought in from the several towns, three hundred shot of nine pounds weight, three hundred shot suitable for a swivel gun of small size, and one hundred weight of grape shot, to Captain Joseph Foster, for the defence of the Town of Gloucester, he giving a receipt in behalf of said Town, to be accountable for the same. Also, Resolved, That the honourable the Council be desired to order the company raised by Captain John Lane, part of which is now at Cambridge, to march immediately to Gloucester, there to remain, for the defence of that or any of the adjacent places which may be attacked by our enemies, until further orders, and to be under the direction and command of the Committee of Correspondence of the Town of Gloucester, and to be under the same regulation with the forces raised for the defence of the sea-coast. [2]

Representatives Foster, Singletary and Morton were a committee to procure the shot. Those of nine-pound weight were for what appears to have been Cape Ann's one and only cannon, which was still not in serviceable condition. Where the powder was to come from, the Lord only knew. General Washington needed every ounce he could lay his hands on for the task of containing the British in Boston and ultimately driving them into the sea. Nevertheless, he had Cape Ann and its strategic importance to the defense of the coast much on his mind. He was afraid Lane's company alone would not be sufficient and directed Adjutant General Horatio Gates to order Major Robert Magaw with a battalion of riflemen to Gloucester:

Headquarters, Aug. 16, 1775.
Sir--You are to proceed with the detachment of riflemen under your command to Cape Ann, where you are to endeavor, not only to protect the inhabitants from all attempts of the enemy, but to do your utmost to distress and annoy any detachment from the ministerial army that may be sent from Boston to plunder or destroy that settlement. Upon your march and during your residence at Cape Ann, as well as upon your march back to camp, you will observe strict discipline, and on no account suffer any under your command to pillage or maraud. Upon your arrival at Cape Ann you will dispatch a messenger to acquaint the General with the state you find things in there, and you will frequently report to the General all extraordinary occurrences that may happen.

I am, sir, your most obt. humble servant,
Horatio Gates,
Adjt. General [3]

Major Magaw and his foot soldiers probably started out for Gloucester that day, for he reported to General Gates:

Cape Ann August 21st 1775
Sir--I wrote to you on the 17th inst that no alarms or appearances of immediate danger had been in this place for some time past. Since the 8th instant when Capt Lindsey Commander of a Sloop of War threw a number of shot into the town--the inhabitants have remained unmolested. On Saturday evening last a Man of War & a Tender

appear'd off this Harbour. We expected an attack. Yesterday they bore away for the eastward & disappeared. The inhabitants have nearly completed a small fort to mount 6 9-pounders. Their spirit seems equal to their abilities. We have neither blankets nor shirts with us. Some of our men are sick owing I believe to want of covering in the night.

> I have the honor &c.
> Robt Magaw Maj
> Rifle Batn Cont Service [4]

The spirit and ability which drew the major's praise were being applied to the rehabilitation of the old earthworks on Watch House Point, christened "Fort Ann" by the men working on it. It would remain almost naked of armament for months, and so would the important redoubt which soon was being raised on Stage Head looking over the harbor above Half Moon Beach, where the pioneers from England had dried their fish in 1623. Works also were shoveled up at Duncan's Point and near the Cut; the exact locations are uncertain. One month after the *Falcon* fight Gloucester still had only one piece of heavy ordnance, which Elephalet Robarts was still trying to get serviceable. On September 8 the town paid him six pounds and four shillings "for makeing careges and weals for the Grate Gun," and two weeks later four pounds and three shillings to Philemon Warner for iron work on the swivels and gun carriages. [5]

While General Washington was under no illusions that he could challenge the Royal Navy, he knew that it would be most difficult, if not impossible, to dislodge the British from Boston so long as they could continue to supply themselves by sea. The key to his strategy was harassment of the enemy's supply lines with stinging hit-and-run attacks from the lairs of Gloucester, Beverly, and Marblehead by sea, while keeping the troops bottled up in Boston by land. But what good was a naval strategy without a navy?

And so, with characteristic prescience, George Washington created the American Navy. He commandeered the schooner *Hannah* of Beverly, had her fitted out as an armed vessel and commissioned her to an experienced and intrepid mariner, Captain Nicholson Broughton of Colonel John Glover's Marblehead regiment. On September 2 General Washington gave Broughton his orders: to sail forth immediately with a picked crew of Marbleheaders from Glover's outfit "on a cruize against such vessels as may be found on the high seas or elsewhere, bound inward and outward from Boston, in the service of the ministerial army..."

Hannah cleared Beverly three days later. One day out, she was chased into Gloucester by a British man-o'-war. This may have been *Lively*, which only a few hours earlier in Ipswich Bay had captured the brig *Unity*, just out of Portsmouth for the West Indies with fish and lumber, and put aboard a prize crew to sail her to Boston.

Lively was not lively enough to catch *Hannah*. America's one-boat navy laid low for the night inside Eastern Point. Next morning she darted out and intercepted *Unity*. Captain Broughton triumphantly escorted the retaken prize back to Gloucester and notified General Washington of this first capture by a regularly commissioned Continental vessel.

So let Beverly and Marblehead vie for birthplace of the United States Navy. Gloucester cradled its first prize. The legitimacy of the prize for the purposes of condemnation, sale and division of the spoils was another matter. *Unity* was, after all, an American-owned vessel, retaken from the enemy and not subject to confiscation. So ruled General Washington, anyway. About ten days later *Hannah*'s disgruntled crew mutinied and refused to sail her out of Gloucester. Thirty-six of them were arrested and marched to Cambridge under a guard of soldiers from Beverly. Their accused ringleader, Joseph Searle, was flogged and drummed out of the army. Washington let the rest of them off with remitted sentences. *Hannah* remained at Gloucester without a crew until fifty more officers and men from Glover's regiment arrived to man her out.

The New England winter was lurking in the north, and town meeting on September 12 voted to provide Captain Lane's defense company with barracks and stove wood, an order which implies that Major Magaw and his unit had returned to

Cambridge. Yet the neglect of Lane's men persisted. Within a week he submitted a petition to the Provincial Congress, probably through Joseph Foster, complaining that most of his seventy-nine men had received neither pay nor their issue of coats and blankets.

Lane's problems were typical of those which dampened the enthusiastically patriotic country units that marched to Cambridge during the early months of the war. John Lane himself came from Buxton, twelve miles west of Falmouth (Portland), Maine. He had already seen twenty years of military service. In May he had been ordered to the Penobscot region to escort a delegation of Indians to Watertown to negotiate a treaty with the Provinical Congress, and to enlist a company of fifty-six men while he was there. He left Lieutenant Gilman to recruit in the Penobscot Bay area and told his other lieutenant to do likewise at Falmouth. Gilman signed up forty-nine men whom Lane took to Falmouth by boat and thence overland to Cambridge, where he wrote his lieutenant at Falmouth to bring his recruits on to Cambridge. Upon their arrival, the twenty-eight from Falmouth were ordered to Gloucester. After the *Falcon* fight, Captain Lane was directed to complete his company at Cape Ann.

Not until he had put these separately enlisted units together and called the roll did he realize that his two lieutenants, unbeknownst to each other, had enlisted twenty-one more than his quota, which put him short on his requisitions. To further complicate Lane's dilemma, Captain Foster had already given the first twenty-eight their forty shillings advance pay for a month, plus twelve more to buy a blanket, and had mustered all seventy-seven as ordered by the Provincial Congress.

This first winter of the war on Cape Ann would be a hard one, and the Provincial Congress on September 27 directed its committee of clothing to deliver seventy-seven coats to Captain Lane, and instructed the receiver general to forward £ 147.8 to Captain Foster to cover a month's advance pay for Lane, his lieutenants and the other forty-nine, and their twelve shillings-worth of cold comfort for blankets if they could find them.

While the representatives were endeavoring to provide for the defenders of Cape Ann, fate in the form of a heavy fog (so

—124—

said one account) crept up on the coast and delivered provender for the defended. Colonel John Stevens reported the event to General Washington:

Sept. 28, 1775

We the Committee of Safety for the town of Glouster beg leave to represent to your Excellency

That yesterday morning a brig was discover'd at anker within Thatchers Island--Captains Somes & Smith in a boat went alongside and asked where from, and where bound, was answer'd from Quebec for Eustatia. They asked what they did there, the answer was they wanted water--Sd Somes & Smith taking them to be enemies came ashore, and invited men to go off in boats and seize her, which they did, and Mesrs Isaac Pool & Samuel Wonson was very active and assisted much in bringing the vessel into Sandy-Bay, which is on the easterly part of our Cape Ann, and found on board her 68 sheep, and 45 oxen, which we have brought ashore to graze--

Captain Wallace who was Master of the brig with ten of his men we now send to your Excellency by the conduct of Lieut Daniel Lane and wait your Excellencys orders & are your Excellencys, etc.

John Stevens Chairman

Capt Isaac Somes mentioned above will wait on your Excellency with Capt Wallace's instructions which his owners gave him at Quebec. Mr. Isaac Pool mentioned above we are informed has got a parcel of letters & papers that was found in the brig and has carried them off without letting the Committee know of them, but we suppose he intends to wait on your Excellency with the same.[6]

Dolphin was the name of the captured brig, and the *Boston Gazette* reported that the livestock was a present from Sir Guy Carieton, Governor of Quebec and commander of the British forces in Canada, to General Gage. *Dolphin* lay anchored near Oakes Rock between Thacher's and Emerson Point when the boats, which had put out from Long Cove, now Rockport Harbor, came up quietly on her, Trojan horse fashion, the armed Cape Anners concealed below decks. Captain Isaac Somes had sailed many a voyage for Joseph Foster, as we have seen.

When the prize had been sailed around to the Wheeler's Point wharf in the Annisquam River, the oxen were hoisted ashore, driven to the harbor and auctioned off in front of Prentice's tavern. "According to the custom of the Canadian French, these cattle had been worked by the horns; and it is said that the purchasers found it difficult to make them draw with the yoke."[7]

After a few days the Council in Watertown decided no harm could come of releasing Captain William Wallace, his crew and passengers, and advised the Gloucester committee of safety to return to him his cabin furniture and clothing, and to the crew their personal effects. General Washington was requested to provide safe passage through the army lines into Boston for the passengers, the wives and children of two soldiers in the Fifty-ninth Regiment of regulars. The committee of safety was told to deliver *Dolphin* to the Commander-in-Chief for conversion into another armed vessel, but by some accident she heeled over, filled and sank in Squam River while her ballast was being taken out; she was never raised, and seventy years later some of her bottom timbers could still be seen in the sand.

Sometimes fate wanted a nudge in the right direction before delivering her bounty. Such a helpful change of course towards Portsmouth was applied to the ship *Prince George* by a fast-thinking fisherman offshore of Cape Ann. Captain Richard Emmes was eleven weeks out of Bristol, England, with 1892 barrels of flour for the king's men in Boston. It was the morning of October 2:

> Last Monday arrived in Piscataqua River a ship from England, intended for Boston. It appears that the day before her arrival she was in company with the *Raven*, man of war, bound to the same place, but parted with her in the night. Meeting with a fisherman, to the eastward of Cape-Ann, the crew requested some directions what course to steer for Boston; the *honest* fisherman, pointing toward Piscataqua River, tells them *there* is Boston. The crew shape their course accordingly, and soon very

luckily found themselves, with their ship and cargo, under the guns of a battery lately built by the people of New Hampshire. The commander of the battery, with a number of men, very *humanely* goes on board to their *assistance,* and offers to pilot the ship up to Portsmouth. I can't go there--says the captain of the ship--I am bound to Boston. But you must, replies the other; and immediately ordered her to be got under way, and soon carried her safe into wharf, where she was taken proper care of by the people of Portsmouth. [s]

10

A CLOSE CALL

Astonishing, deplorable, unconscionable though it was, Yankee mosquitoes had stung *Falcon*, smothered *Margaretta*, regained *Unity,* swarmed all over *Dolphin* and misled *Prince George*. A single summer of war had scattered straws enough on the water to show the set of the tide: the whole Royal Navy simply could not play cat to a thousand mice, nor watch every hole on the American coast. It was as the wiser heads in Parliament had predicted.

To the haughty officers of Admiral Graves's fleet the cutting-out of a stray unarmed merchantman from home was one thing--fortunes of war, and all that--but to clip the talons of a *Falcon,* that, egad, was an affront not to be borne, and these prideful products of English class boiled at the insult and paced and pouted in their wardrooms, downed their glasses of Madeira and swore, 'Od's blood, that no, it should *not* be borne. Cast in such a mold was Lieutenant Henry Mowat, R.N., commander of HM Armed Vessel *Canceaux,* six guns, with a complement of forty-five.

The rebels had sorely tried Lieutenant Mowat's patience. First his ship had run aground in the Piscataqua River in January. With the moderation of the weather early in April, Admiral Graves ordered *Canceaux* to the dock at Halifax to have her bottom checked over for damage, directing Mowat to put in at Falmouth to protect a new naval vessel on the ways from the threatening behavior of the citizenry. The hope the admiral expressed to General Gage that *Canceaux*'s presence in Casco Bay "will be some check to the common disturbers" proved too sanguine. On April 24 the Falmouth customs commissioners were driven by the wrathful patriots there to flee on board of her, and on May 5 Mowat felt so threatened himself by the look of the armed men milling about on the shore that he employed Linzee's oft-used maneuver, sprung his cable and hove broadside to the town. *Canceaux*'s log told the rest of the story:

> May 9. Fresh breezes and clear Wr AM Capt Mowat and Doctor Baillie went ashore to walk and were intercepted and taken prisoners by some armed men. At 2 PM hove taught the spring, the ships broadside to the town, fired 2 guns as signal   at 9 came on board the Captain and Doctor.

> May 10. AM exercised at small arms -- a shot was fired from the shore and entered the ships side. Kept at arms all night.[1]

In three more weeks the contagion of rebellion was inflaming Portsmouth, where HMS *Scarborough* swung at anchor in the Piscataqua. Captain Andrew Barkley had stopped two sloops from Long Island with provisions and sent them to Boston under convoy of *Canceaux*, causing such a fuss in Portsmouth that the customs men there thought it wise to follow the example of their colleagues at Falmouth and took shelter on the man-'o-war. Captain Barkley wrote Graves on May 30:

> ...I send these two vessels round under the protection of the *Canceaux*, for if I had sent them singly by themselves, there were arm'd boats all ready to pursue them and likewise expresses have been sent to Newbury and Cape Ann to fit out vessels to intercept them, as therefore it is morally impossible for me to send any vessels that may be stop't with provisions round to Boston without having an armed vessel to accompany them there otherwise they will be seized and the people in them very ill treated, if not put to death. I don't know any other scheme, that will have a greater effect in bringing the people of this Province to a due sense of the duty that they owe to the Mother Country than that of stopping their provisions...[2]

To his regret, Lieutenant Mowat missed the pleasure of distributing his share of round and grape among the uncouth horde of seditionists grubbed into Breed's Hill; *Canceaux* was in the royal dock at Halifax, hove down for repairs, and did not return to Boston, which was by then under siege, until the end of July.

August droned in, and the Gloucester patriots clipped the claws of the *Falcon.* By the end of September there was some closely guarded activity at the king's docks in Boston. The sloop *Spitfire* and armed transport *Symmetry,* veterans of June 17, were undergoing secret alterations. Both were crawling with carpenters during the day, while under cover of night certain bulky equipment and quantities of warlike stores were being put covertly aboard. Eyes that were not meant to see, did. Selectman Timothy Newell, for one, reported in his diary on October 3:

> This morning two bomb ketches and several armed vessels with some soldiers sailed on a secret expedition, it is said to demand a ship belonging to Portsmouth, retaken by our whale boats, & carried into Cape Ann--also to demand of that town 40 seamen which they took from the man of war--if not delivered in 24 hours to bombard the town. [3]

Newell's information was premature, but not by much. The Portsmouth ship and the man of war were *Unity* and *Falcon.* The British navy was getting up a mission of revenge, although two days after its supposed sailing the supposed expedition against Cape Ann had not left Boston Harbor. But intelligence reports persisted that something ominous was in the offing. General Washington was so alarmed that he wrote John Hancock in Philadelphia and sent dispatches post haste to all the major seaports on the coast to the effect that he had learned an enemy squadron was scheduled to sail secretly from Boston on October 4, armed with two mortars, four howitzers and other artillery intended for the bombardment of a town whose identity he could not discover.

Washington did not know the half of it. Four more days passed, and the naval vessels which had been the objects of so much activity had not moved from their moorings. And then, at one in the morning of October 9, four of them raised sail, silently slipped their cables and passed through the fleet in Nantasket Roads, the wind fair for the eastward. In the lead was *Canceaux* ... then *Halifax,* six guns, thirty men under Lieutenant John De la Touche, lately arrived from Halifax, one of two schooners Admiral Graves had purchased and fitted out as warships ... and *Spitfire* and *Symmetry,* decks rearranged and reinforced to support the weighty mortars and howitzers and cannon which could serve only one end: to hurl flaming bombs ashore for the purpose of burning a town to its cellars and visiting a special kind of horror on the inhabitants.

For two days, since October 6, Lieutenant Mowat had carried his orders from Admiral Graves in his pocket. He had been given the command of this squadron, his superior explained, because of his years of experience charting the coast to the eastward of Boston and his "late spirited and judicious conduct at Falmouth." His mission was to "proceed along the coast, & lay waste burn and destroy such seaport towns as are accessible to his Majesty's ships."

The squadron's first objective was to be the harbor of Gloucester,

> that town having fired in the month of August last upon his Majesty's Sloop *Falcon,* wounded her people and taken many prisoners; you are to burn destroy and lay waste the said Town together with all vessels and craft in the harbour that cannot with ease be brought away. Having performed this service you are to take advantage of wind and weather, or any other favourable circumstances, to fall upon and destroy any other town or places within the limits aforesaid, and all vessels or craft to seize and destroy.

> My design is to chastize Marblehead, Salem, Newbury Port, Cape Anne Harbour, Portsmouth, Ipswich, Saco, Falmouth in Casco Bay, and particularly Mechias where the *Margueritta* was taken.. [4]

Graves cautioned Mowat that he had too few marines along to attempt to land and hold ground. Consequently he should risk no lives where there was not a strong likelihood of success; he was to accomplish what he could and then withdraw before the Americans could assemble and cut him off. And he must avoid running aground or placing his four vessels in a position where they could not put to sea at all tides, wind permitting.

Log of his Majesty's Armed Vessel *Canceaux,* October 9, 1775:

> Sailed at 1 AM. At 3 hove to & double-reefed topsails. At 6 fresh gales & squalls, close-reefed topsails & handed the mizzen topsail. At 10 Cape Ann was NNW 7 or 8 leagues, & bore up for Cape Cod. [5]

Those squalls were the salvation of Gloucester.

Lieutenant Mowat tried, albeit lamely, to explain later to Admiral Graves the failure of his first objective:

> The morning after leaving the harbour [of Boston], the *Canceaux* with the other vessels, were brought to off the entrance to Cape Ann Harbour, with an intention of going in the moment that the day appeared; but to my no small mortification a strong gale from the northward reduced the vessels under their low sails, so much so, that the *Symmetry* and *Spitfire* went almost broadside to leeward: finding myself in this situation, I judged it expedient to secure a harbour, and accordingly directed the course for Cape Cod, where we anchor'd in the evening of that day.
>
> The next morning the wind shifted to the southward of the west, we got under sail, and at day break the following morning [October 11], we were close in with Cape Ann. Upon viewing the Town, Mr Grant the Artillery Officer, gave it as his opinion, that the houses stood too scattered to expect success, with the ordnance and stores of his department, and in particular from the small number of carcases, and the uncertainty of their goodness.
>
> On considering the ill consequences of a disappointment in the first attempt of this expedition, and the advantage of encouragement it would afford the rebels, I thought it most prudent to make choice of an object, where the certainty was more secure; tho it was not without reluctance I passed this port, as your orders directed me there first, as well as the

favourable opportunity of attempting Squam at the same time, which I certainly should have done, had the number of troops been sufficient to have landed...[6]

Twice in succession the fates had intervened for Cape Ann...once in the guise of one of those sudden and tempestuous northwest squalls which burst forth upon the harbor of Gloucester with such unexpected violence from the western hills when winter waits in the sky ... once more in the person of the cautious Mr. Grant, so uncertain of the *goodness* of his fire bombs as he gazed upon the town he had been directed to destroy, so deep inside the uncertain shores of the great harbor, already aflame with the foliage of a New England October and defended by an enemy inflamed with a fervor that was beyond any certainty of calculation.

So Lieutenant Mowat and his squadron passed Gloucester by. At eight on the morning of the eleventh, Thacher's Island was northeast by north three miles. Another hour, and *Canceaux's* studding sails were set as the breeze piped up. At ten Mowat ordered *Halifax* by signal to chase a sail to the eastward, standing under Cape Ann... "she proved a schooner with salt. All her people had quit her." By four in the afternoon, Halibut Point bore southwest four miles. They had dropped Cape Ann and were in Ipswich Bay "in company as before--fresh breezes and fair weather."[7]

Under ordinary sailing conditions Mowat's squadron should have arrived at Falmouth the next day, but it was not until October 16 that the four warships came to anchor before the town, broadside, springs to cables. The *Canceaux* commander had an ultimatum rowed ashore: the selectmen were given two hours "to remove without delay the Human Species out of the said town."

The hours ticked by. Mowat stayed his hand until nine-thirty the next morning, when he gave Falmouth what he had been ordered first to give Gloucester. The bombardment ended at sunset, when three-quarters of the town lay in ashes.

The admiral's expedition to chastize Marblehead, Salem, Newburyport, Gloucester, Portsmouth, Ipswich, Saco and Machias was back at anchor in Nantasket Roads on November

2. Lieutenant Mowat, Graves reported to the Secretary of the Admiralty, was "extremely concerned the badness of his vessels and stores prevented his doing more than destroy the Town of Falmouth."

General Gage had embarked for England on October 10, the day after Mowat sailed on his grand assignment. General Howe succeeded him to the command of the British forces and wrote Lord Dartmouth with a hint of disparagement on November 27:

> Before the departure of General Gage, an expedition was concocted by the General and Admiral for the destruction of Cape Ann and Falmouth, two sea port towns on the coast to the eastward, that were distinguished for their opposition to Government...[8]

Some time between Mowat's revenge on Falmouth and the beginning of November, Gloucester took stock of her predicament, her nakedness to the ravages of bombs and carcasses. She looked to her fleet, her all, bottled up at the wharves gathering barnacles and grass, and took a remarkable step recorded by Colonel Stephen Kemble, British Deputy Adjutant General in Boston, in his journal on Nevember 2, 1775:

> Lieut. Grant [perhaps the Mr. Grant who shied away from Gloucester], who was there, says there is a boom or strong chain thrown across the harbour at Portsmouth, which is raised or lowered by windlasses on each side, that all the vessels from Cape Ann are in Newbury (Merrimack) River, and the mouth of it shut up by driving piles or stakes into the bottom, except a small passage, which is left open for vessels, where a raft is moored, to be sunk occasionally...[9]

Newburyport also built forts on the Salisbury shore of the river and on Plum Island and moored a floating battery in the stream. The town spent £ 2433 on these defenses and sought reimbursement after the Revolution, claiming it had thereby prevented the British from entering the river and destroying two Continental frigates under construction early in 1776, and "at the same time rendered it a safe assylum for vessels belonging to Boston, then in the power of the enemy, & of those belonging to Marblehead, Cape Ann & other exposed maratime towns."[10]

Gloucester owed much to her neighbors, for she had scant resources of her own except bedrock determination. "A company of five and thirty came from Ipswich to this town to assist in fortifying our harbour," Parson Fuller wrote on October 30, and the next day: "We had a general muster in order to view arms." The thirty-five may have been the Ipswich men who paused on Chebacco common, hiking to help defend Gloucester, and heard a mighty prayer from the coldsteel Calvinist John Cleaveland. The chaplain roared out "...that the enemy may be blown..."--"to hell and damnation!" shouted an over-excited soldier--"...to the land of tyranny from whence they came," he concluded unperturbed.[11]

A few days before the Ipswich reinforcements arrived, the Gloucester committee of safety forwarded an urgent plea to General Washington, most likely by the hand of Joseph Foster, "with respect to affording some necessaries of defence to Cape Ann." On October 30 Washington wrote Speaker James Warren of the General Assembly from Cambridge: [12]

> Sir: At the instance and request of the Committee of Cape-Ann, I despatched Major Mason to survey & make a report of such works of defence as were already constructed there, & how far any new one might be necessary. From his observations & account, I find that a battery may be erected, to the great advantage & security of the place; but the small stock of artillery, belonging to the Army, prevents me from supplying the materials for this purpose. I have therefore thought proper to acquaint you with the circumstances of the case, that you may make the best provision for this necessity; and have also sent Major Mason down to you, that particular inquiry, if desired, may be made. Be pleased to communicate this information to your honourable House.
>
> I am, etc.
> George Washington [13]

This was a disappointment, but Joseph Foster must have lobbied with effect among the other representatives at Watertown, because on November 4 the House resolved:

That his Excellency the General be desired to direct Major Mason to proceed to the Towns of Concord, Worcester, Lancaster, and Leicester, there to view the cannon now in those towns, and such and so many of them, being the property of this Colony, as he shall judge fit for use, and necessary for the defence of said harbour, the Town of Gloucester have leave to remove to that place; and that it be earnestly recommended to the Selectmen or Committee of the towns aforesaid, in whose care any cannon, not the property of this Colony, may be, and viewed as aforesaid, that they deliver them to the Town of Gloucester, on this important occasion, if needed.

And that Major Mason, or the Selectmen of the Town of Gloucester, have liberty, on the credit of this Colony, to procure, from any town or person who may have it to spare, two barrels of powder, to be replaced as soon as the state of this Colony will admit of it, and if not replaced, such town or person to receive pay therefor out of the Colony Treasury, at a rate not exceeding five shillings per pound; and said Gloucester to be accountable therefor to this Court.

That Mr. Batchelor wait on General Washington for the purpose above mentioned; and that the Selectmen of Gloucester be served with a copy of this Resolve. [14]

However, to ask was not necessarily to receive, and Gloucester's last resort remained the specter which arose in Mowat's imagination, as he peered into Gloucester Harbor, of the trap which had snapped on Linzee--a trap he was well acquainted with from his experience on the coast survey. Each new British encounter with American vessels, for which the trap was a refuge, augmented British caution. On November 21 HM Schooner *Hinchinbrook,* in the command of Lieutenant Alexander Ellis, was off Eastern Point:

Standing jest off Cape Ann harbour at ½ past 1 PM. Saw a schooner off Cape Ann at 2. We discovered she was one of the Rebel privateers bound into Cape Ann harbour. Chas'd her and fired several shot at her. Work'd into Cape

Ann harbour after her. At 3 left off chase, the privateer running into the upper harbour where there was no possibility of gettg at her. Standg off & on. [15]

General Washington's *Hannah* the while was cruising in pursuance of his orders and of such vessels as might be found in the service of the ministerial army. On November 13 she sent into Gloucester a fine little prize, the sloop *Speedwell.* Captain Broughton and his Headers were still congratulating themselves when further examination revealed that the owner of *Speedwell* was none other than General Nathanael Greene, Washington's right hand man at headquarters. His Excellency notified Continental Agent William Bartlett at Beverly that he "does not wish to have any thing to do with her," and the Gloucester committee of safety advised the embarrassed Captain Broughton to reimburse General Greene for his confiscated cargo of provisions and the expenses *Hannah*'s overzealousness had cost him.

Lee (left) escorts captured *Nancy* into Gloucester Harbor November 29, 1775. The stars and stripes patriotically hoisted by the latter-day artist had not, in fact, been created yet.

11

COLONEL FOSTER

Everybody was looking for *Nancy*.

General Howe, bottled and corked in Boston, was looking for her with growing nervousness because she was a 250-ton brig burdened with an enormous cargo of guns and ammunition for his soldiers, and she was overdue from London's Woolwich Arsenal in company with a transport full of gunpowder.

Admiral Graves was looking for her because General Howe had applied the heat to him. On November 12 Graves wrote his superior that he had ordered Lieutenant Mowat in *Canceaux* to sail out in search of *Nancy*; if perchance she had fallen prey to those Cape Anners and was hid away in Gloucester Harbor, and he could not recapture her, he was to set her on fire. But adverse winds kept *Canceaux* caged in Boston Harbor.

General Washington was looking for her. Word of the enemy's anxiety had filtered through the lines to him by November 26. Out there offshore somewhere, wallowing around in the grey Atlantic, might be the answer to the prayer he had addressed to Congress at Philadelphia concerning his "great want of powder, lead, mortars, indeed most sorts of military stores. A fortunate capture of an ordnance ship would give new life to the camp, and an immediate turn to the issue of this campaign." [1]

The Commander-in-Chief put out urgent word to his nascent navy to sally forth on the lookout for *Nancy*. At Beverly, as soon as Captain John Manley of Marblehead could finish taking provisions aboard the armed schooner *Lee,* which Washington had just now turned over to him, he made sail, and clear of Baker's Island sent a lookout aloft.

In fact, the only man, friend or enemy, not looking for *Nancy* was her master, Captain Robert Hunter, who already knew where she was--or thought he did--ploughing through rough seas and squalls off the American coast in company with the powder ship. [2] On November 27 HMS *Mercury,* twenty guns, fell in with *Nancy* and signalled her to keep in convoy to Boston. The message, however, did not get through, and the ordnance brig and her intended protectress were separated by the storm.

Nancy and the powder ship were still lumbering through the swells toward Boston on November 29, ten miles east of Cape Ann, when a shout came down from *Lee*'s lookout, and the search ended. *Nancy* was lightly armed and struck to the Americans without a shot. Captain Manley put a prize crew aboard and bore off in pursuit of the powder ship. At that moment his lookout sighted a pair of enemy warships on the horizon. Manley prudently took his bird in hand and made for Gloucester Harbor, where not long before nightfall he slipped her in to Freshwater Cove, behind the cover of Dolliver's Neck on the western shore. [3]

One look below on their prize, and *Lee*'s jubilant crew knew they had committed the grandest larceny of the war. Gloucester converged on the cove, and out of the wild excitement a messenger leaped into the saddle and urged his steed down the Salem road for Cambridge on the gallop.

General Washington received the "agreeable account" that night, and his reflex reaction was that the fleeing powder ship, having surely witnessed *Nancy*'s capture, must by then have carried the word ahead to Boston. Obviously the British would go all out to recover her. "Cape Ann is a very open harbour," he wrote John Hancock the next morning, the 30th, "and accessable to large ships, which made me immediately send off Colonel Glover and Mr. Palfrey, with orders, to raise the Minute Men & militia of that part of the country, to have the cargo landed without loss of time, & guarded up to this camp. This I hope they will be able to effect, before it is known to the enemy, what port she is carried into." [4]

Colonel Glover moved instantly. That night he ordered a ton of bread and beef carted down the thirty miles from Cambridge to Gloucester, then followed himself, passing the word to his staff that General Washington wanted every wagon and team of horses and yoke of oxen in the area pressed into service. Within twenty-four hours, or close to it, Glover was at Freshwater Cove with four companies.

As the tackles were sent down *Nancy's* hatches, and the captors hauled up on them, they could scarcely believe their eyes: two thousand muskets, bayonets and infantry accoutrements; a hundred thousand musket flints; sixty-two thousand pounds of musket shot; seven thousand round shot, twelve and six-pound; twenty thousand one-pound shot; bomb carcasses; four siege mortars, including a brass giant with a thirteen-inch bore; two six-pound cannon; eight thousand fuzes; several barrels of powder, and a great variety of the implements of war, lacking only powder and cannon in proportion to the small arms and round shot.

This easy windfall, this bounteous response to General Washington's wishful thinking, was taken out of *Nancy,* got ashore in Freshwater Cove behind the screen of Dolliver's Neck and loaded on the wagons which were rattling in from the countryside around, without detection by the normally inquisitive warships of its rightful, or wrongful, owners. On the third of December the great wagon train from Gloucester, convoyed by Colonel Glover's exultant guards, rumbled into the patriot camp at Cambridge.[5]

"Such universal joy ran through the whole," wrote one officer who witnessed the triumphal procession, "as if each grasped victory in his hand: to crown the glorious scene there intervened one truly ludicrous, which was old Put [General Israel Putnam] mounted on the large mortar which was fixed in its bed for the occasion, with a bottle of rum in his hand, standing parson to christen, while god-father Mifflin [Major Thomas Mifflin, Washington's quartermaster] gave it the name of *Congress.* The huzzas on the occasion I dare say were heard through all the territories of our most gracious sovereign in this Province."[6]

The capture of *Nancy* was the biggest boost to American morale since the *Falcon* fight. Edward Green wrote his brother from Cambridge that "Generall Gates says was he to have made out an invoice for our purpose, he would not have add'd one article more. This ship Howe has been at his wits end about this 10 days past." [7]

George Washington called it "this instance of Divine favour; for nothing surely ever came more apropos." Speaker Warren wrote John Adams in Philadelphia from Watertown the day the wagons rolled in:

> Providence seems to be engaged for us. The same spirit and determination prevails to conquer all difficulties. Many prizes have been taken by our cruisers, and a capital one last week carried into Cape Ann. Of very great value perhaps £ 20,000 sterling, a brig from England with a cargo consisting of almost every species of warlike store except powder & cannon. 2000 very fine small arms with all their acccoutrements, four mortars, one which Putnam has christened & called the *Congress*, the finest ever in America. Carcasses. Flints. Shells. Musket balls. Carriages etc etc. These are principally arrived at head quarters & the great mortar is a subject of curiosity. I hope we shall be able to make good use of them before long. [8]

A committee of the General Court had traveled down to Gloucester to study its military predicament at about the same time that two four-pounder cannon were received from Worcester--the only fruits of Major Mason's efforts to persuade inland towns to let down their defenses for the sake of raising Cape Ann's. [9] The arrival of the vulnerable *Nancy* in his harbor soon after prompted Colonel John Stevens on November 30 once again to remind the legislators that good wishes did not win wars:

> We beg leave further to request, that if you think this harbour worthy of defence, you would be pleased to grant us further assistance; as we have a number of redoubts without cannon, we pray you would order us four nine-pounders and two eighteens, with their implements, and a proper number of rounds for each.

> We pray, also, that Captains Bradbury Saunders, and William Pearson, of this town, may be commisioned to

inlist a suitable number of men, as artillery men, to manage said cannon; that----------------may be appointed a Field-Officer, to command the troops stationed here, and the Militia, when necessary; and, honourable sirs, we are humbly of opinion, could we have one hundred men sent, in addition to those already stationed here, exclusive of artillerymen, or have liberty to inlist them where we can find them, on the same terms of the sea-coast men, might be sufficient to make a good defence, otherwise we fear what our fate may be.

But we leave the matter to the great wisdom of the honourable Court, to act as they think fit, referring for particulars and the great importance of this port to the general cause we are engaged in, to the honourable Committee sent by the Court to view our situation, and should only add, that our necessity for some speedy relief must apologize for troubling the honourable Court so often.

But last night was brought into this harbour, a brigantine, loaded with ordnance stores, from Great Britain, by Capt. Manly, of a privateer, of great value and consequence.

We therefore, now stand in need of instant assistance to defend so valuable a cargo, as the enemy will endeavor to regain it. [10]

Half a loaf was all the General Court could spare, nevertheless. On December 2 the House resolved that in view of "the importance of the Harbour of Gloucester to this Colony, the exposedness of the same to the enemy," there ought to be two additional companies of fifty men each, one of them artillery men, enlisted "to complete and defend the fortifications already erected and erecting." It further voted that a general officer be given the command of the Gloucester forces, with the authority to call up the neighboring militia in an emergency, the company officers and the general to be elected by the General Court at a future date.

Nothing was said in this resolve about cannon. The two new companies would supplement Captain Lane's, which had been stationed at Gloucester full strength since after the *Falcon* fight. Lane had had to plead again with the General Court; in November his men had still received only a month's pay and were "needy." As a half measure, the legislators on November 10 allowed the town £ 206.5 for billeting Lane's seventy-five soldiers from August 16 to the end of October at five shillings a man a week.

Had John Stevens and Joseph Foster and their comrades on Cape Ann realized the full measure of the frustration of their enemies at this juncture they might have relaxed somewhat. British reaction to the capture of the floating arsenal intended to enable the ministerial troops to break the rebel siege was glum. Listening gloomily to the Yankee huzzas which the brisk wind of approaching winter carried across the Charles River to his headquarters, General Howe wrote home to Lord Dartmouth that "the circumstance is rather unfortunate to us, as they are now furnished with all the requisites for setting the town on fire, having got a large quantity of round carcasses and other stores, with which they could not have been otherwise supplied." [11]

Howe was angry that *Nancy* had been sent across without a chaperone, and so was Tory Peter Oliver, Jr., who complained in a letter from Boston to his expatriate father-in-law, Thomas Hutchinson, in London, that "to send an ordnance brigg of such a value out so poorly mann'd and arm'd looks very odd. We have 8 or 10 pirate vessels out between the Capes, and yet our Men of-Warr are chiefly in the Harbour." [12]

A British officer writing home was more sniffishly explicit:

> This vigilent officer [Admiral Graves], instead of sending his squadron to protect the store-ships and transports from England, has, with the utmost prudence, ordered the ships of war in this harbour to be secured with booms all round, to prevent their being boarded and taken by the Rebel whale-boats; and for some time past he has never sent a single ship to cruise off Cape Ann, because the Rebels have had some cannon mounted upon it: no doubt the parliament will thank him on his glorious return for so effectually preserving his Majesty's ships... [13]

Having inherited Gage's quandary, Howe -- as Gage had -- looked seaward for relief, to Admiral Graves...but with no greater expectations. Howe regarded Mowat's abortive expedition to chastize the seacoast as a mere "concoction" of Graves and Gage; but he knew his relief must depend upon the navy, one way or the other, and he urged on the reluctant admiral the necessity of seizing Gloucester and Marblehead harbors before Boston could be secure. On November 26, as the unprotected *Nancy* neared the coast with the ordnance the general was relying on, Graves replied that although Marblehead was defended by a battery of twelve guns and Gloucester was partly fortified, he had a plan:

Frigates cannot be in either, without being exposed to certain destruction: at Cape Anne the outer road is foul, narrow & greatly exposed, and a ship once into the inner road cannot get out again without a leading wind; the enemy would naturally forebear annoying her while the wind continued favorable to depart, but the moment it became contrary the worst consequences might be apprehended: nearly the same danger attends lying at Marblehead.

It is indeed beyond dispute that the rebels have several small cruisers in the Bay, who have every advantage over the Kings ships in point of sailing; & being light vessels, drawing little water, the whole country their friends, can lie under the land, &, upon observing a vessel or two unguarded, dart upon them suddenly, & carry them off even in sight of the King's ships.

Every vessel in his command, the admiral declared, had standing orders to go into Gloucester and Marblehead harbors and capture or destroy American craft, but he had "no hope of their succeeding."

On the other hand, if the general would place three hundred soldiers at his disposal, he told Howe, he believed that with two frigates and siege guns he could sail into Marblehead, seize the irksome battery there and burn the town.

Gloucester would be more difficult. Yet, "I submit to your Excellency's consideration whether we could not with a thousand men seize and keep possession of the peninsula of Cape Anne. The harbours would then be ours." [14]

Howe ignored this proposition.

Again Graves advanced it, carefully shifting the initiative this time onto his superior. It was December 13, and *Nancy* lay in Freshwater Cove, stripped of every last musket flint:

> Altho' fully sensible of the distresses this garrison will be subjected to by the rebels taking its supplies; yet it is impossible entirely to prevent it with the men of war alone at this season. All that I can do is to place the Kings ships in the most likely situations to fall in with vessels expected to arrive, and these are, I think, off Cape Anne, within Salem Bay, off Marblehead, and thence to Cape Cod. The cruizers are now under orders to spread themselves on these stations, and to rendezvous in Cape Cod Harbour in gales of wind easterly. But, without our having possession of Marblehead and Cape Anne Harbour also, it is impossible for ships to keep on their stations or prevent the rebels from making further captures. If your Excellency thinks it advisable to attempt seizing the peninsula of Cape Anne, every assistance the fleet can afford shall be chearfully given. [15]

A few more days passed, and the admiral appended to his copy of this second letter to Howe: "But to this proposition, thus repeated, the general made no reply."

By October of 1775 the Congress in Philadelphia had conceived the United States Navy officially on paper and initiated a search for vessels suitable for conversion to the Continental service. The colonies were advised to do likewise at their expense for the protection of their coasts against "all unlawful invasions, attacks, and depredations" by their "unnatural enemies."

Massachusetts took the lead. At Watertown the General Court on September 28 created the Committee to Consider the Expediency of Fitting out a Number of Armed Vessels. The members were Colonels Azor Orne of Marblehead, Jonathan Grout of Petersham, and one Thompson, and Messrs. Story,

Cooper, James Sullivan of Biddeford, Maine, and Dummer Jewett of Ipswich. On October 6 Captains Joseph Foster of Gloucester and W. Cutter of North Yarmouth, Maine, and Elbridge Gerry of Marblehead replaced Grout, Sullivan and Jewett. On the ninth they recommended that a committee be appointed to prepare a privateering act. Five more days, and a bill for establishing a number of armed vessels, drawn up evidently by this same committee, received its first reading in the House. Two more weeks, and on the first of November it passed the General Court, and Massachusetts was in the business of privateering.

The act erected the ideological rationale for the seizure of vessels in the service of the enemy and for the fitting-out of private armed vessels in Massachusetts ports. It spelled out the procedure for commissioning their commanders and required owners to post bonds guaranteeing an explicit code of behavior and honor on the part of captains. It created admiralty courts at Ipswich and Plymouth and a jury system to govern the condemnation and sale of prizes and cargoes at vendue. The risks would be high, and so would the rewards: net proceeds to the captors after costs; prize money to be split between captors and owners in the case of retaken American vessels, unless they had been already condemned by the enemy prior to recapture, when they were to be treated as regular prizes, winner take all.

Captain Foster's long experience as mariner, merchant, soldier, politician and evader of the British customs doubtless was of value to his colleagues in the framing of this historic legislation.

The first bond officially issued under the Massachusetts privateering act was dated December 7, 1775, for the armed schooner *Boston Revenge,* Captain Stephen Mascoll. The second followed on the eleventh, for the armed vessel *Gamecock,* Captain Peter Roberts of Newburyport. On the thirteenth Congress authorized the construction of thirteen Continental frigates. The third Massachusetts privateer, schooner *Dolphin* of Salem, was commissioned on December 15.

The Bay Colony's fourth privateer was the twenty-ton armed vessel *General Ward* of Gloucester, Captain Mathew Kelly,

commissioned on December 19. Her owners were Ebenezer
Parsons and Captain Joseph Foster, merchants of Gloucester,
and Timothy Jackman of Rowley, gentleman; they posted a
bond of five thousand pounds. [16] So it can be said of Joseph Foster
that he was a man to put his money where his mouth was, as he had
proven ere this.

Captain Foster's other legislative responsibilities in the closing
weeks of 1775 reflected the House's recognition of his knowledge of
the West Indies trade. Someone had spread it that Elias Hasket
Derby, the Salem merchant and a member of the House, "had,
contrary to the Association of the Continental Congress,
imported coffee and other things from the English West-India
Islands," and Foster was asked to head a three-man committee
to journey to Salem, conduct a full inquiry and "direct the
attention of the said Derby to his duty in this House." After
several weeks *King Derby*, as Salemites had crowned the
powerful shipowner, was found "not culpable."

Meanwhile, Foster was on a six-member committee of the
House and Council charged with fitting out ten vessels to be
laden with provisions and goods, at the colony's expense and
risk, to send to the non-British West Indies in the hope of
acquiring arms, ammunition, sulphur and saltpeter for the
manufacture of gunpowder, and German steel for making
gunlocks. Three weeks later the House directed the receiver
general to advance the committee eight thousand pounds on
account.

General Washington's mosquito squadron had been using
Gloucester as a hiding place from which to buzz unguarded
enemy vessels, [17] as Admiral Graves had so gravely deplored.
Not a week passed, with winter coming on, but fresh evidence
of the truth of his unhappy assertions about Yankee harbors
and the sailing abilities of Yankee schooners found its way into
the record...for instance, the log of HM Schooner *Halifax*,
December 18:

> Fresh gales and clear weather. In chace of 3 rebel
> schooner privateers. Cape Ann NE 11 miles. At 2 [PM]
> one of the schooners parted compy wt the others and
> hauld her wind in shore. Gave chace to her, the other two

getting in to Cape Ann Harbr. Fired several shott at the chace. At 5 she got in under the Battery at Marblehead.[18]

Next day, Parson Fuller wrote in his diary: "Our privateers brought a sloop into our harbour laden with wood designed for the besieged ministerial troops in Boston."

Ten more days, December 28, HMS *Fowey,* twenty guns, Captain George Montagu:

> The entrance to Cape Ann NE by E 1 mile. At 7 AM came here his Majesty's Schooner the *Hinchinbrook,* took out our pilot and sent theirs on board. At 8 saw 5 rebel privateers in the Eastern Channel, weighed & gave them chace. After firing several 6 pounders at them they took shelter in Cape Ann.[19]

Such futile cat-and-mouse games were no more a test of British naval strength, to be sure, than was Gloucester's victory over *Falcon* a portent of American capability in repelling an amphibious landing. Graves might be timid, and Howe recalcitrant, but Britain had other commanders, and other fleets and armies. The lion had hardly yet aroused himself to respond to the first tentative twisting of his tail. With Boston at stake, the New England waters were the scenes of the first skirmishes of the struggle at sea. Nothing signifies the sheer magnitude of the colonial challenge, its absurdity, any better than the brave proposal of the General Court on December 28, when faced with expiration of enlistments in three more days, to hold the involuted coast (except for Boston) clear from Buzzards Bay to Casco Bay and beyond with a mere twelve hundred men mustered for another year.

The strongest detachment of these "Sea-Coast Forces" was to be stationed at Cape Ann. The legislators had thought better of their first grandiose plan to put a general in command of three companies there, and now amended that resolve to raise the companies to four, aggregating two hundred and fifty men, under a colonel with the added authority to order the commanding officer of the neighboring regiment of militia to his assistance in case of attack. Only one larger contingent was to be levied, four hundred men in five companies at Falmouth, but they were to guard the "neighboring places in the Province of

Maine," a large assignment. The other units were to be divided among Martha's Vineyard, the Elizabeth Islands, Plymouth, Marblehead and Kittery.

Pay was to range down from nine pounds a month for colonel to thirty-six shillings for privates, and no man passed muster unless he had equipped himself at his own expense with "a good, effective fire-arm, cartridge-box, blanket, and knapsack, half a pound of powder, twenty bullets, and four flints." Any officer or soldier who within two months of passing muster failed to get hold of a bayonet and belt and one-quart canteen was liable for a fine of six shillings a month. Each man's daily provisions allowance was to be "one pound of wheat flour bread, or one pound and a quarter of other bread, one pound of pork, or one pound and a quarter of beef; and where salt fish can be had, they shall be allowed one pound of fish one day in seven, instead of one day's allowance of meat; also one shilling and eight pence per week to purchase milk, butter, peas, and other sauce, soap, and vinegar." [20]

The General Court next proceeded to the election of the colonel to take charge of Cape Ann's defense, and his officers. It was Saturday, December 30, three in the afternoon:

Mr. Sullivan came up with a message from the House, to inform the Board that the House were now ready to come to the choice of a Field-Officer, with the rank of Colonel, to command at Gloucester, by joint ballot of both Houses, if agreeable to the Honourable Board.

Mr. Holten went down with a message to the House, to inform them that the Board were now ready to proceed to the choice of a Field-Officer, to command at Gloucester, agreeable to the foregoing proposal.

In Council: Ordered, That Benjamin Lincoln and John Taylor, Esquires, be a Committee on the part of the Board to count and sort the votes, who reported that the number of votes were:

On the part of the Board	9
On the part of the House	70
Total	79

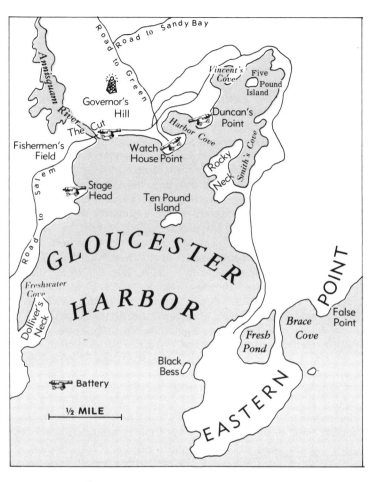

Forty made a vote; and Captain Joseph Foster had 70, and was accordingly chosen. [21]

Daniel Warner and John Lane, who already had militia commands in Gloucester, were elected first and second captains. Bradbury Sanders, Colonel Foster's associate in the *Falcon* fight, was picked for third captain, with special responsibility for "Fort Ann." William Pearson, the sea captain beached by the war whom the committee of safety wanted in charge of the earthworks at Stage Head, was fourth captain. Within a month or two, Captain Lane had been transferred into the Continental Army and was succeeded by Daniel Giddings, Foster's brother-in-law. Young Jeremiah Foster, the colonel's nephew, was elected Giddings's second lieutenant in March, when the General Court was asked to rerank the Gloucester captains, as "some difficulty has arisen," no doubt consequent to Lane's replacement by Giddings, who was accordingly assigned fourth place.

Colonel Foster's command took in at least forty miles of Cape Ann coast and may have extended as far as to include Chebacco [22] and Manchester, whose committee of correspondence two weeks after his commissioning asked the General Court's leave to raise a company to be under his orders. Since he couldn't be at Cape Ann and Watertown at once, Representative Foster moved on January 4, 1776, that the House direct Gloucester to choose someone else to represent it; the town deferred action until its March meeting, however, and did not elect its old standby, Peter Coffin, to succeed him until April 3.

With the defenses of strategic Cape Ann finally under the unified command of the man who had proved his mettle in the repulse of *Falcon* and her landing party, General Washington on January 1, 1776, appointed Winthrop Sargent, Foster's old friend, merchant, ex-sea captain, to the post of Continental Agent at Gloucester; Cape Ann was to be an important base in the war at sea.

Sargent's primary instructions from Washington were to transact the business of the armed vessels which were to be fitted out at the Continental expense, and to supply them with all the necessaries whenever they put in to Gloucester; this meant having on hand at all times twelve barrels each of beef and pork and twenty of bread, to be replenished from the commissary at Beverly. He was to board all prizes brought into Cape Ann, send their papers by express to headquarters at Cambridge, inventory their cargos and take precautions against their embezzlement. Because Gloucester Harbor was not considered safe for laying up prizes for any length of time, he was to have them sailed up to Beverly in care of Agent William Bartlett.

To his agent at Gloucester George Washington offered an inducement, and an admonition: Sargent's commission was to be two and a half per cent on auction sales of prizes and on provisions supplied Continental vessels...and he was to treat all prisoners for whom he had any responsibility "with the utmost humanity and tenderness." [23]

In those few words, the tall Commander-in-Chief at Cambridge said much about himself.

12

THE DIFFICULTIES
WE LABOR UNDER

"If we are compelled to make the last appeal to heaven," the men of Gloucester swore that dark day before Boston dumped the tea, "we will defend our resolutions and liberties at the expense of all that is dear to us." Brave words, these, and they had made good on them with their blood at the redoubt and behind the rail fence on Charlestown heights, and again, in seven weeks, on their own doorsteps. And yet there was a deeper implication to the defense of American resolutions and liberties, and a more tormented sacrificial commitment involving all that was dear to them, than the honest readiness of Gloucestermen to die gloriously for what they were fired up about in town meeting on a December day of 1773.

Six months after Lexington the selectmen for the first of many times were instructed to borrow funds to buy the poor the necessities of life and to provide them with work. "A deep feeling of anxiety and gloom pervaded the town," wrote historian Babson. Three out of four of the working men of Cape Ann were seafarers now cut off from their livelihood by the enemy blockade, and although many were off in the army, and a few privateering, "there still remained a distressingly large proportion of our people, whose productive industry this year could not secure them against dismal forebodings for the coming winter."[1]

How large a proportion, and how dismal those forebodings, and how far and wide had Cape Ann's plight been broadcast are implied in Parson Fuller's succinct diary entry, five days before Christmas: "Four Quaker gentlemen came from the southward to this place to relieve the poor."

Their gift of money inspired the Gloucester town meeting early in January of 1776 to delegate a committee "to take up two proper vessels to send to the southward for grain for the benefit of the town," to find masters and men willing to hazard the blockade and to provision and insure them. Letters of credit to Virginia were sought, but the project moved so slowly that by March 11, when the town authorized four hundred pounds of insurance on the Virginia-bound vessels of Captains William Ellery and William Coas, the selectmen were being pushed to buy or borrow, somewhere, two hundred bushels of corn for the needy and to join with Marblehead in pleading for an abatement of the 1775 tax to the Province on the grounds of virtual bankruptcy.[2]

Heartstricken by the conditions they found in the suffering seaport which already had endured so much in a war that so far had caused the other colonies little more than inconvenience, the good Quakers returned to their brethren for a second subscription. Others came forward, too, and on April 3 Gloucester voted

> that this town acknowledge with the highest gratitude and thankfulness, the receipt of a second donation of a sum of money for the relief of the poor inhabitants of this town from the benevolent Society of the Friends in Pennsylvania and New Jersey, by the hand of their Committee who delivered the same into the hands of the Selectmen to be distributed according to the instructions of the donors.
>
> That this town returns their sincere thanks to the compassionate donors of a sum of money sent by the hand of Mr. John Murray for the relief of our poor which he lays out in provisions and distributes among them according to their necessities.
>
> Also that the thanks of this town be given to Capt. Andrew Giddings for his generous donation of four barrels of flour to be distributed among our poor.

More would be heard from John Murray, much more. He was thirty-four years old at this time, an English preacher who before coming to America in 1770 had been converted from the to-hell-and-be-damned Calvinism which the evangelist George Whitefield had preached up and down New England to the more reassuring interpretation of eternity offered by James Relly, an estranged Whitefield disciple. Relly held that John Calvin's threat of eternal hellfires as the reward for irredeemable sin was false doctrine, a corruption of Scripture; in his view, Christ's sufferings had restored the race to grace — meaning that ultimately, though they must suffer intermediate punishment, all sinners will at last be universally saved.

Debt-ridden and despondent after the death of his wife and child, John Murray sought a new life in America and brought Relly's Universalism with him. While preaching in Boston in October of 1774, he was invited down to Gloucester by the Whig-and-Tory brothers, Winthrop and Epes Sargent, who agreed theologically, if not politically, in their shared enthusiasm for Relly's optimism. Murray preached twice in the First Parish meeting house in November and December, but thereafter the pulpit was barred to him by the ailing Reverend Samuel Chandler, whose Calvinist soul was shocked by this liberal heresy. Joseph Foster was an early member of the small group of Gloucester Universalists who from that time on met in various homes.

On the urging of some of the officers of the Rhode Island Brigade who already were followers of his, Murray in May of 1775 had accepted appointment as chaplain of their unit, stationed then in Jamaica Plain near Boston. When George Washington took command of the Continental forces, the Reverend John Cleaveland of Chebacco was a leader in the movement of chaplains, all of whom were of the established Congregationalist sect, to pressure the general to remove Murray. This so angered Washington that in September he appointed Murray officially as the chaplain to all the Rhode Island regiments, and ordered that "he is to be respected as such."

However, Chaplain Murray was not long in the military life. He resigned in poor health and returned to find Gloucester in the same plight which had so distressed the Friends from the southward. When he was well enough that fall, he travelled to Cambridge and raised a subscription, "a very large sum" by his own account, among the Continental army command and other friends, for the relief of Cape Ann. General Washington headed the list with a donation of ten pounds, then each of his major generals with five pounds, and each brigadier with three.

In Gloucester John Murray doled out his fund with the advice of the selectmen. He estimated that "upwards of a thousand individuals ... in consequence of this very providential and seasonable support, were enabled to get through the worst winter they ever experienced through the war; that he never had any advantage of a pecuniary nature for himself, but, on the contrary, was thirty dollars out of pocket, happy that he had it to dispose of."[3] It was this act of benevolence for which Gloucester thanked him at the beginning of April, 1776.

Mr. Chandler had died after a lingering illness in March of '75, and the Harbor Parish was without a pastor for a year until April 2, '76, the day before the town meeting officially thanked John Murray. On April 2 a majority overrode the Universalists (town and Congregationalist church were one in these days, it must be remembered) and invited the Reverend Eli Forbes, a man with due respect for the powers of brimstone, to settle as Chandler's successor. Murray's backers, led by Winthrop Sargent and Colonel Foster, and including Captain Bradbury Sanders and John McKean, the customs smoker, made a last effort to work within the system and on April 4 wrote Forbes urging him not to settle in Gloucester. His doing so, they argued, would split the First Parish apart doctrinally and force them to take steps "disagreeable" to all concerned. Moreover, they pressed (not entirely disingenuously), this was the worst of times to move into town:

> For many years past, our trade, and particularly the fishery, by which our chief dependence is, has greatly declin'd, that, except a very few persons, we have been carrying on both trade and fishery to a very great loss; that many of us have sunk thousands; that we have large debts outstanding which

will be entirely lost. Our fishery at present is at an end, and merchandize abroad very dangerous and precarious; several of our vessels taken, others missing; our tradesmen and labourers dependent mostly on the trade for their subsistence. Should the publick dispute continue much longer, our fishery must be entirely ruined, and then, of course, all other business of any consequence here must fail, as we are at such a distance from the country that it will be in vain to expect anything therefrom in our trade. We are greatly in arrears in our taxes of every kind for two years past; new and heavy ones increasing daily; most of our people gone; not the least expectation but we shall be put to the flight again. Two or three of our principal traders left the parish; more intend it.

Some of us remember the Spanish and French Wars at different periods, with other sore calamities; but never did our eyes behold such a Gloomy Aspect as our affairs wear at this season...[4]

Eli Forbes was a man of forty-eight, a graduate of Harvard, a Congregationalist, a veteran of the French and Indian wars as soldier and chaplain, a missionary to the Indians for a while, and he was not easily dissuaded from a course once set. He replied to the Universalists that he hoped he would do nothing to increase the burdens of the town and admonished his doctrinal adversaries "that the gospel always carries its own reward and a blessing along with it, and those places that have neglected the settlement of the gospel and its ordinances fall a prey to every deceiver..." In two months Reverend Forbes was installed, and the Universalists walked out of the First Parish.

The Sargent-Foster letter of April 4 had in a general way described the gloomy aspect of Gloucester's sacrifices on the altar of liberty. At the end of the month, the town's leaders, desperately looking to the General Court for a tax abatement, came up with some hard facts in an "Estamate of the Loss on Income & the Trade of Cape Ann from April 1775 to April 1776:[5]

80 sail of fishing schooners worth	
300 £ Now worth 150 £ each	£ 12000
Meterels for cureing fish lost wholley	6000

```
Loss on the income of 80 sail
    fishing vessels at 100 £ each                   8000
30 sail merchant men worth
    400 £ each   Now worth 200 £ each              6000
Loss on the trade of the above vessels
    60 only of which have made one voige       [no figure]
10 vessels and cargos taken by the enemy
3 large boats taken by ditto
11600 of superfind feet wharf useless
48 warehouses useless
130 of the most valuable houses shut up
180 families partly supported by the town
40 poor wholy maintainied by the town
233 widows
1059 boys under age no employ
2081 females
Building fences etc damaged   Eaquel to one years
    rent of the same   300 familys moved 4 miles
    out of town at great expence
Expence building forts etc before
    any soldiers ware in pay
The town much indebt & obliged to hire
    large sums of money to support the
    poor & supply the familys of those
    gone in the service of the State   Not
    being able to gether taxes of those
    who are gone.
```

With Gloucester for their model, Salem, Sandwich, Martha's Vineyard and perhaps other towns composed their own litanies of distress this spring; the Vineyard's is specifically identified as having been submitted to the "Massachusetts Committee for Abating Taxes," implying a concerted drive to influence the General Court.

It was not all gloom that first winter of the war. If there was not a brighter side, there was a less dark one. Washington's little squadron and a persistently proliferating pack of privateers darted, pounced and disappeared, much to the irritation of the few of his fleet Admiral Graves grudgingly spared from guarding Nantasket Roads. The reinforcements from England which General Howe hoped would spring him from his Boston prison were not seen on the horizon, and more and more of the ships bearing provisions and supplies for his relief had a confounded way of evaporating as they approached the coast, only to turn up in some rebel seaport like Gloucester.

There was the ship *Jenny,* two hundred tons, Captain William Wood, England for Boston, with fifteen hundred blankets, a hundred casks of oatmeal (that stuff Dr. Johnson said was for horses in England but in Scotland supports the people ... whether in Boston meant for English horses or Scottish soldiers, the invoice did not state), a number of pairs of shoes, a quantity of coal and a hundred bolts of "oznabrigs," jargon for osnaburg, a coarse flaxen fabric woven in Osnabruck, Germany. That first commissioned Massachusetts privateer, *Boston Revenge,* captured *Jenny* and carried her into Gloucester.

Captain Wood, it developed, was an old friend of Robert Hanson Harrison, General Washington's secretary (and a future justice of the United States Supreme Court). On January 26 the Massachusetts Council requested the Gloucester committee of safety to permit Captain Wood, his mate and eight crew members of *Jenny* the freedom of the town. On February 1 Captain Wood wrote Harrison from Gloucester asking him to intervene to have his parole extended so that he could travel to Cambridge; he wanted to see what could be done to regain his vessel ..."the committee in this town has used me in every respect like a gentleman & desired me to write to you on this occasion."

On the thirteenth Washington's secretary vouched for his friend before the Council, and in four days Wood was permitted to "pass & repass at pleasure from and to Cambridge & Newburyport." The courtesies of warfare and old friendships were not forgotten by the gentleman from Virginia. [6]

There was the brig *Henry and Esther,* mysteriously swallowed up on January 26 crossing Ipswich Bay from LeHave, Nova Scotia, for Boston. Not a big haul, mind you, but Captains Daniel Waters and Samuel Tucker of Washington's armed schooners *Lee* and *Franklin* had themselves a brig which they nipped into Squam Harbor, and they had the supreme satisfaction of knowing that sixty-two cords of wood, a hundred and fifty butts of water and forty suits of soldiers' bedding would neither warm nor wet the lobsterbacks that winter. Captain Nellis was treated with the gallantry due his station, and *Henry and Esther* was advertised on June 6 to be sold at James Prentice's tavern "with all her appurtenances, some second-hand rigging, two cables, and a few casks of porter."[7]

There was no slapping the General's mosquitoes.

Log of HMS *Fowey,* January 30, Baker's Island southwest half a league (a "part" is a four-hour watch in the three-watch cycle from midnight to noon or noon to midnight):

> At 10 sway'd up the topgalt masts. Clap'd a slip buoy on the small bower cable & sliped it, hove up the best bower and gave chace to 4 privateers to the eastward. First part fresh gales with sleet, middle moderate with rain, latter light airs & fair. At ½ 1 PM the privateers took shelter in Cape Ann Harbour.[8]

Rough as that first winter was on Cape Ann, it was not a candle to the discouragement which took hold of George Washington in the middle of January. Surveying an army shrunken by the expiration of enlistments and shriveled by a shortage of funds, arms, powder, clothing, food and pay — all the tools of war — and brooding over the failure of Benedict Arnold's expedition against Quebec at the end of December and the prospect of British reinforcements arriving at Boston any day, he wrote despairingly to his old friend, Joseph Reed, that "if I shall be able to rise superior to these and many other difficulties, I shall most religiously believe, that the finger of Providence is in it, to blind the eyes of our enemies; for surely if we get well enough through this month, it must be for want of their knowing the difficulties we labor under."

Then enlistments accelerated. Ten regiments of militia arrived in Cambridge. New supplies of powder were turned up. Henry Knox struggled into camp with the captured cannon dragged heroically through the snowdrifts from Ticonderoga and Crown Point. Impatiently, Washington laid his plans to seize and fortify Dorchester Heights, overlooking Boston and the British, as soon as the ground had thawed and could be worked with pick and shovel, and readied an armada of small craft for an invasion across the Charles River from Cambridge. On March 1 he called in his reserves of militia from the country around to assemble in Roxbury for the assault.

He was ready, at last.

On the evening of March 2, 1776, the cannon of the Continental forces entrenched around Boston opened fire on the enemy strongholds. The barrage was returned briskly, and for most of the night the reverberations of the cannonading rolled across Boston Bay and told the coast and the country that something momentous was under way. But what? Was Howe preparing to break out, or Washington to break in?

By the next morning, March 3, the word must have reached Cape Ann that this was indeed the long-awaited attack on Boston, and the hills would have been clustered with people hoping to get a look at any naval action that might flare up offshore.

They were not disappointed. His Majesty's Brig *Hope*, armed with six guns and carrying a crew of thirty, was cruising about fifteen miles southeast of Cape Ann when at one in the afternoon they spied four sail to the northward and gave chase. The wind was fresh, and *Hope* took three hours to run them down. It was Captain Manley's fleet of armed schooners. *Hope*'s log does not explain why ninety minutes elapsed, but at 5:30 Lieutenant George Dawson engaged them.

The battle lasted only thirty minutes, but the skies were clear, and spectators on the heights of Cape Ann had a panoramic view of it. "Got damaged by them," is the cryptic entry in *Hope*'s log. "One man wounded and several rops shot away and shot in the hull." Yet Dawson gave no quarter. At six, with night coming on, his supposed prey left off and bore away for Gloucester Harbor. Dawson did not follow, but hauled his wind to the eastward to nurse his wounds. At eight that evening Cape Ann was three or four leagues to the northwest, and *Hope*'s tars were clearing the decks and repairing ripped rigging. The bombardment of Boston had resumed for the second night; they watched the flashes in the dark sky to the westward, and their hearts pounded to the ominous roll of explosions across the water.

During the American bombardment, wrote one participant, "our people splet *the Congress* [the thirteen-inch mortar from *Nancy*] the third time that they fired it," as the inexperienced gunners did three or four others. Distracted by three nights running of barrage, the British looked out on the quiet of the morning of March 5, the sixth anniversary of the Boston Massacre, and saw to their chagrin the army and guns of General John Thomas looking back at them from an unbelievable earthwork which had materialized out of the murk on Dorchester Heights.

With many misgivings, General Howe did the only thing honor and duty would allow him to do: he ordered Lord Percy to embark from Castle Island with twenty-four hundred troops and assault the Heights. But a sudden violent storm arose. The attack had to be postponed, and then cancelled as Howe accepted the futility of his position. If he could no longer hold Boston, he must leave it. On March 6 he gave the order to prepare to evacuate. Eleven thousand British regulars and eleven hundred Tories put the sieged town in an uproar as they plundered, destroyed property, spiked cannon and dashed through the narrow streets to the waterfront with loads of legitimate luggage and loot for ferrying out to the fleet.

Having no reason not to suppose that their destination remained as securely as ever a possession of the crown, the people on board the English merchant ship *Stakesby*, from London, made their landfall at Cape Ann on Sunday, March 10, and met their downfall sailing into the courteous clutches of Captains Manley in *Hancock,* Daniel Waters in *Lee,* Samuel Tucker in *Franklin* and John Ayers in *Lynch*. The General's commanders politely but insistently took the three hundred-ton transport in hand and signaled Captain James Watts that a prize crew would be over directly to assist him in getting into Gloucester.

The night was dark, and it was thick-o'-fog. *Stakesby* and *Hancock* approached the Back Shore, hearing surf, but seeing nothing. Somewhere off to starboard must be the tip of Eastern Point. The *Stakesby* prizemaster eased her to come in around to Gloucester Harbor, when with an awful scraping and crunching of timbers they hove up on the rocks of Bemo Ledge at the entrance to Brace Cove. They had mistaken the outline of the shore from which the reef of Bemo reaches out, for the real end of Eastern Point a mile beyond, and discovered to their dismay why local mariners called this bluff the False Point.

All aboard clambered over the side and waded ashore through the surf.

Hancock may have been close enough astern of *Stakesby* that she followed the prize onto the rocks or even collided with her. If so, Manley's schooner was got off, because Winthrop Sargent, Washington's agent in Gloucester, mentioned in his initial report to his chief on the incident two days later that Manley "damaged his vessel verey much. Lost his bowsprit but is refeted." Most of *Stakesby*'s cargo was a loss, Sargent wrote, but "I shall dow all in my power to save what I can ... I should be glad to know what I shall dow with the Capt & sallers as they have know ship to cheap on bord." He enclosed her invoice and two letters intended for General Howe.

Colonel Foster hiked over to Brace Cove with a company to guard the wreck and take off the undamaged spoils. By the third day, Wednesday forenoon, they had salvaged, according to Sargent's second accounting to Washington of March 14, "all the sails & most of the rigen from the ship with about 50 cask of porter & two fine cabels & two ankors."

Wednesday afternoon HM Brig *Hope* was still on station off Cape Ann. A week earlier she had taken two sloops, one of them *John*, owned by Daniel Rogers of Gloucester and bound into Ipswich from Virginia with flour, Indian corn and wheat. Lieutenant Dawson was on the lookout for more prizes and another crack at Manley's squadron. It was one o'clock:

> Fresh breezes and clear wr. Out reefs TS [topsails]. Up T-G [topgallant] yards. Saw a vessel, on shore on the East Point of Cape Ann, with a number of the rebels on bd. Sent the Master, in a boat mand & armd to hir. On the approach of our boat the rebels quitted hir. Found hir to be a transport named the *Stacksby*. Stove a number of casks of porter and set hir on fire. 9 PM boat returned.

Winthrop Sargent's report to General Washington of the next morning offers some explanation for the evident failure of Foster and his men to attempt to repel the boarding party sent in from *Hope*. The wreck itself was indefensible, and too far out on the reef to be defended from shore:

> Last night Capt Dosson had the impedence to run in & set fier to the ship, it being high warter. Our guns would not reach him & she is burnt down to the warter. This low warter if the storm seases we shall sea what we can git out of the ship. The poor Capt Whatts has lost all his venter, being about 150 £ starling. The reason of his not cumming befor, he was unwell. [9]

On March 17, the British and the Loyalists withdrew from Boston to the ships, without a shot fired. The winds were contrary, and the fleet lay at anchor in Nantasket Roads waiting for a fair breeze. Washington's army entered Boston on the twentieth. Worried about the enemy's next move, Colonel Foster on March 24 invoked his authority to summon the neighboring regiment of militia to his assistance in an emergency; he wrote Colonel Jonathan Cogswell of Chebacco, commanding officer of the Third Essex Regiment from Ipswich, Rowley, Topsfield and Wenham:

> Gloucester, March 24, 1776.
>
> Sir — As our enemies' fleet is now lying in Broad Sound in Boston, and the wind fair for them to come to this place if they are so minded, it is therefore necessary that we stand on our guard, and as your regiment is at so great a distance it will not be prudent to wait till the enemy appears in sight before notice is given you.
>
> I have taken the advice of the committee in this town and considered the difficulty that would attend the sending your whole regiment to this town unless the enemy were actually landed.
>
> I have therefore thought it best that you send one company of seventy-five men, officers included, to my assistance, well armed and accou'red with one week's

provisions each, tomorrow morning as soon as possible, which may prevent a general alarm, and this will be your sufficient warrant for so doing.

> I am your humble servant,
> Joseph Foster [10]

In spite of fair wind, General Howe did not finally make up his mind to issue the humiliating order for three more days, until March 27. Log of HMS *Chatham:*

At 3 PM made the signal & weigh'd, made sail & hoist'd in all the boats. At 4 the light house NW 1 mile. At 6 in company with HM Ships *Centurion Lively Savage* & *Tryal* schooner with sixty six sail of transports & other vessels. [11]

Winthrop Sargent was up early next morning to write his final *Stakesby* report to General Washington, in his own unique style and with an afterthought which fairly breathed relief: [12]

Sir — Wen I rote you last I was in hops of saving tne bigest part of Capt Watts cargow but, the storm cumming on direcley after the ship was on fier, that the cask stove against the rocks as sune as thay struck the shoar. Thare was not one cask saved. Sum of the cask which I thought was portor is veneger & grout. Should be glad to know weather I must libel what is saved.

Last night at sundown the fleat about seventy sail past our Cape stearing about E [by] S distant about six Leags.

19 bals of porter	2 cabels
6 hogsd of do	3 ankers
<u>17</u> quart cask of do	1 horsor
42	2 oyrn haths
9 hogsed veneger	3 coppors
2 bals of grout	Sail & running rigen
	2 boats
	Sundry blocks
	3 hogs

The Boston Loyalists were not unanimous in their choice of Halifax and the rigors of Nova Scotia. New York was a stronghold of Toryism, and one Jolly Allen, a shopkeeper ("Black Jolly Allen," James Warren called him) herded his wife and seven children, four fellow Tories and seventeen other women and children, household goods, clothes and casks of Delft and glassware on board the sloop *Sally* the afternoon the British fleet sailed, hoping to take refuge there. *Sally* belonged neither to Black Jolly nor to Captain Robert Campbell, but to David Pearce of Gloucester, and she had been cut out of its harbor by *Hope* ten days after Bunker Hill battle and brought to Boston.

One day out, *Sally* was wrecked on the back of Cape Cod. The selectmen of Provincetown reported that all aboard were "in the most miserable condition," some sick with the smallpox, out of fresh water, and Campbell the only one who knew how to sail. A few weeks later, the bona fide skipper of *Sally*, James Jordan, who had escaped from Boston after her capture, petitioned the General Court on behalf of David Pearce that her rightful owner be delivered the "remnant" of his sloop, her sails and rigging.

As the vast British fleet of warships and transports sailed off to the eastward, Washington's little navy followed at a safe distance, like jackals waiting to pounce on a stray from the herd, which is how Captains Manley and Waters happened to take the brig *Elizabeth*, fifteen leagues off Cape Ann, on April 2. They were positively gleeful when they discovered they had bagged Crean Brush, a notorious collaborator and a "cursed villain" in the eyes of his fellow Bostonians, with seventy other Loyalists, a dozen British soldiers and a cargo of goods valued at twenty-four thousand pounds, much of which Brush was suspected of having plundered from his patriot neighbors.

Elizabeth was taken to Portsmouth, and a number of her passengers to Gloucester, creating further problems for the General's conscientious agent, who wrote Washington on April 7:

Sir — The bayer of this has under his gard a number of prisoners & Toreys taken by Comodor Manley & Captain

Warters. The prise is sent to Portsmouth. I mack know dout you have had acount of before this reaches your Excellence. Thar names you have below. Thare is two women & sum children left hear which is not abel to travel. Should be glad your Excellence would send me answer to what I roat you last about Capt Wattss goods and what I am to dow whith the prisoners for I have thirtey hear now upon expences.

I remm, etc.
Winthrop Sargent

PS Sence I rote he above Capt Tucker heve carr the prisoners to Marvelhead ware thay well be sent to head quartr. Will not carrey the women & children for fear of the small pox so I am forc to porvide for them hear. Should be glad of your order in regard to the above. [13]

Washington had left for New York on April 4, and Sargent's letter was a month catching up with him. When it did, he replied through General Ward at Boston that those in Sargent's charge at Gloucester who were prisoners of war should be confined somewhere inland; as for the Tories, "the General Court are the proper persons to take cognizance of them."

The Commander-in-Chief permitted Captains Watts of *Stakesby,* Nellis of *Henry and Esther,* William Wood of *Jenny* and John Robertson of *Nelly* to return to England in a vessel they were buying for that purpose. They had commanded merchant ships taken as prizes, and this was, after all, a gentlemen's war.

13

YANKEE HEROES ALL

Having squeezed the British out of Boston, General Washington was bound that they should stay out. Before he had completed the removal of the main body of his army to New York in mid-April of 1776 to comply with what he considered Congress's untimely order that he defend it against an expected invasion, he gave General Artemus Ward, whom he had left behind as commander in Massachusetts, explicit instructions to set up an alarm system should the British attempt to reoccupy Boston.

Cape Ann was the key to it. Here warships approaching from the eastward would first be sighted. "No time should be lost in fixing with the General Court or Council upon proper signals for alarming the country upon the appearance of a fleet," Washington wrote Ward on April 4. "For the purpose of gaining as much time as possible I think the alarm ought to be given from Cape Ann, or Marblehead, & forwarded by signals to Boston & thence into the country--this matter should not be delayed." [1]

It took twelve days. On April 16 the General Court ordered beacons erected on Governor's Hill at Gloucester (ever after Beacon Pole Hill, at the summit of Commonwealth Avenue), at Marblehead, Boston and on Blue Hill in Milton; when an enemy fleet was discovered, the selectmen and the two commissioned officers closest to hand were to "fire three alarm guns, set the bells ringing and cause the beacons to be fired with all expedition."

Gloucester town meeting promptly directed the committees of correspondence and safety to consult with Colonel Foster about establishing watches at strategic locations around Cape Ann. He was nearly three weeks delayed in fully implementing these instructions because on April 22, mindful of General Ward's preoccupation with securing Boston against reoccupation, the General Court stepped in arbitrarily and ordered one of Foster's four companies--that of his brother-in-law, Captain Daniel Giddings--to march to Boston immediately and pitch in with pick and shovel.

To rob Gloucester for the sake of Boston was not to the liking of Joseph Foster the military man, and there is no doubt that Joe Foster the recently resigned representative from Cape Ann set about some political spadework himself, because eleven days later, on the third of May, the General Court reversed itself:

> ...whereas it appears to this Court that the men stationed at Gloucester are not more than sufficient to guard and defend that place: Therefore resolved, That the Resolve for ordering the company of men aforesaid to march to Boston, be, and hereby is, declared null and void, and that the company aforesaid remain in the station they were fixed at Gloucester aforesaid, till the further order of this Court.[2]

Colonel Foster now could concentrate on his end of the alarm network. He wrote Lieutenant Joseph Lane, in Captain Pearson's company, on May 9:

> Sir -- You are hereby ordered and requested forthwith to march with the party of five men under your command whose names are as follows: Daniel Haraden, John Atkins, Caleb Lane, Joseph Somes and Joseph Davis to Squam, where you are to keep a watch at the entrance of the harbor night and day, which watch is to be properly released at your discretion. You are to give said watch orders to inform you if they discover any vessels or boats that attempt to land on that shore, or that appear to be an enemy. After you have inquired into such information as you may receive from the watch, if you judge it needful you are to fire three guns to alarm the inhabitants there and send one of your party to me

with an account of what occasioned the alarm, after which you are to endeavor to prevent the enemy from landing. You are furthermore to visit the watch at the Cape [Sandy Bay] and Chebacco side under Corporals Brown and Emerton once a week or oftener, and see if they keep a good watch agreeable to the orders they have received from me, which you are to demand when you visit said watches and see if these men attend their duty and make a return to me every Tuesday when you send for your allowance of provisions. Fail not.

Joseph Foster

N.B. You are to practice your party in the manual exercise all opportunities.[3]

The Continental Congress no less than the Massachusetts General Court continued jealous of civilian prerogative over the military. On April 17, pursuant to a vote of the whole body, the committee on fortifying ports (John Adams, Benjamin Harrison and William Whipple) requested General Washington to prepare and submit detailed plans of the harbors, forts and ordnance at Gloucester, which commanded the eastern approach to Boston, and New London, Connecticut, at the entrance to Long Island Sound and New York.

Washington had no quarrel with the principle of civilian control, though he was daily more restive under constant Congressional meddling in his almost overwhelming job. He ordered Colonel Richard Gridley, his veteran chief engineer who had designed the works at Breed's Hill and Dorchester Heights, to make the survey at Gloucester and sent Colonel Henry Knox, the Boston bookseller turned artillery expert, off to New London.

No one knew better than Joseph Foster how long he was expected to be on ends, but how short he was on means. His influence comes through in the letter Isaac Smith wrote from Salem on May 22 to the leading member of the congressional committee on fortifying ports, John Adams, whose wife Abigail was Smith's niece. Even if a British fleet could be stopped from rendezvousing in Nantasket Roads, where a small squadron remained at anchor, Foster's old friend and partner pointed out, there may be a dificulty as great iff they should make C. Ann a harbour as they would then stop all coasters coming which now do get along, but iff C. Ann was well fortifyed which by nature is best able with proper batteries to defend itt self of any I know. Indeed M Hd and Salem are well cituated, and iff properly fortifyed would keep out almost any thing, but C. Ann would be the safest harbour for them... [4]

From Philadelphia Adams replied on June 1:

....Cape Ann, I am sensible is a most important post, and if the enemy should possess themselves of it, they might distress the trade of the Colony to a great degree. For which reason I am determined to do every thing in my power to get it fortified at the Continental expence. I cant be confident that I shall succeed but it shall not be my fault if I dont.

I am very glad you gave me your opinion of the utility of that harbour and of the practicability of making it secure, because I was not enough acquainted with it before to speak with precision about it... [5]

The hub of Boston squeaked louder than the rim of Gloucester, however, and was closer to legislative ears in Watertown. One of Peter Coffin's first moves upon returning to the General Court in April to succeed Joseph Foster had been to get through a resolve on May 8 directing the commissary general to deliver two eighteen-pounders to Gloucester. But again the Boston delegation and friends on the committee for fortifying the harbour of Boston stepped in. Two eighteen-pounders to Cape Ann! They were "doubtful whether the safety of the Colony" would admit of it and persuaded the House on May 31 to send down two eighteens *or* "two other cannon, such as said committee may judge may be best spared, consistent with the safety of the Colony...together with the carriages, spunges, and all other appurtenances, and one hundred balls for each cannon, suitable for the same." In the meantime, to Foster's relief, five casks of powder, 537 pounds, arrived from Newbury and were stored at Samuel Rust's place at the head of Little River. [6]

Among the squadron General Howe left behind in Nantasket Roads, to intercept transports and store ships whose masters were unaware that Boston had changed hands, was the new frigate *Milford*, twenty-eight guns. She was a recent arrival from England, and Captain John Burr had been learning a thing or two about the weatherly qualities of the New England schooners which were poking their prows out of their harbors, now that the most of the British fleet was at Halifax...and about the seamanship of the men who sailed them....and about the perils of Gloucester Harbor...to all of which his log testifies:

April 3 -- Cape Ann NNE 6 or 7 leagues...Light airs with rain, gave chace, fir'd 8 shot at the chace. Proved to be a pirate schooner from Cape Ann Harbr, where she got in.

May 14 -- Thatcher's Isld NNE 2 leags. Saw a sail under the land. Out reefs and gave chace. At 11 found the chace to be a rebel privatr. Hove in stays & fir'd 2 nine poundrs & stood off...Mode [rate] and fair. Discovered a rebel privateer coming out of Cape Ann Harbr. Fir'd 5 three poundrs & 10 nine poundrs.

May 27 -- Cape Ann Wt 8 leags. Fresh breezes & hazey, latter light airs. At 1 PM saw some privateers standing in for Cape Ann. Made sail and gave chace. ½ past lost sight of them. Shorten'd sail and brought to.

Close calls. The word went up and down the coast to keep a weather eye out for *Milford* and be ready to run. Isaac Smith told John Adams that the new frigate "goes exceeding fast." [7]

On the bright blue morning of June 6 *Milford* was cruising in Ipswich Bay at latitude 42.50, twelve nautical miles east northeast of Cape Ann. People on shore at Sandy Bay had the impression from that distance, not recognizing her, that she was a clumsily worked merchant ship, probably shorthanded, and an easy pigeon. Lieutenant Mark Pool urged them on and talked Captain John Rowe into putting aside his suspicion that she was a British warship playing decoy. They rounded up about twenty fishermen, farmers and workmen at the dock, piled into two small fishing boats with their muskets and set out after the prize.

Just as this two-boat flotilla of fearless fools embarked on the high seas of Sandy Bay under the command of the two Bunker Hill veterans, a friendly sail rounded Halibut Point from Ipswich Bay which proved on hailing to be the 120-ton privateer brig *Yankee Hero*, seventeen guns, pride of Newburyport since her maiden cruise in February when she brought home a barque and a brig. The *Hero* was provisioned for six months but manned by only a skeleton crew, and Captain James Tracy was bound for Boston to complete his complement of 120, possibly intending to recruit at Gloucester on the way.

The Cape Ann musketeers came alongside, and a joint enterprise was agreed upon then and there. Fourteen of them climbed aboard, which raised the privateer's force of fighting men to forty. The boats were sent back. The strange sail now bore east southeast about fifteen miles out to sea. The wind was westerly, and Captain Tracy crowded on all canvas.

When *Yankee Hero* had reduced the distance separating them to six miles, Tracy was aghast to discover that their intended victim was a British frigate. He put about to run for shore, but in ten minutes his westerly died on him, as the offshore breeze so frequently does on a warm day off Cape Ann, leaving the *Hero* in the lurch. Then just as characteristically, it piped up from the south. The frigate took the air first, being now to windward, and came up on the American like a banshee, figuring to cut her off from shore. And then the wind backed fresh from the westward again, and *Yankee Hero* took it and hauled for Cape Ann, the frigate in her wake.

For an hour they chased, closing in on the Back Shore of the cape, and when the pursued-turned-pursuer (which was indeed the much-feared *Milford*) came within half a mile of *Hero*'s stern Captain Burr put his bow chase guns into action; but Tracy reserved his larger fire and replied only with his swivels.

The distance narrowed. Alive with armed men from her decks to her tops, the frigate pounded through the seas, smashing away the *Hero*'s wake, running her down like a fox on a hare, firing the bow chasers, closing in on the Americans, foot by foot. When *Milford* was on his broadside, Tracy knew he had to fight or strike his colors. *Yankee Hero* opened up with all

The foundation stones of Perkins Story's long-abandoned operation are laid on those of Jeremiah Foster's sawmill at Chebacco Falls, Essex. Looking downstream.

High tide on the Essex River here at the Landing meets the fresh water of Chebacco Falls. The sea is three miles through the meandering marsh.

Joseph Foster's house at lower left, restored in 1973, contrasts with the rising YMCA. Beyond are Harbor Cove, the Fort (Watch House Point), the outer harbor, Ten Pound Island, Eastern Point and the Atlantic. View from City Hall tower.

Typical of Cape Ann vessels in the Caribbean and European trades, the topsail schooner *Baltick* departs from the West Indies on November 16, 1765. She was built up the Merrimack River in 1763.

The Foster House, host to a dry goods store, crowds the Broome Tavern to its left on Middle Street. At right is Dr. Dale's three-story colonial manse. View from the Unitarian Church steeple, 1871.

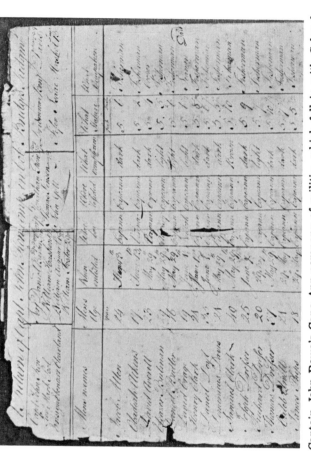

Captain John Rowe's Cape Ann company of militia, which fell in with Colonel Bridge's Middlesex Regiment and dug through the night on Breed's Hill, was long on fishermen and short on stature.

John Linzee of the Royal Navy and his Boston bride, Susanna Inman, not long after their marriage in 1772.

As in the miniature, Linzee in this portrait by Sir George Chalmers wears the coat of a British naval lieutenant.

From behind these dunes Peter Coffin and his men repulsed the boat from *Falcon* trying to land on the beach at right, August 5, 1775. The rocks of Farm Point are beyond. Not much had changed by the 1890's, when the photograph was taken.

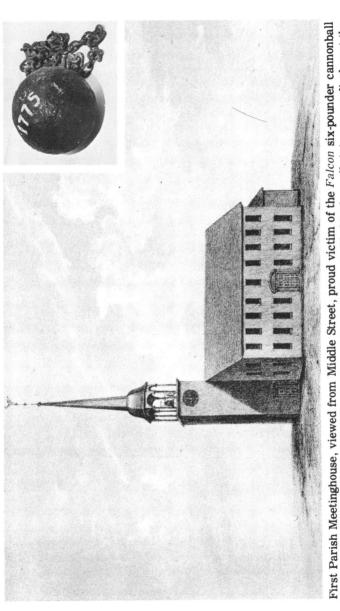

First Parish Meetinghouse, viewed from Middle Street, proud victim of the *Falcon* six-pounder cannonball which hung for years in the vestibule after being discovered embedded in the wall; it is now on display at the Cape Ann Historical Association.

The Head of the Harbor in 1847, by Fitz Hugh Lane. Rocky Neck and Ten Pound Island rise behind the brig which is half-hidden by the sheds on Five Pound Island in the middle foreground. The fleeing West Indiaman

Her captors grounded the British ordnance brig *Nancy* deep inside Freshwater Cove on November 29, 1775, probably by the wharf at the foot of Waterside Lane at far left. In the 1850's Fitz Hugh Lane painted this calmer scene from the western lee of Dolliver's Neck.

Lieutenant Henry Mowat
Commander of *Canceaux*

Brace Cove, Eastern Point, 1850's, probably by William Niles. The prize transport *Stakesby* wrecked on Bemo Ledge at left, March 10, 1776.

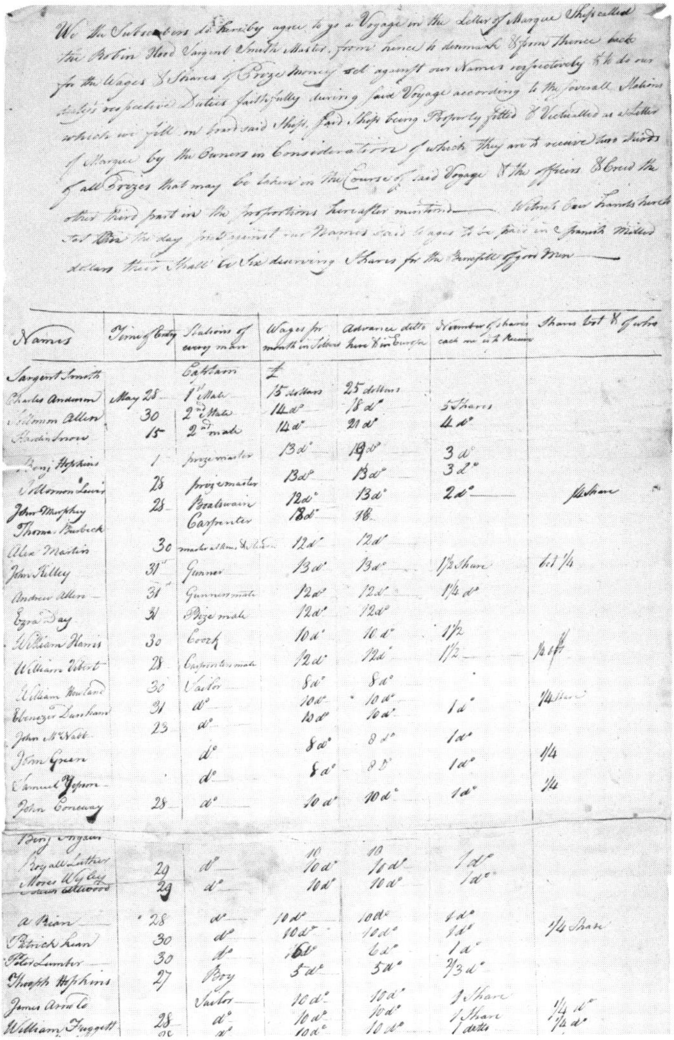

We the Subscribers do hereby agree to go a Voyage in the Letter of Marque Ship called the Robin Hood Sargent Smith Master, from hence to denmark & from thence back for the Wages & Shares of Prize Money set against our Names respectively & to do our duty's respective Duties faithfully during said Voyage according to the several Stations which we fill on board said Ship, said Ship being Properly fitted & Victualled as a Letter of Marque by the Owners in Consideration of which they are to receive two thirds of all Prizes that may be taken in the Course of said Voyage & the officers & Crew the other third part in the proportions hereafter mentioned — Witness our hands hereto set this the day fixed against our Names said Wages to be paid in Spanish Milled dollars there shall be Six deserving Shares for the Benefit of good Men —

Names	Time of Entry	Stations of every man	Wages per month in Silver	Advance ditto here & in Europe	Number of shares each one is to Receive	Shares lost & of who
Sargent Smith		Captain	£			
Charles Anderson	May 28	1st Mate	15 dollars	25 dollars		
Sollomon Allen	30	2nd Mate	14 do	18 do	5 Shares	
Hardin Snow	15	2nd mate	14 do	21 do	4 do	
Benj Hopkins	1	prize master	13 do	19 do	3 do	
Sollomon Lewis	28	prize master	13 do	13 do	3 do	
John Murphy	28	Boatswain	12 do	13 do	2 do	[illegible] share
Thomas Burbeck		Carpenter	18 do	18		
Alex Martin	30	master at Arms [illegible]	12 do	12 do		
John Kelley	31st	Gunner	13 do	13 do	1/2 Share	lost 1/4
Andrew Allen	31st	Gunners mate	12 do	12 do	1/4 do	
Ezra Day	31	Prize mate	12 do	12 do		
William Harris	30	Cook	10 do	10 do	1/2	
William Vibert	28	Carpenters mate	12 do	12 do	1/2	1/4 of [illegible]
William Rowland	30	Sailor	8 do	8 do		
Ebenezer Dunham	31	do	10 do	10 do	1 do	1/4 Share
John McNabb	23	do	10 do	10 do	1 do	
John Green		do	8 do	8 do	1 do	1/4
Samuel Jepson		do	8 do	8 do	1 do	1/4
John Conway	28	do	10 do	10 do	1 do	
Benj Ingram						
Royall Luther	29	do	10 do	10 do	1 do	
Moses Wyley / John Allwood	29	do	10 do	10 do	1 do	
A Bean	28	do	10 do	10 do	1 do	1/4 Share
Patrick Kean	30	do	10 do	10 do	1 do	
Peter Lumber	30	do	6 do	6 do	1 do	
Joseph Hopkins	27	Boy	5 do	5 do	2/3 do	
James Arnold		Sailor	10 do	10 do	1 Share	1/4 do
William Fuggett	28	do	10 do	10 do	1 Share	1/4 do
	28	do	10 do	10 do	1 ditto	

Register of the Boston privateer *Robin Hood*, commanded on her maiden voyage in May 1781 by Captain Sargent Smith of Gloucester, assigns shares of prize money among officers and crew.

Captain John Somes
Gloucester privateer commander

Israel Trask
Soldier at ten, privateersman at thirteen

Province of Nova Scotia —

These are to certify that the persons named in the margin, being Prisoners of war and late belonging to the Brig'e Letter of marque Ship the Polly have permission to reside at Windsor in the said Province, and have this day signed a Parole, stipulating to keep in the said Township or within two miles around it, and to behave themselves in every other respect as Prisoners of war ought and should do.

Given under my hand at Halifax in the Province aforesaid the 23d July 1782

H. Turnbull

Dep't Com'y Gen'l for Naval Prisoners

Joseph Foster — Captain

Jeremiah Foster — First Mate

Joseph Foster Jun. — Third Mate

Thomas A. Sergeant — Surgeon

Parole of the captured Captain Foster and his officers, given at Halifax, Nova Scotia, July 23, 1782.

The English barrel organ seized on the high seas by John Somes
still serves the Independent Christian Church (Universalist) on
Middle Street as a silent reminder of its beginnings.

Reverend John Murray

Reverend Eli Forbes

Beaver Dam Farm on the Rockport road in 1924 retains the granite barn of uncertain vintage at left and the house presumed to have been built by Colonel Foster. Roger W. Babson razed them and restored the Babson cooperage of stone behind the house.

main and quarterdeck guns, swivels and small arms, and the battle was on.

Milford log:

> ...at 2 saw a strange sail in the SW in chace of us. At 3 the chace haul'd in for the land. Made sail & gave chace. ½ past fired 4 shot at the chace. At 4 fired 4 shot more at her. At 5 came alongside the chase who fir'd several shot at us on which we came to action...

The American account of the action was published on August 9 in the *Essex Journal and New Hampshire Packet* of Newburyport:

> The ship was soon up along side, and with 12 nine pounders of a side, upon deck, besides forecastle and quarter deck guns, and with her marines, overlooking the brig as high as her leading blocks, kept a continual fire. ["Lieutenant Pool wished to board the ship and carry her, sword in hand, or die in the attempt," according to Babson, "but his advice of this reckless measure was unheeded."] After some time the ship hauled her wind so close, (which obliged the brig to do the same) that Capt Tracy was unable to fight his lee guns. Upon this he backed under her stern, but the ship which sailed much faster, and worked as quick, had the advantage and brought her broadside again upon him, which he could not evade.

Milford log:

> ½ past 5 the chace wore and bore away. We then wore and came alongside of her again within pistol shot...

For another hour and twenty minutes, the *Essex Journal* reported, the overpowering frigate and the outsized, outsailed, outmanned and outgunned privateer fought it out "not a hundred feet from each other, yawing to and fro," when *Milford*'s fire slackened. Tracy again tacked under his enemy's towering stern, and when clear of the

> smoak and fire, perceived his rigging to be most shockingly cut, yards flying about without braces, some of his principal sails shot to rags and half his men to appear-

ance dying, and wounded...In this situation they went to work to refit the rigging and to carry the wounded below, the ship having then taken a broad sheer some way off, and none of her guns bearing; but before they could get their yards to rights, which they zealously tried for in hopes still to get clear of the ship, as they were now nearer in shore, or to part from her under the night, she again came up and renewed the attack, which obliged Capt. Tracy to have recourse to his guns again, though he still kept some hands aloft to his rigging, but before the brig had again fired two broadsides, Captain Tracy received a wound in his right thigh and in a few minutes he could not stand; he laid himself over the arm chest and barricadoe, determined to keep up the fire, but in a short time, from pain and loss of blood, he was unable to command, growing faint, and they helped him below. As soon as he came to, he found his firing had ceased, and his people round him wounded, and having not a surgeon with them, in a most distressed situation, most of them groaning, some expiring. Struck severely with such a spectacle, Capt. Tracy ordered his people to take him up in a chair upon the quarter deck, and resolved again to attack the ship, which was all this time keeping up her fire; but after getting into the air, he was again so faint, that he was for some time unable to speak, and finding no alternative but they must be taken or sunk, for the sake of the brave men that remained, he ordered them to strike to the ship.

Milford log:

...we then continued firing our great guns and musquets for about a glass [hourglass] longer when she struck. She proved to be an American armed brig called the *Yankey Hero* of 17 carriage guns and 12 swivels & 52 men. [8]

"The brig's last gun was filled with pieces of iron, spikes, and a crowbar," someone told Babson. "The latter, being the only missile left on board, was thrust into the gun by Pool, who, when he went on board the frigate as a prisoner, discovered this new implement of war sticking through the bitts of her windlass. It was called, by the British sailors, the 'Yankee belaying pin.' "

Yankee Hero lost four men killed; one of them was Sandy Bay's schoolmaster, Hugh Parkhurst, who had survived Bunker Hill with Captain Rowe. Twelve were wounded, including from Cape Ann Eben Rowe, whose hand was shot off, and Reuben Brooks, who expired in Halifax prison from a head wound complicated by smallpox. *Milford* recorded but a single casualty, a marine shot in the arm.

The victorious frigate took her prisoners aboard, sent over a prize crew and made sail with the fallen *Hero* for Nantasket Roads at nine in the evening.

Unbelievably foolhardy as it all was--a score of Gloucestermen armed with muskets and a few cutlasses, off to capture an unidentified sail on the horizon, and persuading a shorthanded Newburyport privateer to join them in their folly--the turn of those aboard from bravado to bravery when they realized their awful mistake struck fire in the hearts of Americans reading the story in the *Essex Journal* and other newspapers which picked it up:

> Thus was this action maintained upwards of two hours in a low single deck'd vessel, with not half the metal the ship had, against an English frigate, whose navy had been the dread of nations, and by a quarter the number of people in the one as in the other, yet the victors exulted as though they had overcome a force as much superior as this was inferior to them...With justice to Captain Burr of the *Milford*, it must be acknowledged, he treated with humanity and politeness the officers and men that were wounded; but to the eternal disgrace of Britain, and the present king and parliament, let it be recorded, that in this very action above related, upwards of thirty Americans (prisoners in *Milford*) were forced at the forfeit of their lives to fight against their countrymen, and the officers and men of the *Yankee Hero*, that were not wounded, are now detained in several of their ships, and may meet with the same cruel fate -- an exaction that even the Savages have not been known to require. It is to the credit of the *Hero*'s men that not one would enter upon the ship's books, though not only urged by every persuasion, but by threats.[9]

While Cape Ann people took to the high ground to cheer the chaser, watched her chased, and with consternation turning to dismay saw her finally chastened in unequal combat, another Yankee captain, unnoticed, was attempting to win with guile what James Tracy was losing with guns, lives, spikes and a crowbar.

Some weeks before this futile encounter the British ship *Lady Juliana*, from Jamaica for London with a cargo of rum, sugar, mixed goods and currency (some said $1000, some $20,000), was captured by the Pennsylvania privateer sloops *Congress* and *Chance*. Her captors put a prizemaster and crew aboard of her, with orders to take the *Lady* up the coast to Cape Ann; why Gloucester is not known, but her captain and his wife and all hands who elected not to stay on as prisoners were put ashore at Havana.

Coming up on Boston Bay from the eastward, *Lady Juliana* (now in American hands, but flying British colors) fell in with a Scotch vessel, the transport *Anne*, 230 tons, Captain John Denniston, astray from a fleet of thirty-one sail carrying thirty-five hundred reinforcements to Boston, and innocent of any knowledge that General Howe and his entire army and most of his navy had abandoned the town for Halifax.

Captain Denniston hospitably invited this unnamed Yankee prizemaster aboard for breakfast, taking him for the legitimate master of *Lady Juliana*. He informed his guest that he had for passengers ninety-five soldiers in a light infantry company of the Seventy-first Highlanders under Captain Hamilton Maxwell, and thirty-five tars for the fleet, and was bound for Boston.

What a coincidence, responded the quick-witted Yank. So was he bound, for although he was loaded for London, he had changed his mind and thought he might get a better price from General Howe's quartermaster.

Hmmm, mused Captain Denniston. He had to admit he was a stranger to the coast. Would his breakfast guest consider leading him into Boston?

The wily prizemaster didn't see why not, and returned, chuckling, to his prize.

Lady Juliana had almost lured the gullible *Anne* into Gloucester Harbor on the sixth of June--the same day if not hour that *Yankee Hero* and *Milford* were chasing around off the Back Shore--when Captain Denniston espied two American privateers and leaped to the conclusion that he had been seduced into rebel waters. He wore ship and ran for it. *Anne* almost escaped the trap, but next day she was captured and escorted into Marblehead by three of General Washington's schooners, *Lee, Warren* and *Lynch.* [10]

Meanwhile *Lady Juliana* arrived in Gloucester with her rich cargo and the news that *Anne* had given her the slip and within hours would undoubtedly be in the safe custody of Commodore Banks's squadron in Boston Harbor, telling all. There seemed a strong chance that the British commander would attempt to regain such a valuable prize, an anxiety only heightened by *Milford*'s show of prowess against *Yankee Hero* a few hours earlier. A messenger was sped to Watertown and the General Court for help.

Next morning, June 7, the Massachusetts Council resolved that somebody should do something immediately to secure the *Lady* against a foray by the enemy to retake her, "the harbour of Gloucester in our opinion not being in such a state of defence as to protect the prize should the enemies men of war attempt to take her out."

The House of Representatives, which only a week earlier couldn't spare Gloucester two eighteen-pounders, had a total change of heart. All fired up over the dramatic events of the previous day down at Cape Ann, the members adopted a resolve hastily submitted by Peter Coffin and John Low, two of Gloucester's delegation of five representatives:

That the Town of Gloucester be supplied with the following pieces of cannon, viz: four twenty-four-pounders, four nine-pounders; and out of those that have one or both trunnions off, four six-pounders, properly stocked, with the necessary apparatus for each cannon; also with forty rounds of shot, ten of which to be double-headed, for each cannon, and likewise with ten barrels of gunpowder; and that the Commissary-General be, and he hereby is, directed to deliver the same to Peter Coffin and John Low, Esqs., they giving a receipt to be accountable to this Court for the same.

And it is further resolved that a company of matrosses, to consist of fifty men, including officers, be raised to manage the cannon stationed there, to be under the command of Colonel Foster, and on the same pay and regulations as the company of matrosses stationed at Marblehead; said company to serve till the last day of December next, if not sooner disbanded by this Court. [11]

The House elected William Ellery captain, and Benjamin Somes first lieutenant of this paper company of matrosses, or artillery privates. That they were recruited, and that the cannon materialized, are indicated by the choice of George Sayward in October as second lieutenant "of the company of matrosses stationed at Gloucester."

It was a fleet of transports carrying units of Scots Highlanders as reinforcements for Howe that Commodore Banks had been looking out for from his anchorage in Nantasket Roads, the fleet from which *Anne* had strayed, and they were all at sixes and sevens, and ones and twos, coming onto the New England coast. Two days after *Anne*'s capture, in the mid-afternoon of June 9, HM Brig *Hope* stood up to three sail to the northeast and found that two were from Glasgow with Highland lads. As for the third..."chaced a rebel schooner in to Cape Ann that was indevouring to decoy the above ships in to Cape Ann. Fired 8 four pdrs shoted [shotted: loaded with ball and powder] at the rebel schooner." [12]

Five more shiploads of Scots troops made it past the American marauders and joined the fleet at Nantasket Roads. General Ward's forces had moved out to the harbor islands with cannon in a determined effort to make Boston untenable for Banks, and on the morning of June 14, 1776, they opened fire on his fleet. The warships responded with little effect. The commodore concluded the time had come to say goodby. He ordered the signals aloft in *Renown*, his flagship. *Renown*, *Hope*, the captured *Yankee Hero*, two small schooner prizes and eight transports weighed anchor and made sail. Going out, they blew up the Boston lighthouse and spoke *Milford* with three more transports of Highlanders in convoy. Out of range, finally, of the American shore batteries, the last of the British in Boston cleared The Graves for the last time--three warships, three prizes and eight transports.

They sailed off for Halifax at eight in the evening, two years to the day from the day Parliament closed the port for dumping the tea. But the welcome sight by no means quieted American anxieties that what the enemy gave up without a fight he might not return one day with an armada to take back, for Howe lurked at Halifax, and no one knew where he would strike, though strike he must, and soon.

The legislature delegated a committee to survey the situation of coastal defenses between Boston and Newburyport. It completed its evidently hurried report on June 19. Marblehead, Salem and Newburyport were praised for the state of their fortifications, but not Gloucester. The committee declared Cape Ann to be of prime strategic importance, and deplorably vulnerable:

> The importance of the Harbour of Gloucester is so great as in the judgment of your Committee to demand a very early and serious consideration. They have a fort erected called Fort Anne with ten ambozeurs in which they have 1 24 pder with three nine pounders, honey combd [metal-flawed] and not fit for use if possible to be avoided. No 2 is a four gun battery in which is one 9 pder that is not good and one 6 pounder fit for use. No [illegible, but probably 3] is a four gun battery lying on a neck of land between No 1 & No 2 and not of so much importance as No 1 which is a five gun battery & has one 24 pounder & 1 nine pounder. Besides these there is a battery erected which has no guns, but in which a feild piece or two might be of great service. They have about 240 men, 100 shot for the large cannon and one thousand wt of powder for the while.[13]

The only identifiable location in all this confusion is Fort Anne, on Watch House, later Fort, Point. The four batteries referred to presumably are the same described by Babson as having been thrown up after the *Falcon* fight on an eminence near

Watch House Point, at Stage Head, Duncan's Point and near the Cut. The "neck of land" may be Watch House Neck. The committee counted only twelve cannon among twenty-eight embrasures, and it disdained all but four of these--two twenty-fours, a nine and a six. It thought Gloucester should be supplied immediately with a number of heavy ordnance and stores, and "that some measures be adopted for the speedy filling up the Sea Coast Companies stationed there in the room of those who have enlisted or shall enlist on board any of the Continental or Colonial armed vessells."

In Philadelphia John Adams was true to his word to Isaac Smith and his own loyalty to Massachusetts. On June 24 his Congressional committee on fortifying ports recommended that Gloucester Harbor be strengthened with ten twenty-four pounders and ten eighteens and "that the Commanding Officer in the Eastern Department be directed to order an engineer to dispose of said cannon to the best advantage for the defense of that harbor, and also to order a sufficient number of troops there to do the necessary work," all to be at Continental expense.[14]

Congress might ordain, but man could refrain, as the long war would amply demonstrate before it was won. The onward surge of battle soon made the number and merits of honey-combed cannon defending Gloucester Harbor a matter of declining moment.

A companion sign of the seeming indifference to grand events which would be taken as a point of proud perversity by generations of Gloucester people yet unborn occurred on June 21, the week after Boston Harbor emptied itself of the last of the British; it caused the selectmen in some irritation two days later, on Sunday, to issue a proclamation which they command-ed to be read from all the pulpits in town after divine service:

Whereas the inhabitants of this town has been warned to assemble on the 21st day of this month, to act on a matter of the greatest Consequence that was ever laid before this or any other town in America: and as the number then convened was no ways sufficient to determine the sence of the Town, with respect to this momentious affair--To know, whether, should the Honble Congress for the Safety of the Colonies, declare them independent of the Kingdom of Great Britain, they the said inhabitants will solemnly ingage with their lives and fortunes to support them in the measure.

We therefore earnestly desire all the inhabitants of this town who are qualified for voting to assemble at the Meeting House in the First Parish in Glocester tomorrow the 24th inst. at three o'clock afternoon in order to give their representatives their advice and directions with respect to this Important Business.

On Monday afternoon at three, those free, white, male landowners of Gloucester who were of age and were not off with the Continental Army or at sea aboard a privateer or too old or too ill or too apathetic to attend, assembled in the House of God on Middle Street which had withstood Captain Linzee's cannon-ball. Town Clerk James Porter recorded their proceedings in the town book:

June 24--Voted to determine the votes of the voters walking. 125 walked from the east side of the House to the west side by which they voted in the affirmative, that if the Honble Congress for the Safety of these Colonies declare them independent of the Kingdom of Great Britain, they do solemnly engage with their lives and fortunes to support them in the measure.

Those that were contrary minded was desired to walk to the eastward but there was none that did.

Voted that a copy of the above vote be given to the Representatives as directions from their Constituents.

The next entry in the town book of Gloucester, carefully, boldly penned, is the Declaration of Independence. Until that momentous moment, the call to town meeting had each time been preceded by the command to the constable, in an elegant hand..."*Anno Regni Reg Georgii 16*--In His Majesty's Name you are required to notify and warn the Freeholders..." From that day forth Gloucester was summoned to self-rule *In the name of the government and people of the State of Massachusetts Bay.*

As expected, General Howe returned...not to Boston, but to New York, which fell to the British that autumn of 1776. The tide of war moved south, not again to redden the waters of Massachusetts. For Cape Ann the shift of battle portended a new phase: Gloucester would go to sea on the offensive in a role for which the old seaport was properly fitted by tradition, and inclination...privateering.

14

PRIVATEERS AND PRIVATION

The glad sight of the last of the British squadron in Massachusetts Bay hull down off Cape Ann for the eastward and Halifax on June 14, 1776, was Gloucester's and the rest of the coast's encouragement to take seriously to privateering. Until that day, so long as enemy warships might be out there over the horizon, few merchants were about to hazard their capital; since Foster and Parsons sent *General Ward* bravely forth with one gun at the end of '75 , not one armed vessel had been commissioned out of the port.

The unwillingness of the owners to risk their all until the odds improved does not mean that Gloucestermen shirked a fight at sea. Witness the Sandy Bay crowd that took out after the frigate of twenty-eight guns with flintlocks and cutlasses. And there were the men aboard the privateer sloop out of Salem, fourteen guns and a hundred crew, and a fist-shaking name, *Tyrannicide.*

Tyrannicide was ghosting along off Baker's Island on June 21, just under way from Salem, giving Captain John Fisk a moment to note the more leisurely aspects of the war in his log:

At 6 in the morning caught sum cod fish. Calm. At 12 wind breazed up to the southward. Bore away for Cape Ann Harbour. At 6 came to ankor in Harbour. Let the Cape people go on shore to git their clothing. Fair pleasant weather. [1]

Not a sign that a week earlier *Tyrannicide* had defeated the eight-gun enemy packet schooner *Despatch* in an hour's bloody battle...nor that Captain Fisk's youthful lieutenant was a former townsman of his Cape Ann people, a certain Jonathan Haraden, born and brought up in Annisquam and removed to Salem. Four years hence this Haraden would command the privateer *General Pickering* in one of the most dramatic engagements of the entire war, with *Achilles* off the coast of Spain.

Midsummer arrived, and General Howe leapfrogged Boston from Halifax to New York, which he intended to make his future seat of operations and the base of an inland wedge to cut New England off from the other colonies. Howe's invasion relieved the pressure from Massachusetts Bay. British warships were more rarely seen on patrol now, and between August 2 and September 2 it suddenly seemed feasible for Gloucester to embark earnestly on the business of harassing less-well-protected British merchantmen.[2]

The first of her privateers in this new phase of the war was a converted fishing schooner of seventy tons burthen with the obnoxious name of *Britannia*. Colonel Foster was of the opinion that the time was ripe for another flyer and went in on her with Winthrop and Epes Sargent and John Winthrop, Jr., a son of the famous Harvard scientist; he had worked in a Gloucester countinghouse after graduating from Harvard in 1765, returned to Boston and now was back at Cape Ann.

The owners signed Captain William Coas as commander and Coas Gardner, mate, with fifty men. They renamed her *Warren*, honoring the fallen hero of Bunker Hill, and armed Gloucester's second commissioned privateer with four four-pounders, four three-pounders, twelve swivel guns and four small bronze mortars called cohorns. Coas's commission was dated August 2, but sailing was delayed, as John Winthrop advised the Council, by lack of gunpowder. He was given permission to purchase seven hundred pounds of it from the public stores, which he pledged he would pay for in cash or by an equal weight of saltpeter.

Warren probably had taken on her powder and cleared Gloucester when *Langdon*, another converted fishing schooner, sailed with fifty men and high hopes. She was commissioned to Captain Jacob Allen on August 28 and carried twelve swivels and six carriage guns, one of which burst in the act of firing an overexuberant salute to the town as they stood out of the harbor, injuring two men. It was *Langdon*'s sole claim to fame. She embarked two months later under Captain Samuel Robinson on a second cruise, and may never have fired another gun, in earnest or in fun.

But *Warren* struck it rich her first time out. Captain Coas crisscrossed the shipping lanes from the West Indies and waylaid three merchantmen bound for London. Prize number one, the four hundred-ton ship *Picary*, Captain Brookholt Cleaveland, was brought into Gloucester on September 14. She was from Tobago with 325 hogsheads of sugar, 161 bales of cotton, indigo, and enough Madeira (168 pipes of 110 gallons each) to make pickled picaroons of all her captors.

In Boston John Bradford passed on the good news of "Johnny" Winthrop's first successful venture to John Hancock in Philadelphia, in an ingratiating postscript to a letter of September 30: "Ive wrote to Mr. Winthrop to pick out a pipe of the best wine for your private use..."[3]

Gloucester was settling down to celebration of *Picary* and her liquid lading when in around Eastern Point sailed *Warren*'s second rich victim, the brigantine *Swallow* of 120 tons, which had departed Tobago for London in ballast topped with ivory ("elephants teeth") and gold dust she had taken in trade on the coast of Guinea, supposedly having sold a human cargo to the Caribbean planters.

Warren's third capture was her richest. John Somes, brother of Isaac, brought her in as prizemaster on September 30. She was the five hundred-ton ship *Sarah and Elizabeth*, from Jamaica for London, creaking and groaning with 394 hogsheads of sugar, 180 puncheons of rum, twenty casks of indigo, seventy live tortoises, six casks of tortoiseshell, fifty bags of cotton, much mahogany and a great quantity of silver plate and currency. Wrote Babson:

Her captain's name was Foot. She was captured in the night. The captain's wife and a number of ladies were on board, who were greatly terrified, under the apprehension that if any resistance was made they might be murdered by the Yankees, whom they supposed to be Indians; and, by their crying and screaming, induced the captain to surrender without firing a gun. The next morning, when he saw to what an insignificant craft and small force he had surrendered his fine ship, which he could have defended easily and successfully, he became completely unmanned, and gave vent to his mortification and regret in tears. [4]

Captain James Foot and his lady remained in Gloucester that fall and early winter of 1776 and 1777 and were so well liked by their captors that they returned him half the value of his adventure (or venture, a personal speculation in goods on a voyage) and refrained from bidding against him when his vessel was condemned and put up at auction. Thus he got back *Sarah and Elizabeth*. This encouraged him to ask permission of the Massachusetts Council to take twelve or thirteen of his crew and sail her back to Jamaica. He had been in the Jamaica trade since his youth, and seven-eighths of his vessel was owned by planters on the island. He told the Council he believed that several Gloucester people would testify to his good character and "unexceptionable behavior" while among them.

Foot certainly had made good friends at Cape Ann. On February 24, 1777, the Council approved his projected voyage provided that he put into New York on the way down and endeavor to obtain the release of as many Massachusetts men held prisoners there as he had members of his crew. He not only agreed but volunteered to return directly to Massachusetts if he failed. The Council granted him a parole, and nothing more was heard of him. The man must have been as good as his word. [5]

Warren had followed *Sarah and Elizabeth* into port, and within three weeks, on October 21, 1776, set sail again under a new commander, Captain John Colson. She took only a small West Indiaman, and on her third cruise eleven months later, under Captain Silas Howell, was captured and brought into New York.

Another Gloucesterman as ready to look the lion in the jaws as *Warren*'s Coas was Isaac Somes, who had sailed for Foster before the war. Soon after his commissioning as commander of Johnny Winthrop's sloop *Union*, ten guns, on September 2, he sailed out of Gloucester with a crew of sixty-five and crossed the Atlantic, fixing to raise some hell off the coast of Portugal. He did. Babson credits him with a ship bound for Lisbon with fish and a salt-laden brig which he sent back to Cape Ann. The British Admiralty records, however, credit *Union* with more than fish and salt: they preserve the report of a French vessel that off "The Rock" (Cape Roca, north of Lisbon) she had been stopped by

a North American armed vessel which forcibly put on board of her 11 sailors, part of crews belonging to two English vessels which she had seized on 12th Nov. about 25 leagues W. of said Rock. This pirate is a sloop called the *Union*, belonging to Cape Ann, of 10 carriage guns, 8 swivels and 40 men comd. by Isaac Soams. She had capt. 3 other ships of which 2 sent to Cape Ann, another in ballast let go [6]

Winter had shrivelled all but the brown and rattling oak leaves when Captain Philemon Haskell put to sea in mid-November in David Pearce's schooner *Speedwell*. How he proposed to take a prize with only three guns and to spare anyone from his crew of twelve to man one, is a mystery but he did...not one but three English fishing vessels with partial fares and much salt which was welcomed in Gloucester, where its scarcity (so much having always been imported from Cadiz and the West Indies) had driven people to set up evaporating works at Norman's Woe, the Cut and Squam--a sign, too, that the fishing was coming back since the war moved south.

Two of these prizes of *Speedwell*'s, *Dolphin* and *Phenix*, are called brigs by Babson, who says they were sent to the West Indies and both captured. If this was the same *Phoenix* which was commissioned as a schooner with four guns and a dozen men under Captain William Card on November 21, seven days after *Speedwell*'s commission, it was some kind of a record for the start of a cruise, taking of a prize and her conversion from a fishing brig to a privateer schooner.

The third of *Speedwell*'s prizes, the brig *George*, was fitted for a voyage to Bilboa, Spain, in the course of which she brought back, by circumstance unknown, John Beach, an Englishman who would make his mark on Gloucester. Beach bought the Sanders house east of the First Parish meeting-house.[7] Between his new home and the church he built a ropewalk which extended all seven hundred and fifty feet from Middle to Back (Prospect) Street, long enough and with thirty feet to spare to twist out an anchor cable for the vessels of his adopted town. *Speedwell* sailed again in the summer of '79 when she was caught in a bad gale and had to jettison all six of her guns. She crawled home, did *Speedwell*, and nothing more is known of her.

Judging from the state the selectmen reported Gloucester to be in after the first twelve months of war--a hundred and eighty families partly supported by the town, forty poor wholly on dole, 233 widows, 1059 boys without work, in a population of some five thousand--the approach of the winter of '76 and'77 was regarded with dread and desperation. In such a frame of mind were the selectmen when they called the freeholders together on November 21 to consider "the distressed circumstances of the numerous poor families, who are not able to get employ and are destitute of food, cloathing and fuel to defend them against the inclemencys of the winter, and make provision for them as they see proper, as the selectmen has no money or stock of supplies in their hands."

Even the grist mills of the town had gone to ruin. The meeting debated what to do about them, so that if corn could be found it could be ground "without loss, or cause of complaints."

And then there was the town's quota required of it for the Continental Army. Enlistments were lagging. Again the free-holders met, early in December, and bleakly approved a six-pound bounty for recruits. The till was empty, said the treasurer. So another tax was voted.

And the indigent? Gloucester met for the third time and instructed the selectmen to borrow two hundred pounds for relief or accept the equivalent in goods. Two days before Christmas the voters gathered for the fourth time in a month and warned the owners of Ring's tidal grist mill at Riverdale to get it working by the first of March, under the direction of "a faithful millar," or forfeit their rights to the stream.

Still and all, the secular charity which flowed so glacially this yuletide from the cheerless interior of the First Parish Church was warmer than the Calvinist variety that the Congregationalists of the Harbor extended to that jovial prophet of universal salvation (a false one, Parson Chandler had said), the Reverend John Murray. Bitter as was the winter on Cape Ann, it was less frosty than that searing of the puritan soul brought on by the suspicion of a new idea.

"The spirit of liberty mounted very high in Gloucester," recalled Mrs. Judith Stevens, daughter of Winthrop Sargent and the future wife of John Murray, writing of this time, "and for the purpose of influencing the ignorant, the teacher was proclaimed a PAPIST, sent out by Lord North to aid the purpose of an obnoxious ministry. Anathemas, and sometimes stones, followed his steps as he passed the streets." [8]

In the dead of that Cape Ann winter, on February 27, 1777, John Murray was peremptorily summoned fom his sickbed in Winthrop Sargent's house to appear before the Gloucester committee of safety, of which his patron was a member, but not at this time Colonel Foster, another supporter. His friends advised against his compliance, since only five of the seventeen members made a quorum, and those sitting were known to be zealous in their enmity of him. But Murray insisted; he had a sure sense of drama and a nice appreciation of the uses of martyrdom when not carried to extremes. The tone of the star chamber (if a Murrayite who took notes is to be granted credence) was established by one of his interrogators, who declared: "I conceive we have sent for this man to know from whence he came, who he is, and what business he has here; this is a time of difficulty, we are at variance with England, he calls himself an Englishman, we do not know what he is. He associates with a great many whom we look upon as enemies to this country, and they go to hear him, converse--I think--I cannot call it *preaching.*" [9]

Murray answered softly but stood firm. He supposed that neither Captain Winthrop Sargent nor General Washington were enemies to their country, which, upon his arrival five years before, he believed to be "a land of civil and religious liberty--every charter and every law made among yourselves breathed a spirit of toleration. I felt assured I should be allowed liberty of conscience; my intentions were upright."

The committee of safety could not, one member of this minority observed threateningly, "be answerable for anything that might be done by a mob, and it was not in their power to prevent it, if he did not, without delay, leave the town."

"I am not afraid," replied the preacher, laying his outspread hand upon his chest. "The worst this mob can do, is to deprive me of a life which I have been many years quite willing to resign. Sir, I commit myself and my cause to the Ruler of Heaven and of Earth." [10]

Saying which, he walked out.

This inquisition occurred less than two weeks before town meeting on March 10, "the aim of which," his devoted Judith claimed later, "(lest the friends of the promulgator should take the alarm) was most illegally shrouded in silence." The vote seems to bear out her accusation that the meeting was loaded; it was fifty-four to eight to approve the action of the rump committee of safety in "desiring Mr. John Murray to depart this town in five days from March first." Murray's followers included some of the leading (and richest) men in Gloucester. They were not intimidated. He remained and went about his preaching and conversing.

"Alas, alas!" deplored staunch Judith, "how tyrannical is the dominion of prejudice! In this instance it precipitated men, respectable men, who in the common occurrences of life had uniformly preserved a decent reputation, upon a procedure the most absurd and unwarrantable." [11]

Joseph Foster was discharged as Colonel of the Sea Coast Forces defending Cape Ann on November 19, 1776. No reason is recorded, nor does it appear that he had a successor. The logical explanation for his return to civilian life is the probable transfer elsewhere of the units under his command with the shift of the war away from New England and the relaxation of coastal defense. A couple of days before Christmas the town asked him to turn over *Falcon*'s bullet-riddled boats which had been in his custody since April of '76; the selectmen wanted to sell them for what they would fetch, the town treasury being equally as shot. Colonel Foster failed to comply. The March of 1777 meeting which was rigged by Murray's enemies put Foster on a committee to look for some way of alleviating the distress of the poor and elected Captains William Ellery, John Smith and Jacob Allen (good Congregationalists all, and members of the committee of safety) to demand of him *Falcon*'s boats and of Winthrop Sargent her anchor and hawser which he, likewise, had been holding; the three were directed to sell these souvenirs of the attack, proceeds for the benefit of the poor. They didn't get about their assignment until May 24, with results noted on the reverse of a copy of their vote of instructions:

> This day we the subscribers waited on Col. Joseph Foster agreeable to the within directions and business. We received for answer from him that the town owed him and when the town would settle his account and give him security for what they owed him he was ready to be accountable for the boats...and furthermore we waited on Capt. Winthrop Sargent and received for answer that the town owed him for the things he had that was Capt. Lynzey's.

Wm Ellery, John Smith, Jacob Allen

Two days after receiving this rejoinder from Foster and Sargent, who must have enjoyed a chuckle over it, the town requested the selectmen to pay the Colonel anything due him, a transaction which was not consummated until February 24, 1778, when they remitted him £ 25.19.4 for his account rendered.

Warren's first cruise had profited them so handsomely that Joseph Foster and the other owners in the spring of 1777 threw in with Captain Bradbury Sanders and William Pearson and bought at auction the salt brig which Isaac Somes and *Union* had taken off the coast of Portugal in November. They rerigged and renamed this prize the brigantine *General Mercer* (after one of Washington's commanders who had been killed fighting bravely at the Battle of Princeton in January), armed her with fourteen guns and gave the command of her to Captain James Babson of Gloucester.

On May 21 *General Mercer* and a crew of a hundred sailed from Boston with the Boston brigantine *Fanny*, Captain John Kendrick, and seven other privateers in a squadron dominated by two of the new Continental frigates, *Hancock*, the flagship of Captain John Manley, and *Boston*, commanded by Captain Hector McNeill. It was a dubious experiment, trying to make a naval squadron out of a mixture of frigates and privateers, and it failed. Six days out, all but one of the privateers had gone their separate ways and were not seen again. On June 7 Manley captured the British frigate *Fox*, but was taken himself, with his prize, a month later in an engagement with three enemy warships in the course of which *Boston* escaped. Manley landed in a prison hulk in New York Harbor. He was exchanged in March in 1778, court-martialed for the loss of *Hancock* and acquitted.

After getting separated from the squadon, *General Mercer* and *Fanny* sailed to the coast of France and took two British sugar ships on August 13 which they tried to enter at Nantes under the guise of Dutch vessels from St. Eustatius. The deception was discovered, and the prizes were confiscated in the French Court of Admiralty, "yet notwithstanding," as an American account subsequently reasoned, "His Most Christian Majesty the King of France having in his great Goodness been pleased to order the sum of four hundred thousand livres, French money, to be paid to the owners."

This munificent offer of the young Louis XVI quite likely was a result of his formal alliance with the United States early in 1778. In August of that year the other owners of *General Mercer* appointed Foster their agent (John Grenell and Adam Babcock of Boston representing *Fanny* as agent-owners) to collect on the royal pledge. The Massachusetts Council on October 17 certified the facts and authorized John Holker, Agent General of the Royal Marine, and Consul of France, to pay the claimants according to the order of Louis. At the rate of exchange, the four hundred thousand livres was about $75,000 in silver, divided between the owners and crews of the two vessels.

That was one channel by which Yankees made fortunes privateering, and one reason why the new American navy, with its low pay and hard discipline, had recruiting problems.

While *General Mercer* and *Fanny* were keeping company after slipping away from Captain Manley's chaperonage, Cape Ann was in high excitement over the fitting-out of Gloucester's first home-made privateer, the brigantine *Gloucester*. David Pearce and his associates had built her and gave her to Captain John Colson, who had cruised in *Warren* the previous autumn. She had fourteen guns and a big crew of 130. Colson was commissioned on June 28 and again on July 17. Probably the first cruise was a shakedown. *Gloucester* may have sailed in July with the brigantine *Fair Play*, of Newburyport but commanded by Captain Isaac Somes of Gloucester, and the brigantine *Wilkes*, also built by David Pearce of Gloucester, under the command of John Foster Williams of Boston; both were commissioned the same day.

Besides launching three privateers on the ocean wave, the seventeenth of July launched firstborn Mary Foster on the seas of matrimony, and a joyful commissioning it was, joining together two old-time Chebacco neighbors, Fosters and Wades. Mary was twenty; handsome Nathaniel Wade was twenty-seven, probably a major by now, home on furlough from General Washington's army. As a young captain he had led the Ipswich minute men up Breed's Hill, and back down again, and since then had fought in the battles of Long Island, Harlem and White Plains with the Commander-in-Chief.

Gloucester stood out Gloucester Harbor under her cloud of canvas and out of sight around Eastern Point, with the hopes and hearts of all Cape Ann. To the eastward she sailed, and sent back her first prize, the brig *Two Friends*, captured with a cargo of wine and salt. Soon followed another brig, *Spark*, fish and salt, sailed back by Isaac Day.

And that was it. Never again a word or a sign of Gloucester's *Gloucester*, not a plank or a shred of sail. Less the two prize crews that providence spared, more than a hundred went down in her. Three brothers in one family, the Worley boys...in one stroke, sixty Gloucester wives made widows.

To the mourners, the following winter was one of unutterable grief; which was somewhat aggravated by the tales which superstition bore to their dismal firesides, that the fate of their friends had been indicated by signs from the invisible world. It was currently reported, and believed by many, that one dark night, about the time it was supposed the ship was lost, a ball of light (called, by seamen, a corposant) was seen to move about the town in a mysterious manner, and approach successively the homes of all who were on board of her; remaining a few moments at each of them, to indicate the melancholy fate that had befallen the ship and her unfortunate crew. [12]

A more real and dreaded sign from the invisible world moved through Gloucester in a mysterious manner this winter, the smallpox. The election of a committee of which Foster was a member in March 1777, to provide the town with a pesthouse betrays the presence of the disease. The isolation "hospital" was built on a remote stretch of the old road through the woods above Freshwater Cove, near Solomon Parsons's house. Strange to say, a year later, in April 1778, the disease had slowly taken hold but still was not epidemic; twice that month the town rejected inoculation.

Despair pervaded Gloucester this fourth spring of the war. In May the General Court pressed the town for its quota of clothing for its men in the army. In a gesture of futility, the people voted to assess themselves six hundred pounds which they did not have, to buy the wanted goods which were not available. The selectmen asked the voters to donate shirts, stockings and shoes for 137 men, and the voters asked the selectmen to tender the town's excuses when the General Court wanted to know why it had failed to meet its obligation.

This widespread feeling of depression naturally dampened the privateering spirit. The catastrophic loss of her namesake knocked the wind out of Gloucester's sails for a whole year. The only recorded ventures in which Cape Ann was concerned for the twelve months after the middle of July, 1777, were the departure of *Warren* in September on the third cruise which ended in her capture, and of the Newburyport-owned brigantine *Civil Usage*, fourteen guns and twelve swivels, commissioned to Captain John Smith of Gloucester on March 28, 1778.

Captain Smith sailed with seventy-five men, some or all from Cape Ann. Not long out, he chased a large and well-armed transport with eight hundred on board. They engaged. "He continued the fight with great bravery and spirit," wrote Babson. "till it was made certain that he must haul off or surrender. In the early part of the engagement, he received a wound from a musket-ball, in the throat; and while remaining on deck during the action, as he attempted to swallow some water, he could only prevent the liquid from taking a wrong direction by pinching his wound with his finger and thumb."[13]

Captain Smith expired in agony. Not so his lieutenant, who was struck full in the head by a cannonball; Nathaniel Allen was standing beside him when it happened. Withal, *Civil Usage* got better usage than *Yankee Hero* and managed to bear off and escape. Young Allen had left the army to try privateering, and this was perhaps all the taste of the game he wanted.

Some of these fellows were incurable. Mark Pool, for one. He fought with Captain Rowe's company at Breed's Hill, then talked him into taking on *Milford*, as we have seen, was captured, escaped, made his way back to Cape Ann, and now, in August of '78, was marching off at the head of his own company of Gloucestermen to join with other units of volunteers from Boston and North Shore ports in General John Sullivan's unsuccessful campaign to drive the British from Newport--unsuccessful because the Comte D'Estaing would not bring his French fleet back in support of the assault after it was scattered by a storm.

Winthrop Sargent was no less incurably venturesome, in his own way, than Mark Pool...he and his friend David Pearce. After the loss of Pearce's *Gloucester* and the capture of *Warren*, in which the Sargents held a large interest, Captain

Sargent set about the building of a great (for Gloucester) ship of 220 tons, a venture in which he is said to have been joined by Pearce. She was documented on August 14, 1778, ten days after her principal owner had put Gloucester back in privateering, after an absence of a year, with the commissioning of the schooner *Hawk* on her only known cruise, under Captain Coas Gardner. The new ship mounted eighteen guns. Her command, and the responsibility for a crew of 150, were given to Captain William Coas, who had taken *Warren* on her first lucky cruise; Coas Gardner had been his mate then (they were related through Captain Coas's mother, a Gardner). Her owners named their privateer ship *General Stark*, after gaunt John Stark of New Hampshire, defender of the rail fence at Breed's Hill who was this summer in command of Washington's northern army. A brave name for a brave ship, they hoped..."There, my boys, are your enemies, the redcoats and Tories!" General Stark is supposed to have exclaimed as he led his men into the Battle of Bennington a few months before the launch of the *Stark*. "You must beat them or my wife sleeps a widow tonight!"

Probably *Hawk* and *General Stark* cruised off together this August. How *Hawk* fared is not known. The *Stark* made a second short cruise before the winter lay-up, sending back a schooner laden with salt and the ship *Providence* laden with nothing...practice runs, perhaps, for bigger stakes. [14]

Colonel Foster traveled to Philadelphia in September. He met with the congressman from the Essex district, Dr. Samuel Holten of Danvers, a physician-turned-politician who had practised briefly on Cape Ann twenty years back and married a Gloucester girl, Mary Warner. Dr. Holten noted the occasion in his diary on September 14: "Congress sit till after 8 in the evening. Colo. Foster dined with us. He came from Glocester in Mass. & brought me a letter from Sister Sukey."

A clue as to his guest's business is Dr. Holten's entry of a fortnight previous, on August 27, that "the consul of France and 10 other Gentlemen of distinction dined with us by invitation. We had a grand, elegant dinner." The French consul was the same John Holker whom Foster was trying to convince through the leverage of the Massachusetts Council that he should turn over the four hundred thousand livres which His Most Christian Majesty had offered the owners of *General Mercer* and *Fanny* as indemnification for the condemnation of their prizes at Nantes in August of '77. Foster may have been hoping to discuss the matter with Holker in Philadelphia or to obtain Dr. Holten's intervention with him. He may also have used the opportunity to lobby in behalf of John Manley, who had been acquitted in court martial for the loss of *Hancock* and was in town trying to pry a new command out of Congress until the middle of August, when he returned to Boston.

While Foster was away, the smallpox erupted in Gloucester like a smouldering underground fire suddenly bursting into flames. More and more nervous citizens were sneaking inoculation in spite of the town's ban; thereby they endangered others during the infectious stage of the procedure. Town meeting on September 22 fell back on a half-measure: the selectmen and the committee of safety should permit the inoculation of those who had been "extraordinarily exposed" on the condition that they remove to a properly isolated location.

Still it spread. After another month the town gave in altogether, realizing that inoculation was the only hope in the face of what was now a full-blown epidemic. The town meeting approved the homes of Zebulon Stanwood, Peter Coffin, Enos Dodge, Barnabas Dodge, Solomon Parsons near the pest house above Freshwater Cove, David Plummer and James Pearson, all spotted around the parishes, as inoculation hospitals. Captain John Fletcher, one of the founders of Tyrian Lodge of Masons, was thanked for his brotherly offer of a hundred pounds to pay for inoculating the poor.

Two private armed vessels sailed in December from the pox-ridden port, and the assumption is that all who signed papers displayed pockmarks as badges of mutual protection and reassurance. The first was David Pearce's brigantine *Success*, commissioned to Captain Solomon Babson on the eleventh. In spite of her formidable sixteen guns, she was manned by only twenty for a voyage to the West Indies. Captain Babson was looking for neither trouble nor prizes, but trouble he found;

Success was captured on her homeward passage. On December 17 Isaac Somes cleared in the two hundred-ton ship *Sky Rocket*, owned by Daniel Sargent and Ebenezer Parsons. She, too, was armed with sixteen guns, but Somes had ninety men aboard, and he *was* looking for trouble; there is no record that he succeeded any more than *Success*.

The house of Bradbury Sanders at Rose Bank, east of Vincent's Cove, was in a settled part of the Harbor and was for that reason not among those approved as inoculation hospitals. The exclusion did not bother Captain Sanders, a fact which did bother his neighbors, who bitterly demanded a special town meeting on the matter. It was held six days before Christmas in the bitterly cold Middle Street meetinghouse to consider "that a number of persons are inoculated with the smallpox and remain in Capt. Bradbury Sanders house to the exposing the persons and families of a large neighborhood and interrupting their safe passing in the highway for the purpose of religion or commerce notwithstanding the town has approbated proper places of regulations for persons who are desirous to be inoculated."

After fretting for two days, the selectmen called the people together again. Sanders's defiance was denounced as "disagreeable to the town." He was told to clear his house of the smallpox immediately, and the doctors in the town were warned that they would be prosecuted if they inoculated or visited patients contrary to the rules. Isolation and inoculation were the only weapons, and Gloucester's leaders made no bones about their reluctance to entrust the supervision of either solely to the local doctor. The result was a truly desperate effort to manage a worsening public health crisis by plebiscite. Thus this same meeting voted that citizens who had been exposed to Mrs. Crosman would be inoculated if they removed to the homes designated as hospitals.

A miserable Christmas was endured. Congress had set aside December 30 as Thanksgiving for 1778, and on that day the pronouncement that all Cape Ann dreaded to hear was read from the pulpits: the epidemic was out of control; the selectmen and the committee of safety "had done all that was in their power to prevent the spread of the smallpox but to little or no purpose and desire the town's directions what further should be done.''

Next day, the people who dared came to the meetinghouse with fear and foreboding. Caught between the devil they knew and the devil they didn't, they reversed themselves and decided that inoculation should continue for only two more weeks. Then they ran for it.

Voted that the meeting think it not possible to prevent the spreading of the smallpox.

Voted that it is recommended to each parish in the town to confine the smallpox to as small limits as it can.

15

SIX SMALL CHEEZES
&
PART OF A PAIL OF BUTTER

Through the winter and into the spring of 1779 "that loath-some disease" rampaged over Cape Ann. The pesthouses ran out of room, and the homes reserved as inoculation hospitals had to bar their doors. The authorities threw up their hands. The parishes were left on their own. How they managed was their business. Sandy Bay met and voted to ban inoculation in homes without a permit, on penalty of thirty-three lashes.

There is no record of the toll. It is said that of 110 who were inoculated in one village, two died. Several old people and children succumbed at Sandy Bay, among them Caleb and Ebenezer Pool, Mrs. Abigail Rowe and the widow Elizabeth Clark; they were buried in tarred sheets near the shore west of Whale Cove. The smallpox hung around until as late as July 22, when the widow Ruth Andrews died of it.

The most prominent victim of the worst epidemic in Cape Ann's history died under ironic circumstances on January 7. Epes Sargent, Senior, had returned from virtual exile in Boston to face the harsh music in the place of his birth. Babson claims that the stubborn old Loyalist was inoculated against his will under the pressure of a town vote calling for a general inoculation, that "he had a presentiment that the disease would prove fatal to him, and therefore desired an exception in his favor; but the authorities were inexorable, and he submitted to the fate he apprehended." If his inoculation was in truth forced on Sargent, it was with a singularly malevolent intent against this outspoken Tory, because there is nothing in the records to indicate that the procedure was ever made compulsory. [1]

One curious turn to the epidemic found its way into the town records. On March 1 the selectmen paid Benjamin Webber "for smoaking people that came out Capt Manley and half a day work on Pest House." After failing to win a naval assignment from Congress, John Manley had reverted to privateering in the ship *Cumberland,* commissioned to him on December 14, 1778, only to be again captured, this time by the English frigate *Juno* in January. Manley was partial to Gloucester Harbor and may have put in there before sailing into the arms of *Juno.* If he gave his crew shore leave, they naturally would require a thorough prophylactic "smoaking" to insure, supposedly, that they didn't carry the pox back aboard.

The cold broke, the snows melted into mud, the sun rose higher by the day. The smallpox spent itself on its last victim, and Gloucester had not died, for Gloucester could not help awakening to the spring and to the vernal urge of the tides, as it always had. Spring of '79 came on the land, the beginning of the fifth year of the Revolution, and it quickened the pulse and lifted aloft the never-earthbound hopes of the Gloucestermen for luck ... only in these times the dreams were of opulent English merchantmen floating on the surface of the sea, not of fat mackerel schooling underneath.

One of these seasonal optimists was Thomas Sanders, seven years out of Harvard College, educated to be a schoolmaster. But first he thought he would teach the British a lesson; to accomplish this high purpose he was commissioned master of *Tryal,* a schooner boat so-called, armed with four swivel guns and manned by eighteen men. So states his commission. Babson states, however, that *Tryal* had a dozen each of guns, men and oars and a single sail, and "a small place built up forward to receive the arms and ammunition ... The crew went ashore every night to encamp and cook." Our historian must have been in error; a lightly armed open boat could hardly have cruised as far as Canso, Nova Scotia, as he claims, capturing three coasting vessels, one of which was retaken and the other two brought back to Gloucester.

Tryal passed into other hands. Captain Sanders came into the command of the shallop *Speedwell* (as Babson has it, for there is no other record of her existence). He decked this craft over as he had *Tryal*, with four swivels mounted around the hatch coaming, which his twenty-five fighting sailors, braced with small arms, made their fortress on coming to action. Sanders pushed his luck as far as Nova Scotia's Gut of Canso, where he was chased by British cruisers and taken. [2]

Even the good ship *General Stark* had been laid up over the winter of the smallpox, and with the first break in the weather the spring refit was hurried along. On April 5 this privateer sailed on her third cruise out of Gloucester. Captain Coas had some first-rate masters in their own right for officers. Captain James Pearson was his sailing master, and Duncan Piper, who had saved his skin by piping up during the *Falcon* fight, was his third lieutenant. Coas had a crew of 135.

After losing a man overboard in a gale while crossing the Grand Bank, the *Stark* shook off this ill sign by taking a brig from Limerick with a cargo of beef, pork and butter which they sent back--and welcome it was--to Gloucester. Near the Azores the *Stark* fell in with two vessels which revealed themselves, upon being engaged, to be a ship of twenty-eight guns and a brig of fourteen. The American took a shot through her mizzen mast, five through her ship's boat and another in her quarter before hauling off for the eastward and away. Next they crossed with the British ship *Porcupine,* fourteen guns, which struck to the *Stark* without a shot. Evidently in an expansive mood, Captain Coas stripped his prize of her light sails and her guns and let her go. He mounted six of *Porcupine*'s quills on his half-deck, and with this extra fierceness captured an English brig out of Bristol and a sloop bound for Oporto, Portugal, which he stripped; then he took off the sloop's crew and sank her.

Venturesome, but so far not very profitable. Coas sailed *General Stark* into Bilboa, Spain, to refit before embarking for home. But here at Bilboa, suddenly, his victory over the Bristol brig turned pyrrhic with a vengeance; one of her crew he had taken aboard as a prisoner came down with the yellow fever.

Thirty of *Stark*'s men sickened with it, and Coas had to hire a house on shore for a hospital, where several died.

One day while he was bossing the work on his vessel, and waiting for his sick men to recover, and wondering how he was going to fill out his complement, he was hailed from the wharf. Who should it be but young Ignatius Webber, Jr., and two fellow Gloucestermen, stranded in Spain, wanting to work and fight their passage home.

When last seen, Webber had sailed from Gloucester for Spain in his father's vessel with a cargo of corn a few days before the British marched out to Lexington and Concord. It happened that they outsailed the news of war, sold their corn, carried a cargo of lemons to London, and after a close escape from the press gang made a deal to fly the British flag over a load of salt for Annapolis Royal in Nova Scotia. Almost across, they were stopped by HMS *Rainbow*, whose officers felt they were suspiciously far to the westward for a Canadian destination. Their true identity was discovered and they were imprisoned at Halifax. Ignatius was exchanged in a cartel, returned to Gloucester, signed on with the privateer *General Arnold* of Newburyport, which took a prize and put him aboard as master. But not for long, because they fell in with three British cutters, which retook the prize and brought it into Oporto. Webber and two shipmates escaped and with the help of the French consul made their way to Corunna, Spain. It was a hard trek, most of it barefoot after they wore out their shoes, and they slept under shelving rocks and trees. At Corunna they heard *General Stark* was at Bilboa. They took passage in a patache, disembarked and walked into the arms of their townsmen, as Webber wrote in his *Narrative:*

> The coast of Biscay about this time being infested with Guernsey privateers [these Channel islanders were notorious smugglers and freebooters], a thousand dollars reward was offered by the police, for as many as should be brought in. Captain Coose [Coas] consulted his officers and it was agreed that while the ship's bread, etc., was making ready, and his sick men recruiting [recuperating] on shore, to go out and cruise a few days--which we did and returned with a Guernsey lugger.

Upon engaging the lugger, the *Stark* had let go with a broadside which clipped off the legs of the steward and wounded eight other Guernseymen; the steward died next day. Coas brought his prize into Bilboa and sold her for $1600, making the brief encounter worth $2600 with his reward. Webber was joined abroad by several other Yankee seamen and prizemasters who had sold their prizes, and about July 20 *General Stark* sailed for home. Early in August, in Babson's words,

> she made a sail under a cloud of canvas, and came up with her after a severe chase of four hours. The enemy, finding he could not escape, hauled up his courses, and prepared for action. After a brave resistance of two hours, he surrendered to the *Starks,* having first sunk his mail; for the vessel proved to be an English packet from Jamaica, bound home. When he struck, all three of his topmasts were shot away. He had six men killed and nine wounded; one of whom was shot in both legs, and in the head by a musket ball, besides being struck between the shoulders by a splinter. One of the wounded men had his right hand shot off. The prize was put in charge of Duncan Piper, and ordered for Gloucester, where she arrived safe.[3]

The badly wounded man was John Low, who lived to become John J. Babson's principal first-hand source of information on Gloucester privateering.

Ignatius Webber's version of the engagement with the Jamaica packet is of interest:

> On our cruise homeward we took several prizes, amongst which was a ship packet of sixteen guns from New York bound to Falmouth in England. We had a pretty smart action with this ship, for about three glasses, when she struck to the *General Stark*. She rounded to & her three topmasts went by the board (as the action was before the wind)--several being killed & wounded on both sides, and the ships very much cut to pieces in their riggin & sails, the packet in particular. About a week afterwards we got her under full sail again.

Hardly under way, they captured a fish-laden brig from Newfoundland for Lisbon, showing fourteen guns, ten of which were wooden "Quakers," as Babson described them, adding rather redundantly ... "useful sometimes for intimidation, but availing nothing for purpose of attack or defence." Coas took two more fish-brigs and ordered all three to Gloucester. Then he made sail for home himself, having no more spare crew to man more prizes, with twenty on the sick list and eighty-four prisoners. *General Stark* arrived at Gloucester on September 15, 1779.

Gloucester had not been idle that summer either. John Somes hove eight carriage guns aboard the sixty-ton schooner *Wasp* and sailed with forty men in May. They took a brig from Ireland, with a cargo of provisions, and sent her back home to Cape Ann. For her next cruise *Wasp* was commissioned to John's brother Isaac, on August 3. Outward bound, they fell in with the privateer ship *Harlequin* from Salem, twenty guns, and the two chased a Jamaicaman with a cargo of rum. The chase struck to *Harlequin* before *Wasp* came up. Captain Putnam Cleaves had a hundred men with him, but numbers didn't count when they refused to share the prize money with Isaac Somes and his forty: the Gloucestermen hired an ambitious young lawyer of whom more would be heard, Theophilus Parsons, who won their case in court and received for a fee, 'tis said, three hogsheads of the prize rum *Harlequin* had to give up. [4]

The most ambitious American amphibious expedition of the war was mounted by Massachusetts in the summer of 1779. Nineteen naval vessels and privateers under Commodore Dudley Saltonstall of Connecticut and twenty transports carrying two thousand troops commanded by General Solomon Lovell arrived in Maine's Penobscot Bay on July 25. Their mission was to capture the British fort at Castine, in the head of the bay on the Bagaduce River, defended by a small British force and three sloops of war. Lovell was unable to take the fort and sent back to Boston for reinforcements, while Saltonstall twiddled his fingers. On August 13 five royal warships sailed into the Penobscot. The entire American force, with Saltonstall in the lead, turned tail and fled up the Bagaduce, where two ships were captured before the rest were scuttled. Those who were not taken prisoner took to the wilderness. Saltonstall was later sacked from the navy.

One of the scuttled privateers was *Sky Rocket,* Isaac Somes's old Gloucester command, out of Boston on this fiasco. Another was *Black Prince* of Salem, and among her crew was a Gloucester veteran of fourteen, Israel Trask. This young fellow had been privateering in *Black Prince* since 1778, when he was thirteen, and they had taken a whole fleet of prizes in two cruises off the British coast, including a privateer fitted out by the ladies of London and bewitchingly christened *Ladies' Adventure.* Israel had his first go on the high seas in 1777 when he was twelve and sailed with Philemon Haskell in Gloucester's *Speedwell.* He had taken to privateering after he was mustered out of the army when the British evacuated Boston. The truth (which he sought to establish sixty-nine years later in a petition to Congress for a pension) is that he had been encamped outside Boston with General Washington's forces since enlisting at Gloucester in February 1775 in the company of Captain John Low of Beverly--in which his father, Jonathan Trask, was lieutenant--at the age of ten.

After they blew up their *Black Prince,* up in the Bagaduce, Israel Trask stated in his petition,

> I, with many others, escaped to the dense forests and travelled through the wilderness about three hundred miles with a pack on my shoulders containing a small blanket, a square piece of salted pork, a few biscuits, a bottle of wine, and one shirt. The second day of our march, my shoes, made of materials such as at that period of which I write were furnished, and which were new when I left ship, gave way. The distance still to perform ere I reached home was effected on my bare feet ...I believe my arrival home took place in September from the circumstance of meeting some farmers returning from their labors of haying on the marshes between Rowley and Ipswich late in the afternoon. Not meeting with the usual charity in this day's march, the cravings of hunger compelled us to ask them to enable us to break our

fast. They willingly spread before us the remaining fragments of their lunch. Hence I infer that my arrival home was in the month of September 1779, as the practice of mowing the salt marshes in Essex was in that month.

At the end of October *General Stark* was off on one last short cruise before the winter hibernation. James Pearson, the sailing master, took her, results unknown. Webber was not aboard. His father had arrived back in Gloucester in a prisoner exchange cartel from Halifax during the summer and took command of a Boston vessel, for Cadiz. Ignatius, Jr., signed as second mate in the privateer brigantine *Fair Play*, owned in Newburyport but hailing from Gloucester, first under Isaac Somes, then Andrew Giddings, and now, William Parsons. Their destination was Martinique. Webber recalled the voyage in his *Narrative:*

After sailing from Martinico, in beating up between which & Guadeloupe we had a man fall from the main topsail yard into the water. We hove a hen coop over board which he recovered. Being in company with a schooner which was in our weather quarter, she bore down under her jib and took the man up, who received little or no injury from the fall. We had tacked but fell to leeward. It blowing fresh and night coming on, we veered away our deepsea line with a buoy to the end of it. The schooner being in our wake, took it up and hauled about half the line on board, then slung the man with the bight of the line and put him into the water. We hauled up on the line, he helping himself by swimming, we got him on board again without receiving any harm whatever.

We came on our coast the first of January 1780 [sic 1779] and arrived at Gloucester on the 13th inst. In going into the Harbour, it being night, and the land covered with snow which was very deceiving, we ran ashore on the back of the Harbor beach. The tide being in our favour, we got off again without much difficulty. (I was not a little mortified at this circumstance by reason the Captain placed some confidence in my knowledge of the Harbour.)

Small wonder that Webber fetched up *Fair Play* in Brace Cove, as he evidently did (the beach there is the "back of the

Harbour Beach," or Niles). Once again the man at the wheel had mistaken the False Point, as he peered through the murk, for the end of Eastern Point and brought his helm over for what he thought was the entrance to the harbor. *Stakesby*'s prize crew had made the same error in '76; so had many before them, and so would many after.

The winter was extremely severe, as Webber's account attests--quite arctic, in fact. *General Stark,* according to Babson, was frozen into the ice (which extended at one time as far out as from Black Bess on Eastern Point across to Dolliver's Neck) from the middle of December until March 20, 1780, and had her provisions and wood hauled out over it by team. For years "the great snow storm" was talked of and wondered at. Early in 1780, probably in January, various accounts describe the travelling due to the depth of snow and the intensity of the cold as "excessive bad." It began with a northeast gale which screamed in from the Atlantic on and on without let-up; the snow fell with scarcely any respite for twenty-seven days. In Sandy Bay Stephen Pool dug up one of his sheep, still alive; it had been buried for twenty-nine days. Many buildings were drifted clear over the ridges, windows obliterated, and the occupants had to be tunnelled out from the surface to the door.

The last winter, a blizzard of smallpox ... this one, an epidemic of snow, ice and cold ... all laid like a lash on five years of war, deprivation, starvation, suffering and death. The apocalyptical Horsemen pounded across the frozen turf of Cape Ann.

On the last day of 1779 Gloucester again begged the General Court to abate its taxes:

> It represents the taxable polls to have been reduced from 1053 in 1775 to 696 in 1779; that at the commencement of the war all the most active, wealthy inhabitants moved from the town to places of greater security; that there are but 856 acres of arable, orcharding, and mowing land in the whole town, which do not produce enough of the necessaries of life to support the people two months in the twelve; that their privateering adventures had been very

unsuccessful; that of 5000 tons in fishing schooners, merchant vessels and boats, belonging in the town in 1775, the whole amount, improved or not, is now only 2040 tons -- 690 tons having been lost since the last fall, and that all their interest in merchant vessels consisted of one-half of a small ship; that they had a very numerous poor to support--upwards of 750 of that class that lived chiefly on charity; in short that the town was very poor, and that they believed that all the money in town, collected in one sum, would be insufficient to meet the tax set upon it. [5]

Gloucester's plight touched the hearts of her neighbors. The selectmen tried to keep account. At various times during 1779, Nathaniel Tracy, Newburyport's leading merchant and one of the owners of *Yankee Hero,* sent two hundred pounds, [6] while "private gentlemen" in Salem forwarded £ 289 and four barrels of flour. Donations came from Byfield and from Plaistow, New Hampshire. People from Newbury's second parish contributed meat, oatmeal and a small cheese, and from its third parish twenty-one bushels of corn, as well as pork, meal and two cheeses. The upper and lower parishes of Danvers raised eighty-four pounds in cash, Topsfield thirty and Wenham forty-two. Boxford gathered together for the poor people of Gloucester mutton and pluck, "six small cheezes & part of a pail of butter." [7]

Some score or more of women from Sandy Bay, Squam and Up-town Parish by the Green whose men were off in the war watched the small cheeses and part-pails of butter dribbling into Gloucester from the neighbors, and bethought them of the well-stocked stores of Colonel Foster. They marched on the Foster farm at Beaver Dam and demanded that the haves share with the haven'ts. The proprietor was not on the premises, but his younger sister, "Aunt Betty," was and refused them in the absence of her brother. They broke down the door and shared and shared alike in the tradition of their absent fisherman husbands, leaving an account of what they took in case better times should ever come.

The Colonel was angry when he heard of this invasion, but he thought it over, and relented, and then invited the ladies to partake of his stock at the Harbor as well. "The tale of suffering and destitution that the women had to tell so touched his feelings," related Babson, "that he liberally supplied their wants, and dismissed them with words of the utmost kindness and sympathy." [8]

That winter of 1779 and 1780 was the bottom of the American Revolution. George Washington was stymied in the Hudson Valley. The tide of his country's reserves seemed to have run out. His men were freezing, sick, unpaid and rebellious. Congress was bankrupt, and so was Massachusetts, where inflation had wafted the paper currency out of sight, devalued by seventy to one. To meet its 1780 quota for the Continental Army of thirty-two men, and another thirty-eight for the militia, Gloucester voted to borrow $180,000 for bounties, $51,000 for pay and forty thousand pounds to furnish its share of provisions and clothing. The opportunity to go through freezing hell with the Commander-in-Chief, and serve six months without pay in the bargain, did not arouse enthusiasm in a patriotic privateersman who had tasted his sweet morsel of whatever succulent prize he may have been lucky enough to have helped sail gloriously into Gloucester, regardless of how "unsuccessful" the town fathers complained that enterprise had been.

Yet the clouds parted. Spring burst again upon the rugged landscape of Cape Ann. The sweet clethra spread its gossamer veil upon hill and dale. The shad shed its fragrance adrifting o'er the rusty ledge and out to sea. The climbing sun cast sapphires on the waters of the bay. And it was fitting-out time.

The first to make a break for it had been the small brigantine *Lightfoot* of sixty tons. She was built for Winthrop Sargent on the West Parish shore of Squam River by Thomas Moore, a captured carpenter in the crew of *Warren*'s plush prize, *Sarah and Elizabeth,* who decided to stick around instead of returning home on exchange. Bradbury Sanders took *Lightfoot* in February, lightly armed and manned, probably for the West Indies.

In April 1780, as the first dandelions were warily poking their yellow heads through the warming sod, the privateer brigantine *Wilkes* sailed from Gloucester under Captain Job Knights. Israel Trask, now a hardened sea dog of fifteen, was in the forecastle; he had already made a winter cruise off Spain in the privateer *Rambler* (at Bilboa they were visited on shipboard by John Adams, en route to the Paris peace talks with his son, John Quincy Adams) since his homecoming from the Penobscot debacle. *Wilkes* took two prizes, only to fall into the graceful clutches of HM Sloop of War *Fairy* in the West Indies. They were brought to St. John's, Newfoundland. "I was put on board prison ship," he told Congress in his petition, "from which I was ejected at the point of the bayonet with fourteen other men, conducted to the *Vestal* frigate then in port and forced to do duty until the arrival of Admiral Edwards, whose humanity at the instance of a pathetic petition ordered us to be restored to the prison ship where we passed some months suffering with hunger, our chief food a scanty allowance of oatmeal unsifted and made into gruel. We were with some hundred others huddled on board a small brig under the cartel flag and arrived safely at Boston."[9]

Gloucester's third privateer of the new year to cleave the sparkling sea was the ship *America*, commissioned to John Somes on June 9. She probably carried about twenty guns and a crew of a hundred, among whom was the captain's younger cousin, Sam Somes, back to sea after a hitch in the army, and Jim Prentice, the popular and militant tavernkeeper, in charge, it seems, of a small detachment of "marines." Captain Somes and Prentice made a contrasting pair ... Somes dark, stocky, standing five feet six ... Prentice a jovial giant for his day, six feet two.[10]

Late in July the brigantine *Fair Play,* which Ignatius Webber had misguided up on the snowy beach of Brace Cove in January, sailed with six of her twelve guns and a short crew of eight, Captain Elias Davis. It was *Fair Play*'s last documented commissioning and very probably her last voyage, in which case one of her crew was Alexander Parran, the sergeant in Warner's company at Bunker Hill who was shot through the shoulder and lost the use of his right arm. Off Guadeloupe, *Fair Play* was fired on and sunk. Some of the crew and Captain

Davis swam to safety, but not Alexander Parran. After five years, that British musket ball caught up with him, and he drowned.

The tides flowed and ebbed, and flowed again ... the tides and the fortunes of war. On August 28, at about the same time that Parran's note was being called, the Reverend Obadiah Parsons made a notation of more than ordinary interest in the records of Annisquam's Third Parish Church: [11]

> *Died* Samuel Edmundson--died on board the boat, within a few miles of Cape Ann. He sailed in the schooner *America,* Capt. Isaac Elwell, commander, from the West Indies, November 25th, 1779, bound for this town--met with remarkably severe weather on this coast and about the first of January, 1780, when within a few miles sail of Cape Ann, the wind suddenly put in to the northward, he lost the vessel's rudder and was drove off the coast again, and driven hither and thither on the ocean, till the second day August last, when they were taken off the wreck by Capt. Henry Neal, on his passage from Dartmouth, in England, bound for New York. When near Long Island, August 10th, Capt. Neal gave a boat to Capt. Elwell, with provisions, in which he with the survivors of his crew viz: John Woodward, Samuel Edmundson, Jacob Lurvey and Nathaniel Allen, came along the shore and arrived at Cape Ann, August 26th, 1780, landing at Annisquam.

According to Allen, who was a Manchester man, *America* (not to be confused with the privateer ship) traded her cargo of salt fish at Guadeloupe for sugar, cotton, cocoa, coffee, rum and molasses. It was during a violent gale on Georges Bank that a giant sea carried away their rudder, sails and bowsprit. For month after month the disabled schooner ghosted over the sea. They had a week's provisions left, and when that was gone they lived on parched cocoa, "burned-down" rum, a few fish they caught and rainwater. In six months and seventeen days they sighted but three sails, and it was the third that saved them, twenty leagues to the westward of the Azores. The British captain would not take them into New York, which was occupied by his countrymen, but gave them his ship's boat.

They sailed it by day, and beached and slept beneath it at night, until they reached Cape Ann. [12]

"When the land at Annisquam was seen by Captain Elwell and the survivors of his crew, Samuel Edmundson, who was very feeble and lying in the boat, was raised up, and--when told it was Annisquam, his home--he was so completely overcome with joy that he fell back in the boat and died in a short time." [13]

Thirteen months back ashore was too much for Captain Elwell, and on October 3, 1781, he was commissioned commander of William Pearce's brigantine *Friendship*, eight guns. He sailed for the West Indies with twenty men, and they captured a brig full of rum.

When Gloucester town meeting came around in March of 1780, Joseph Foster was going on fifty, and it may have been that sobering thought which turned him again from other preoccupations to public service after a lapse of some time. He was elected measurer of wood, and tithing man, and to the committee of correspondence again, and was asked with Peter Coffin to be a reception committee of two to welcome a delegation from the General Court coming to revaluate the town, presumably as the result of its year-end plea of destitution. Later the two were joined by five others "to wait on the Court's Committee thats a comming to view the Town." The viewers were in for a shock.

This was all routine stuff to Foster. The challenge came on May 8, when he was elected head of a town committee of thirteen members to recommend what action, if any, the freeholders should take to ratify the state constitution. Permanent self-government was the objective. He was in a singular situation.

Early in 1778 the General Court had declared itself a constitutional convention and drawn up a constitution which it blandly distributed to the towns for their expected approval. Theophilus Parsons, descendant of the Gloucester Parsonses, (he who took his fee in hogsheads of rum), was practising law in Newburyport at the time, having been driven out of Falmouth, Maine, when Mowat levelled that town; he thought this a most irregular and irresponsible method of framing the structure of government. Parsons was a student of political theory, and a brilliant one. He dominated a convention of Essex County towns held at Ipswich early in May to consider the matter and wrote its report, curiously entitled *The Essex Result*. It was an enormously influential pamphlet which tore the General Court's proposed constitution apart, mainly for its glaring absence of a declaration of rights and its failure to provide for a separation of governmental powers, and then spelled out Parsons's own conception of "the true principles of government."

Out of this convention Parsons gathered round him the powerful political group called the Essex Junto. Its action, and the cogency of his pamphlet, influenced the towns to defeat resoundingly this first inadequate draft of the Massachusetts constitution. Gloucester rejected it on May 20 by a vote of 109 to 0.

The General Court took the constitutional issue off the table in the spring of 1779; the chastened legislators this time requested the towns to elect their own delegates to a special convention. They did. The delegates met in the First Parish Meetinghouse in Cambridge, 312 of them, on September 1. Gloucester sent Joseph Foster, Winthrop and Epes Sargent, Peter Coffin and Samuel Whittemore. It was that hardest of winters, when travel was so "excessive bad," and frequently but a handful of these shivering founding fathers could be found at work. But they hammered out a document, with the help of John Adams in the early stages and the highminded conniving of Theophilus Parsons and his Essex Junto, and laid it at the mercy of the voting populace on March 2, 1780.

It was for the consideration of this second-draft state constitution which he helped to frame that Joseph Foster headed a committee of Gloucester citizens on May 8. On May 22 the document was read aloud in town meeting, and the question put if the freeholders would accept it. Forty-eight — not a large number to be deciding a question of such supreme importance in a town of five thousand — walked affirmatively to the eastward, and none to the westward, and it was a vote. The Massachusetts Constitution was accepted by the town of Gloucester ... except that "Col. Foster and Capt. Sargent [Epes, Jr., probably] said they objected to it" — and that is the strange upshot of the singular situation in which Foster found himself.

To go back a bit. John Murray's Universalist followers in June of 1776 walked out of the First Parish, as they had threatened they would if Eli Forbes accepted the ministry. This precipitated a campaign by the Congregationalists which grew more acerbic with each passing sabbath, first to cajole, and then to bludgeon them back into the fold.

It was bitter. The anti-Murray committee of safety, for instance, was directed by town meeting (which was dominated by the Calvinists) on April 1, 1778, to let out any lands in Gloucester belonging to "refugees" and British subjects, and to sell the buildings thereon. When John J. Babson wrote that he was not aware of anyone who fitted either category, he forgot the English emigre John Murray, still a British subject as far as is known, a refugee as far as his enemies were concerned, and a landowner; when they tried to run him out of Gloucester in 1776 as a vagrant, a friend presented the preacher with a deed of gift which qualified him as a freeholder, hence not liable to a charge of vagrancy.

The First Parish campaign commenced with expressions of "tender concern" for the Universalist brothers and sisters. In a while they were being taxed with "silent neglect," then with "unscriptural, unconstitutional proceedings." The temperature rose, and they were accused of "contemptuous silence." Finally, "we have waited long in hope that the rules of common decency and good breeding (if no higher motive) would at length have induced you to make some reply, but we have waited to no purpose."

Having waited to no purpose, the First Parish in September of 1778 suspended Winthrop and Epes Sargent, Jr.; Ebenezer Parsons (brother of Theophilus) and their wives; David Pearce; Winthrop's daughter, Mrs. Judith Sargent Stevens; and seven other women. Why Joseph and Lydia Foster and other devoted Universalists were not among the indexed fourteen is not known. They were, however, listed as founders of the Independent Church of Christ, John Murray pastor, in January of 1779. And in May, 1780, Colonel Foster and one of the Sargents, probably Epes, were in the anomalous position, as two of its framers, of objecting to the proposed state constitution in town meeting while refraining from actually voting against it.

If they explained their reasons for this peculiar stance, the fact was not reported in the town records. It is most likely that they took exception to Article III of the drafted Declaration of Rights which laid it on the towns, by means of their taxes, to support the public worship of God and "public Protestant teachers of piety, religion and morality." The article decreed specifically that all church tax money paid by the taxpayer "shall if he require it, be uniformly applied to the support of the public teacher or teachers of his own religious sect or denomination, provided there be any on whose instructions he attends." For all of its fine phrases respecting the rights of conscience, the effect of Article III was to perpetuate orthodox Congregationalism, the established church in virtually every town, as the state church. It placed the whole legal onus of proving their constitutional qualifications on the minority Protestant denominations, mainly the Universalists and Methodists at this period, demanding that in the meanwhile every taxpayer in town, regardless of his religion or absence of it, support exclusively through his taxes his parish church and minister, which were invariably Congregationalist.

Articles I and II of the Declaration of Rights, it should be noted, barred from state office any candidate not avowedly "of the Christian religion." This excluded Roman Catholics on the grounds that they were not true Christians because they declined to disclaim allegiance to a supranational spiritual jurisdiction.

Article III — so vestigial of the old theological authoritarianism (what would John Wise have thought of it?) — provoked heated debate in the towns. All the same, anachronistic as it was, it did not hold up ratification. It was a crude sophistry, this attempt to incorporate the old religion into the new structure of government, and it would not survive long, in great measure as the outcome of the storm which was making up around it in Gloucester.

16

EMBRACE THE FIRST GOOD WIND

After a shore leave of eighteen years during which there is no evidence of his ever having taken the wheel in his own hands and braced himself against a canting deck afroth to leeward with the salty foam of the sea, Joseph Foster went back to it. It was October of 1780, half through the sixth year of a stalemated Revolution (if you were on one side) or Rebellion (if on the other). His last voyage of record was in 1762, thirteen years before the lobsterbacks lock-stepped on Lexington, when he took the schooner *Joseph* to the West Indies with a load of lumber.

On the tenth of October Winthrop Sargent and William Pearson joined Foster in putting up a continental bond of twenty thousand inflated dollars and petitioning the Massachusetts Council for a commission for him. Next day he was officially Captain Joseph Foster of old, with a difference: now he was in the ranks of the privateersmen he had so often staked to fortune, or disaster, since that day in December of 1775 when he had sent *General Ward* to sea with a single gun, number four of the fifteen hundred commissions Massachusetts would issue before the issue was settled.

Captain Foster's command, at long last, was the faithful brigantine *General Mercer.* He had held a share in the privateer back when she sailed off in Manley's ill-managed squadron in '77 to make her fortune in spades off the coast of France. Now she was owned by Winthrop Sargent, and her guns were reduced from sixteen to eight, and her crew from a fighting hundred to a cautious twenty-five. Prizes, surely, were not the object of this voyage.

Why did Joseph Foster choose this uncertain moment to return to the rigors and hazards of a life at sea, magnified by war, when he had been doing quite comfortably ashore for a score of years?

Lord Cornwallis had withdrawn to winter quarters in North Carolina after an indecisive campaign in the south. Benedict Arnold had fled to the British after the fizzle of his treachery in September. And to his annoyance and frustration, General Washington had recently been forced to admit to the Comte de Rochambeau that he was not yet in a position to participate in an assault on New York with the French nobleman's five thousand countrymen newly arrived at Newport.

The naval war, too, was hither and yon. The fleets of America's allies, France and Spain (soon to be joined by Holland), had failed to come to grips with the British naval forces in the West Indies under Admiral Sir George Rodney; with hurricane season in the offing, Rodney sailed for his North American station and arrived at New York on September 14.

So it was perhaps the news that his Majesty's warships had abandoned the Caribbean for the winter that put Colonel Foster powerfully in mind of his old and profitable haunts. Ah, Christmas at Martinique! What a warm thought to stir cold Yankee blood!

Then too, he had married off his second daughter, Lydia, the previous fifth of March to John Osborne Sargent. She was nineteen; John was twenty-three, a son of Epes the Tory of late, Winthrop's nephew. A happy event, yes....but one which brought home to the father of the bride, as it inevitably does, that the years are passing and 'tis time to have a last grapple with the old life. Yes, and he was fifty in July. The sea called.

One remembrance of this evidently uneventful voyage lingers on, wafted faint yet distinct downwind of time: in granting Captain Foster's commission, the Council directed that the naval officer of the port of Gloucester clear the *Mercer* for the West Indies without delay, as her cargo of fish "was unfit for home consumption."

The departure of *General Mercer* marked an acceleration of privateering activity from Gloucester which continued almost without interruption, winter and summer, until the end of the Revolution. Hardly a month passed but at least one and sometimes two or three letters of marque, many of them converted prizes, dropped Eastern Point astern to range the seas ever wider and ever bolder, trading more openly with the allies in Europe and the Caribbean, always with an eye out for a fat and unattended victim as the Royal Navy turned ever more to the defensive.

The *Mercer* and Foster were not out ten days when the brigantine *Ranger* of ten guns made sail under Captain Samuel Babson on October 19, and then the ship *Eagle,* owned in Boston but commanded by Captain Nathaniel Sargent of Gloucester, on November 8. Directly after Christmas the eccentric Englishman John Beach took command of the ship *Gloucester Packet,* the renamed Jamaica packet *Halifax* taken by the *Stark* in '79. She had been refitted by David Pearce with sixteen guns. Beach sailed for Cadiz with forty-five men and captured the brig *Mary* with a cargo of flour. In January 1781 the eight-gun brigantine *Delight* sailed under Captain Moses Hale; then the ship *Polly,* three hundred tons, twenty guns and thirty-five men under Captain William Coas, owned by Winthrop Sargent, and unnamed others probably including Foster. Shortly *Betsey* followed *Polly* around the Point, early in February, twenty guns, Captain Philemon Haskell, 130 men, owners unknown. This many winter departures were unheard of.

Captain Foster could not have returned home in *General Mercer* more than a few weeks when he was commissioned commander of *Polly* on February 20, taking her over from Captain Coas. There is no more information about this voyage than there is about the *Mercer's.* His commission states that *Polly's* armament was cut back from twenty to eighteen guns, and the crew from thirty-five to thirty, "having on board as provisions twenty barrels of beef and pork, and two thousand weight of bread--as ammunition five hundred weight of powder, and shot in proportion." [1]

Numerous encounters had impressed on chaser and chased that speed and the ability to sail closer to the wind were the strongest assets of the Yankee privateers. An exciting trial occurred during a cruise this year of the small (ninety tons) and very fast brigantine *Ruby*, owned in Newburyport and commissioned on April 9 to Captain Benjamin Webber of Gloucester. Among his crew of fifteen was his young cousin, Ignatius, who had shipped to the West Indies once or twice since we last saw him waiting in some embarrassment for the coming tide to float *Fair Play* from the foul berth where he had put her in Brace Cove.

After a quick voyage to Martinique, *Ruby* embarked again for the West Indies. On her homeward passage, in company with the brigantine *Flora* of Boston, she took a large English ship loaded with brandy, gin, wine and dry goods which they manned out and sent to Boston. Again *Ruby* set out for the Caribbean, probably under Captain Solomon Babson, who was commissioned to her on August 9; and now came the test of a full-rigged ship against a brigantine, half-rigged fore-and-aft on the mainmast. Webber remembered it vividly in his *Narrative:*

> As we were running down in the latitude of Martinica one morning, saw a sail to the southward of us. We sprung our loof [sailed closer to the wind] and made sail towards her, she standing to the northward by the wind. We came so near as to perceive she was a ship of war. We bore away and made sail. She gave chace and came up on us considerably. We found she would soon be alongside if we continued before the wind, there being few vessels if any could equal our vessel by the wind, in sailing when in proper trim. We found it was necessary to manouevre. We therefore got in readiness to gibe and bring our vessel on the larboard tack, which we did expeditiously, the ship being nothing behind hand with us. We at first brought her three points to windward of our wake, so that our sails would all draw to advantage, and so continued to loof gradually. We soon brought her into our wake.
>
> She began to fire bow chace guns. We fired stern ditto. We soon brought our vessel within seven points of the wind,

the ship at this time three points to leeward of our wake. We found we were going to windward upon her very fast. She edged away and fired her broadside. Her round shot chiefly passed over. Her grape fell short of us. We received no damage. Soon after she gave over chace, and we arrived safe at Martinica. From the description given of this ship here, she was of twenty guns, belonging to Barbadoes.

A fast sailer, an eager crew, well-served guns, a captain who knew when not to serve them, resourceful and experienced owners--and a powerful dose of luck--these made a successful Massachusetts privateer. And such was the aptly named letter of marque ship *Robin Hood* of two hundred tons burthen. She was built early in 1781 by Joseph Clark for Boston men with close Cape Ann connections and given for her maiden cruise on May 24 to Captain Sargent Smith, a Gloucesterman not yet quite twenty-four years old, the younger brother of the Captain John Smith who died three years earlier of a gunshot wound in the throat when he was so unwisely brave as to engage *Civil Usage* with a transport of overpowering strength.

A hundred and seventy years after *Robin Hood* sailed on that first voyage her papers were discovered under the eaves of a colonial Gloucester house and given to the Cape Ann Historical Association. The account sheets, tallies, receipts, manifests, shipping papers, master's instructions and correspondence, on paper almost as white and supple as the day they were penned, reveal an intimate feel of the day-by-day business of legal piracy in the state which fitted out more privateers than any other in the War of Independence, and of the men who made fortunes at it, and of how they did it.

Robin Hood's builders were wise in the ways of profitable patriotism. Stephen Higginson, Salem-born, took to the sea early, voyaged to Europe, began privateering soon after the outbreak of war and moved to Boston in 1778. He spent the rest of his career in business and public service and was the grandfather of Thomas Wentworth Higginson, the author and reformer. He was at this time thirty-eight, a tough, confident, highly intelligent veteran of the riskiest of all legitimate maritime pursuits.

Daniel Sargent was fifty, a brother of Epes and Winthrop. He stuck with commerce and the fishing business in Gloucester until the war, then moved to Newburyport, and from there to Boston. He owned interests in several privateers, some of them Gloucester-based.

Ebenezer Parsons had shared the ownership of *General Ward* with Joseph Foster. He came from Byfield and was a brother of lawyer Theophilus, but his family roots and a considerable business and vessel stake were at Cape Ann. Eben was thirty-five and associated closely in Boston in the spring of 1781 with another brother, Captain William Parsons, twenty-six.

The Gloucesterman to whom the owners of *Robin Hood* entrusted their new ship and a substantial portion of their fortunes, Captain Sargent Smith, was a mere twenty-three and had only one previously recorded command, the Boston privateer schooner *Peacock* of four guns which he took in the autumn of 1780. Gamblers, all five.

Robin Hood had been framed and planked at Clark's Boston shipyard and was having the deck laid, judging from the earliest entry against the owners' account on February 15, for deck nails. A fortnight after this, William Capen agreed to complete the joinery for either twenty pounds hard money, paper at the rate of exchange when paid, or fifteen hundred pounds in paper taken in molasses at twelve pounds a gallon or in other West India goods at market prices. Thus had inflation restored trade to the barter system.

Alexander Baker and Company billed five hundred pounds for ten days' work "stopping the worm holes," four and a half days paying the vessel's bottom with tar, and four days paying her black work and upper works. Richard Skillin billed sixteen pounds for a variety of blocks, deadeyes, belaying pins, fids, hand pumps and serving and gunners' mallets, and took most of it in ninety-eight gallons of molasses.

Hundreds and thousands of items went into the ship as she took form on the stocks, all of the work well washed down with the rum that nothing in New England could be accomplished without ... 80 gal. Rum us'd build'g ship, £1152...4 Gall Rum

Launching. And there was the fitting-out after the launch, stepping spars (mainmast fifty-eight feet, main topmast thirty-six feet, main topgallantmast thirty-two feet), the rigging of her, stretching on the new canvas, four hundred pounds paid to John Hooton the oarmaker who had been one of the Mohawks on a Tea Party, for twelve sweeps twenty-eight feet long.

Then May bloomed upon the land, and the sea called ... sweet sad siren call of spring on the shore, and the day was in the offing. All was feverish, spring-feverish, all hustle and abustle at the wharf. Tackle was rigged, and new blocks squeaked and new hemp groaned lifting fourteen prodigious guns and carriages aboard, one by one. The quill scratched on down the ledger, column after neat column, down to the business of it now ... cutlasses, muskets, pistols, speaking trumpets, spy glass, fishing line, leads, hooks, log lines, time glasses, spare canvas, "shott of all kinds," fifty pounds of powder bought at Cape Ann, a hundred bought somewhere else...from William Cordwell a bill for musket balls, half-pound powder measures, one-pound powder measures, gun ladles.."3 peoples passage from Cape Ann, £ 36."

For guests aboard, thirty-six pairs of handcuffs and forty-two keys, £ 583. For purposes of deception, Continental and English ensigns, £ 4.12. Readiness to sail under false colors was regarded as a matter of necessity among privateersmen, if not pride.

By the last day of May the whole ship's company of sixty-one, including two prizemasters, had signed on for a voyage to neutral Denmark, and two, David Hawkins and John Camell, had "run away," as noted beside their names. They all took their advance wages in Spanish milled dollars and agreed in writing that the owners should have two-thirds share of all prizes, a third to officers and crew, and "there shall be six deserving shares for the benefit of good men," apparently bonuses for meritorious service. Forty-five signed papers (four with their "X") designating William Parsons their prize agent.

Sargent Smith had received his commission on May 24, certifying that *Robin Hood* was rightly provisioned to serve sixty men with sixty barrels of beef and pork and eight hundred pounds of bread, and fourteen guns with eight hundred pounds of powder and shot in proportion. Except for these stores, the new and untested privateer floated light on her maiden voyage. They had their expectations, but her speed and ease of handling were unproven, and her owners wanted every initial advantage in her first encounter with an enemy. They intended that *Robin Hood* should take a rich prize or two on the outward passage which would test her abilities and at the same time supply her a cargo for Denmark.

On June 2 Captain Smith was handed his orders. Families, friends and sweethearts thronged the wharf. Tearful were the leave-takings. The lines were cast off. *Robin Hood*, all shining and bright (if not in Sherwood green, then in Baker black), was kedged into the stream; her sails, whitest of the white, were unfurled to the climbing sun of spring and filled with the fair breeze. They were off, for fortune, and a knock at the British, they hoped, on a daring voyage into England's back bailiwick, the North Sea, as a war without end moved into its sixth year.

Captain Smith's orders were dated May 29 and signed by Stephen Higginson, Daniel Sargent and William Parsons, but there is hardly a doubt that they were written by Higginson out of the breadth of his personal experience as a master in the foreign trade and privateering. They are so explicit, so lucid, so full of practical guidance, and of warning at every anticipated turn, so revealing of the times, of the crafty *modus operandi* of America's freebooting quasi-navy, as to be a primer of privateering ... not of the blood and thunder, but of the bread and butter of it that made fortunes large and small for the Higginsons of Salem and Boston, the Sargents and Parsonses of Boston and Cape Ann, and the Joseph Fosters and David Pearces of Gloucester--and made of Massachusetts the great maritime state of the new nation.

Boston May 29, 1781

Capt. Sargent Smith

You being the master of our ship *Robin Hood* and ready to sail, our orders are that you embrace the first good wind and proceed from hence to Christian Sand in Denmark. [Christiansand, across the Skagerak, is on the south coast of Norway, which was virtually a province of Denmark.] On your arrival there you will deliver the goods you carry out from here to Mr. John Merchant who goes out in the ship with you, and you will get the ship ready to take in such goods as he shall send down from Copenhagen for you...

We have fitted the ship at a great expense and have sent guns and men enough to enable you to take prizes on your passage and we put great dependence on the prospect of captures in your way out. We therefore would have you look at every vessel you see, if your ship sails very well, which we have no doubt of, and attack all such British and Bermudian vessels as you may meet with and think yourself capable of taking without danger of losing your own ship. You will take care to satisfy yourself as to the force of a ship before you go too nigh her, and when you are doubtful of a vessel's strength, be sure to see that your ship outsails her or delay going very near her till afternoon, so that if she proves stronger than you expected you may have the advantage of the night to escape.

When you get in the track of ships bound from England to Quebeck, New York, Newfoundland and the homeward bound West India men, you need not hurry along but run under easy sail for the better chance of prizes, till you have taken as many as you can man and keep 25 men on board your own ship, then proceed your voyage as fast as you can. You will remember that the American, Dutch, French and Spanish vessels [these were of the alliance against England] which you may retake are by a new regulation all our own. When you get upon the coast of England and Denmark don't be over anxious after cutters if you should see any. They generally sail very fast and are often of much greater force than they appear to be, and very seldom of much value. But every other kind of vessel you may venture to look at, if your own sails fast. Should you meet with any vessel with rice, tobacco or sugar, you will load your own ship out of her, for it will not be worthwhile to part with your men for a vessel of but little value. The same conduct will be advisable if you meet with vessels bound to Newfoundland and having nothing but a few stores. Take all them out, dismantle and dismiss them. We are persuaded that you will meet enough vessels that are valuable to expend your men, and should you meet one that is very much so you will put your best prize master and men on board her. Give them all orders to avoid our eastern shore in coming home with prizes ...

You will be careful to find the best trim of your ship and have her marked after you arrive, both forward and abaft. Be sure not to load too deep when coming home.

Keep her wales free from the water half a streak or three inches at least, and be sure to avoid everything that is large and has any force in your way home, as your vessel will then be too valuable to run any risk. Don't even chase anything unless you are sure that she is small. We suppose that 30 tons of iron will be ballast enough with tea and bale goods. Mr. Merchant will send you down from Copenhagen a memorandum of the goods that are to come home, and you will be very careful that the tea, hemp and other goods that are subject to damage are very well stowed. It will be necessary to have your decks and upper works thoroughly recaulked and then put on a good coat of turpentine. You will have the goods properly dunnaged from the bottom and sides to guard against any water that may run down, and have the heaviest goods stowed at bottom. Be careful and take an account of every package that is put on board with the marks, etc.

Mr. Joseph Winthrop who goes out in the ship will go directly to some other port ["over to England" crossed out] to send you some goods that are to come from thence. These you will reserve room for provided they get over to Christian Sand by the last of September, but if they do not get there by that time you must fill up with goods from Copenhagen if enough should offer or come away without being full by the 10th of October at farthest, for it will not do to make it later than that before you sail.

You must be very careful in passing the Orkneys both coming and going. This passage in thick weather is a little difficult ...

Should you carry any prize into that port or any goods taken out of prizes, they are to be sold and the money laid out in goods and shipped home in the ship by Mr. Merchant, on the joint account of the crew and owners, the officers and men to pay at your return here the same freight as other people ... If you find that Americans are allowed to carry prizes into that port [Christiansand] and you go out from thence to cruise, it must be only for a short time. You must be in again by the first of September to take in your cargo. If you find the ship sails very fast on your passage out, be sure to get as near the same trim when coming home as possible, and make no alteration in the masts or anything else.

You must give your prize master orders not to go into Cape Cod Harbour as the British cruisers frequently go in there, and be careful always to keep copies of your commission by you and give one copy of it with proper orders to every prize master. You must also order them if they should be obliged to put into any other harbour than this to send a man express to us, and not attempt to go out again if it be a safe harbour till he receives orders from us. Direct them to hoist a jack or ensign at the end of the jibb boom, the color to hang down under the boom and pendant at foretopmast head as a signal for us to know them, and you will show us the same signal when coming in yourself.

Be very careful to keep good order on board the ship, see that the sailors are well used and that every man attends only to his own proper business. Be sure not to leave too many prisoners on board any prize, and especially that no officer, owner or navigator is among those that may be left. Use those prisoners that you take on board your own ship with humanity, but don't give them so much liberty as to endanger yourself...

You will write us by the prizes you may take exactly what you think of the ship as to her sailing, etc., as we shall be governed much by that in our conduct as to insuring, and if Captain------should be at Christian Sand when you arrive, write us very particularly by him. If she sails as well as the *Favorite* we shall be very easy about her. [The unnamed captain is undoubtedly Isaac Somes of Gloucester, who was commissioned commander of the hundred-ton brig *Favorite*, owned by Daniel Sargent and others, on December 14, 1779.]

In your passage out don't go too near Halifax or Newfoundland but run over the middle or southern part of Georges and the Grand Bank, nor don't when near the longitude of Newfoundland chace any very large ships, for they have some very fast sailing frigates on that coast, and but very few large merchant men that are bound westward go very near the coast. But if you find your ship sails as well as we expect and you may wish, you can then venture to look at everything even in those places where there are frigates stationed to guard against our privateers.

Should you find the cruisers about the Naes of Norway [Lindesnaes, or The Naze, the southernmost cape of Norway, about forty miles west of Christiansand] so very thick that you cannot get in there, or you should chance to be chased into Holland for protection, you may then go up to Amsterdam and land there upon freight for home on the best terms you can ... If you meet any boats on that coast that you speak with, be sure to inquire whether there is any new political alteration, such as a war between Denmark and England, etc. There is no event that can take place that will hurt you unless Denmark should take a part with England against us and our allies. This therefore you must, if such an opportunity offers, inquire very particularly about, and should this contrary to all expectations happen ... you must then go to Holland unavoidably ...

If you take any prize that has a gentleman passenger on board, keep him on board your ship till you arrive in Europe, and then let him go with Mr. Winthrop after pledging his sacred word that he will procure the release of John Higginson [Stephen's younger brother], who is in Fortune Prison [Forton Prison, Portsmouth, England] and has been there for 20 months, or engaging that if he does not obtain his release he will then return and be your prisoner again. Or let him write by Mr. Winthrop to his friends and desire them to get said Higginson released and sent by Mr. Winthrop on board your ship till Higginson is discharged and has joined you, and then to be immediately discharged and suffered to go home. If you should not take any such person in any of your prizes, you will then detain the captain which you think of the most importance and has the best friends, for the better his companions the more likely the prisoner will be to procure the release of said Higginson. The detaining your prisoner will be, we think, the surest way of effecting Higginson's release, and you will use that method or the sending the prisoner home on parole, as you and the passengers in your ship may think best, all circumstances considered.

As there can be no doubt but they will know in England of your being at Christian Sand and perhaps also the time of your sailing from there, it's very probable that one or two fast sailing vessels may be sent to lay waiting for you. Great caution must therefore be used when you come out. We would have you tarry there till there is a [page torn] and if the weather be thick, the better. Go out so as to pass the Naes two or three hours before sunset and either keep the shore of Norway close aboard or else run away to the westward all night nearly as circumstances may render expedient. If any cruisers should be waiting for you they will probably keep from 5 to 15 leagues to the NW of the Naes, that being the common path. You must therefore endeavour to go either within or without that track before you haul to the northward. It will probably be most safe to go without them.

If you should take a vessel that has a good cable on board about the size of your new one, take it on board the ship for her use and put the old one on board the prize.

PS: May 31. Mr. Winthrop thought of going to England to receive some money due to him and his friends, and to bring it home in British goods, but after examining closely the Resolves of Congress and the Acts of this State, we find that all such goods are strictly prohibited and will be subject to seizure. We have therefore advised him not to think of doing it, and we order you not to receive any such goods from him or any other person as we would not by any means encourage an illicit trade nor subject the ship to seizure. You will therefore notwithstanding what was said about Mr. Winthrop's going to England and your receiving his goods, take no goods brought by Winthrop or any other person from England, nor any but such as are purchased at Copenhagen,

Christian Sand, Gottenburg or some other part of that country.

We are etc.

S. Higginson
D. Sargent
Wm. Parsons

Robin Hood lived up to her owners' expectations and her captain's wish. Somewhere on the high seas, outward bound, they chased down the English brig *Concord* and sent her home with a prize crew. By December 12, the cargo left in her, if not *Concord,* had been disposed of in Boston; a receipt among *Robin Hood*'s papers shows that merchant David Greenough, evidently a minor shareholder, participated in the proceeds. After their arrival in Denmark, supercargo John Merchant sold twenty casks of rice, several of them damaged; evidence is lacking that they were loaded at Boston, and there is scarcely any doubt that Captain Smith transferred them from his prize in mid-ocean, as advised by his owners.

The Boston-Gloucester privateer arrived at Christiansand on or a day or two before July 16 (the day fresh provisions first came aboard), but not without event. Sargent Smith had been unable to steer clear of enemy cutters ... or he had momentarily forgotten his owners' caution not to be "over anxious after cutters." Their agent at Copenhagen by the interesting name of C. S. Black's Widow and company wrote them on November 6 that "the disagreeable affair Capt. Smith had coming in to Christiansand with an English cutter by some guns that were fired on his Majesty's Territory by some of his people, tho' quite against his order, has caused Capt. Smith & likewise Mr. Merchant both detainment & trouble, but we are exceedingly glad to advise you that we at last got everything settled to entire satisfaction."

Thank God for influential agents when six weeks from home in a strange country in wartime! It sounds as if *Robin Hood* engaged the cutter outside Christiansand, overshot the target and violated neutral ground. That his guns were served against his orders is an alibi of the captain's which invites some skepticism. His supercargo's account reveals that Smith paid a fine of forty-five pounds in the admiralty court at Copenhagen.

As a result of the long detention and delay arising out of this embarrassing incident, *Robin Hood* failed to clear Christian-sand for home until about December 8. John Merchant had done his work well. The ship was stowed and trimmed with the thirty tons of Swedish iron as advised by her owners, as well as five tons of hemp, four tons of junk, chest upon chest of the finest tea, excellent dry goods, spices, cartons of wafers, boxes of bird shot and a crate of fiddles and flutes. This sundry cargo was freighted to a number of consignees in New England by Merchant, "Madam Black" and Joseph Winthrop.

Winthrop had obtained goods for home at Gottenburg, Sweden. There is no clue in *Robin Hood*'s papers that he attempted that covert mission to England which caused the owners such wrenchings of conscience as they weighed the profits to be gained thereby against the moral opprobrium of illicit trade with the enemy...and even worse, the consequences of getting caught at it. Whether a gentleman hostage was taken with friends influential enough to trade him off for the long-suffering John Higginson is to be doubted. But it is a fact that Higginson arrived home from prison in England only six months after his brother's vessel. [2]

Robin Hood was back in Boston early in 1782, late, but having secured a worthy prize and a good cargo on a long and hazardous maiden voyage which took her twice through the enemy's home waters. Captain Smith had passed his test with flying colors (Continental or English, as suited his purpose) and was sent off again on a second cruise in the course of which *Robin Hood* bagged and manned for Boston, on May 5, 1782, a British privateer brig of fourteen guns, laden with coffee and cotton.

Another prize taken by *Robin Hood* when Sargent Smith had her is described by Babson as "a British packet of greatly superior force." The enemy was not all that superior, because the historian mistakenly identified *Robin Hood* as a brig of nine guns; she was a ship of fourteen, and the packet mounted sixteen. The American privateer, according to this undated account, overtook the enemy, and Smith shifted all his guns over on his business side and let loose a brace of salvoes. The packet struck. She had a crew of sixty, and forty passengers. The prize was taken into Martinique. The prisoners were exchanged at Antigua for Americans from a captured privateer under the command of Duncan Piper of Gloucester, possibly the schooner *Industry.* [3]

While *Robin Hood*'s merry men were off on the high seas redistributing the wealth of nations in the summer of 1781, [4] Gloucester's most celebrated privateer got under way round-about the sixth Fourth of July. Captain William Coas was back pacing the familiar quarterdeck. *General Stark* mounted more guns than ever before, twenty-two, and carried fewer men, a hundred. The facts of this cruise have never clearly emerged from the fog bank which the *Stark* sailed into a few days out, but they may be reconstructed approximately as follows:

It seems that advance word had reached New England that a fleet of store ships and transports was en route from England for Quebec, because the *Stark* proceeded directly from Gloucester to the Gulf of St. Lawrence to lie in wait. A week after Captain Coas received his commission for this cruise, Captain William Coles took command of the twenty-gun privateer ship *Brutus* of Salem, and he too headed for the Gulf on the same mission. They may have sailed in company, and probably were joined by the ship *America* of Newburyport, still under the command of John Somes of Gloucester.

Entering the Gulf of St. Lawrence, this trio of North Shore privateers sailed into a thick fog. When it lifted, behold, there was the Quebec-bound English fleet! Not a warship around, apparently. The *Stark* took *Detroit, Polly* and *Beaver* and brought them back to Gloucester, where their cargoes were sold for $400,000, albeit in depreciated currency. *America* and *Brutus* cut out three more of the Englishmen each, and so it merited Babson's appraisal as "one of the best cruises ever made in America in so short a time." [5]

On the first or second of October, 1781, Gloucester's greatest privateer clipped confidently out the harbor on one more cruise before the onset of another winter. That master privateersman, Coas, was in command, as he had been on her maiden voyage three years before. One week out, on October 8, *General Stark* was captured in Boston Bay, within sight of Cape Ann, by HMS *Chatham* and taken to Halifax.

Captain William Coas did not languish long in Halifax prison before he boarded a cartel for Boston on exchange. A storm arose, and the ship was never heard from. "He was a man of great enterprise, daring, and bravery," Babson wrote of him, "not without some of the faults of the privateersman, nor destitute of the best qualities of a true-hearted sailor."[6]

Ten days after the capture of the pride of Gloucester, Lord Cornwallis succumbed to the siege of Yorktown and surrendered his entire army of seven thousand men. It had taken six and a half years, but the tide had finally turned.

17

TO THE FINISH

Robin Hood was gathering barnacles in the toils of the Danish naval bureaucracy (affording Captain Smith the chance to have his ship hove down for bottom work) when Isaac Somes cleared Christiansand bound home for Boston and Gloucester early in September of 1781 in the fast brig *Favorite.* He brought a choice cargo and a packet of letters for his owners from the efficient C.S. Black's widow. Somes could not have completed his crossing much before the end of October, arriving in time to hear the bad news of the capture of *General Stark*, and the glad news of the surrender of Lord Cornwallis. [1]

Once home, Isaac Somes was not one to take in the slack when he could better be back at sea, nipping the lion's flank in his own profitable way. He had ever been in demand for such patriotic missions since that first madcap cruise in the sloop *Union*, along around this time of the year in '76, when he had the piratical audacity, as his victims thought, to pick off five prizes almost in the shadow of Buckingham Palace. Captain Somes stood at the head of Gloucester's privateersmen--first in *Union*, then in *Fair Play*, then *Sky Rocket*, *Wasp* and *Favorite*--and he had been back at Cape Ann just long enough to embrace his wife and inquire of his children how their lessons were going when a company, members now unknown, offered him a new privateer ship, just then completing her fit-out.

That the name of his new vessel was *Tempest*, and that a wild-looking figurehead of Jupiter glared out from under the bowsprit, and flashes of lightning streaked across the trail-boards ... these flirtations with fate bothered Isaac Somes not in the least. But they affected Gloucester most direfully, and there was much shaking of heads.

> The religious feeling of the people was greatly shocked at the name given to this ship; and, when they saw the appropriate emblems and devices with which her bow and stern were adorned, they indulged the most melan-choly forebodings concerning the punishment that might overtake what they deemed a daring defiance of the power of Him who rides upon the whirlwind and directs the storm. [2]

Well, the Someses were Universalists...

Someone dubbed the privateer *Terrible Tempest*, which caught Gloucester's morbid fancy and perhaps did not make it any easier to recruit a crew. On November 25 Parson Fuller took ominous note with his usual economy of ink: "A Man of War & a Transport burnt by lightning in our Bay." Next day: "A Sloop taken by the privateers and brought into our Harbour loaded with fish & train oil. A violent storm of snow." On November 29 Isaac Somes received his commission as commander of the ship *Tempest*, twelve guns, crew of forty, most of them from Cape Ann.

If Ignatius Webber's memory can be trusted, *Tempest* sailed on New Year's Day, 1782, for the West Indies in company with Webber himself in a prize brig he and one William Morgan had bought at auction; his father, Captain Ignatius, Sr., in the privateer ship *Mars*, fourteen guns; and two other privateers, one of which was probably the brig *Favorite*, under her new master, Captain Elias Davis of Gloucester, the other without a doubt the good ship *Polly,* off again for a sunnier clime in the command of that rejuvenated old sea dog, Captain Joseph Foster.

If Foster family tradition is to be credited, on the other hand, the West India fleet left Gloucester a week earlier, on Christmas Day of 1781, "when it was so warm that everyone had their windows open, and the ladies wore their summer dresses. The next morning there was a foot of snow on the ground." [3]

Old friends--the masters of *Tempest* and *Polly*--and as the historian relates,

> they kept company till they got into the Gulf Stream, where they encountered a severe gale, attended with the most terrific thunder and lightning. During one brief flash, by which several men on board the *Polly* were stunned, the *Tempest* was seen by Capt. Foster, a short distance off; but, when the next flash enabled him to discern distant objects, she was missed, and never seen again. Capt. Foster supposed that she was taken aback, and went down stern foremost...

> And when, not many weeks after she sailed, tidings were received of her foundering at sea, with all on board, in a violent tempest, the sufferers were looked upon as men who had devoted themselves to destruction by embarking on board of a doomed ship, rather than such as had perished in the ordinary providence of God. [4]

Mars was captured by an enemy frigate and carried into Jamaica, where the senior Captain Webber for the second time in the war tried the hospitality of a British prison. But fate had not yet quite finished with that other pagan craft, nor *Tempest* with fate. Her Jovian jinx flashed forth once more before Babson laid it to rest:

> It was a singular circumstance, that the builder of the ship was killed by lightning the next year after she was lost. [5]

Pressed on all fronts by the allies, England had surrendered at Yorktown all hope of keeping her American colonies, and the boldness of five Gloucester privateers embarking together for the West Indies so soon after the humiliation of Cornwallis testifies to the waning of her strength in the Caribbean.

Faithful servants of the crown fought on, of course, as was expected of careerists. One of these defenders of empire was Captain Henry Mowat, owner of the hand which a wild williwaw had stayed from wiping out Gloucester in the days when Britain rode the crest and her admirals chastized seaports. Since 1779 Mowat had been cozily ensconced on the edge of the Castine wilderness, far up in Penobscot Bay, where he rested on his laurels after taking a major part in bringing about the most humiliating American naval disaster of the war, the suicide of the Saltonstall expedition. He was an able officer. He possessed *sang froid.* Naturally he was a snob. And being a lively chap who enjoyed nothing better than to sport a fine calf in the quadrille, he was unutterably bored with the company of bored subalterns, hedgehogs, raccoons, bears, and the serene sighing silence of the Maine woods.

Anything for excitement, so Captain Mowat gave his midshipman (so says the American version) the command of a brig of fourteen guns with orders to sail out the Penobscot and cruise to the westward until he was off Cape Ann, where he was bound to encounter some fishing boats. He was to seize one of these, man it, and, keeping his brig out of sight, land some hand-picked men at Beverly, Salem or Marblehead. Once ashore, they were to locate a Yankee privateer loaded for a cruise (Mowat had been informed by agents that there were several fitting out in North Shore harbors). When he had discovered such an easy, unsuspecting mark, the midshipman was to cut her out, quietly, and escape with her, under convoy of his brig, back to Castine and the Bagaduce.

The young officer followed his orders to the letter. Toward the end of March he came on the Cape Ann coast, took a fishing boat, manned her with twenty-five of his crew and innocuously landed. The spies were put ashore. They slipped into Gloucester, and according to the *Salem Gazette* of April 11, 1782,

> made inquiry among their friends (of whom, no doubt, they have more or less in every town) respecting our trade and found that the ship *Harriot,* belonging to Capt. David Pearce, was ready for sea with a very valuable cargo on board. The person who made these inquiries confesses that he had been on board several vessels, in order to see their situation and strength; and to prove to the Captain of the brig that he had been on shore, he stole

a hat and two blocks from a schooner, and convinced him that the ship might be cut out, or the stores broke open, as there was no military watch kept in town. They chose the former.

One of Captain Mowat's agents on this underhanded mission, perhaps the hat-snatcher and the chief, was Daniel Somes of proud surname, a scapegrace Gloucesterman who had quit the town and joined the Tories down Maine, where he presumably crossed paths with the Castine commander. Daniel was the youngest brother of Captains Isaac and John. Colonel Foster's efficient watch must have long since been disbanded, perhaps when he gave up his commission. [6]

Harriot was a converted prize, an English packet which struck to a Newburyport privateer late in '78. Captain John Beach had been commissioned her commander on January 21. She mounted sixteen guns and lay at anchor in the harbor, loaded and almost ready to sail for Curacao. [7] Mowat's spies reported that she had only two men aboard.

Treacherous Dan Somes and his counterprivateersmen laid their plans. On March 31 a black craft which looked like a small fisherman sailed casually into the harbor and dropped anchor outside Ten Pound Island; only two or three men showed up on deck at a time, and no one paid any mind to it. They bided their time through that evening and into the night, and a few minutes after four in the morning they quietly weighed anchor, came up alongside *Harriot,* looming in the dark, silently boarded, overpowered the two watchmen, brought in her anchor or just cut the cable, and made sail with nary a sound. Soon, prize and nondescript captor were slipping out by Eastern Point with a fair breeze, no one on shore the wiser.

A bold stroke. There was not a vessel afloat at Gloucester capable of giving chase.

It was the dawn of April Fools' Day when David Pearce arose from bed in his house on Front Street at the head of his wharf, checked the weather at his window, and his vessel. Gone! He was flabbergasted. Where? There she was, just visible beyond the Point and making knots for the eastward in the company of the dark stranger no one had paid any mind to coming into the harbor yesterday.

Harriot's owner flung on his clothes, burst out of his door and sprinted up to the meetinghouse on Middle Street, bellowing all the way. Inside, he seized the bell rope and set up a clamor which tumbled the whole town, Congregationalists and Universalists without discrimination, from their beds and into the streets.

Among those who came running was the bellringer's friend and neighbor, Captain Foster, not long home in *Polly* from the West Indies voyage during which he had witnessed the tempestuous finale of Isaac Somes and all with him. What the hell to do? Go after them! What in, for God's sake? Why in *Polly,* says Foster, aground at the end of your dock there, what else? [8]

Pearce's *Polly*, of course--the only vessel in the harbor at the moment that could match his *Harriot*--but she lay there at the end of his wharf, grounded out in the mud, having her bottom graved; her hold was swept of ballast; stores, guns, ammunition and sails were ashore; her topmasts were struck, her topyards were down, and her rigging was in a heap!

Word of what had befallen *Harriot,* and of what Pearce and Foster intended doing about it, flew through the town, and by seven in the morning the infuriated patriots of Gloucester were dashing about on the Pearce wharf and all over her, preparing their Diana for the chase. Back in the hold was hove the ballast by one gang of volunteers, while another climbed aloft with rigging, topyards and topmasts. By others sails were bent; by others still, powder and shot were hoisted in and guns were swung back aboard. In a trice Captain Foster had himself a crew of a hundred, and as the *Salem Gazette* exulted in the heat of recollection, "the zeal shewn in getting the vessel ready, and the resentment which appeared in every countenance, promised success."

By eleven in the morning the tide was in. *Polly* was afloat. The lines were let go, and as Babson described it,

> the ship began to move from the dock; the men all the while at work on the rigging and in bending sails, and receiving articles from gondolas alongside as she was

moving into the outer harbor. The wind being light, she was assisted by tow-boats in getting out of the harbor. About one o'clock, these were all cast off, and the ship proceeded on her cruise, under command of Captain Joseph Foster; the owner of both vessels, Capt. Pearce, being also on board. The direction which the *Harriot* had steered had been observed; and it was supposed to be the captor's intention to take her to the enemy's station, on the eastern coast. Capt. Foster accordingly took an east-northeast course; and, in the meantime, had his ship put in complete order for action.

All that afternoon, and all night, Foster sailed the course his intuition and long experience had laid out, and at dawn they were vindicated. The shout went up. Ghostly in the dim light of the new day, near the horizon, were the brig and the black fishing boat.

They chased. All morning they chased until they were close in *Harriot*'s wake. And when Mowat's midshipman counted ten guns coming up on him from his pursuer's broadside, he judiciously if cynically parted company with his slower prize and his black Trojan seahorse. He piled on sail and fled. *Harriot* struck without a shot. David Pearce's brother William took charge of her, and together *Polly* and *Harriot* dogged the British brig for the rest of the afternoon. But the midshipman had a long lead, and at dusk Captain Foster called off the chase.

In the meantime, word of the rape of *Harriot* had sped to the near seaports. By two that afternoon Captain John Buffington had his privateer ship *Marquis de La Fayette*, sixteen guns, in hot pursuit out of Salem. About the same hour the twenty-gun ship *Resolution* of Beverly, Captain Stephen Webb, was heading for the rescue into Ipswich Bay from Portsmouth. And an eager bunch from Newburyport began rowing a small armed boat out the Merrimack against the tide. All returned empty-handed.

There were several jolly fellows on board of the [*Polly*], and as provisions, wines, and liquors in abundance had been provided, the night was passed in merriment, and in rejoicing over their success ... and both vessels arrived in the harbor the next-afternoon, to the great joy of the inhabitants.[9]

When enough jolly fellows had recovered from their high spirits, Captain Foster went about preparations for another voyage in *Polly* to the West Indies, this time for Guadeloupe with a cargo of salt fish and lumber. It was late June before he was ready for sea. He had signed as his first mate his brother John's son, Jeremiah, now twenty-seven and probably occupying the house next east to his on Middle Street which Broome once kept as a tavern. His second officer is unidentified. His third mate was his eldest son, Joseph, Jr., just turned eighteen. *Polly*'s surgeon was Thomas Sargent, who had been doctoring Gloucester for fifteen or twenty years.

The most interesting occupant of the forecastle on this cruise was Israel Trask, now seventeen. Since his return from Newfoundland in the prisoner exchange after the capture of *Wilkes*, Israel had been sailing out of Newburyport, first in the brig *Congress*, then in January of 1781 in the privateer brig *Garland*, which was captured homebound from Martinique and taken to Bermuda. Again he was exchanged, and no sooner home than signed on *Ranger* for Martinique, and off to the island a third time in *Lightfoot*, arriving back in Gloucester safely with a good cargo.

No one aboard had reason to suppose that it would not be an enjoyable summer cruise to the Caribbean. The war had been running down since Yorktown. America's nemesis, Lord North, had finally given up and resigned on March 20, and the conciliatory Lord Rockingham within three weeks had initiated peace talks with Benjamin Franklin, the only American commissioner in Paris at the time.

Polly left Cape Ann astern. Captain Foster conned the horizon for unfriendly sails and eyed the trim of his own. His strong right hand was his nephew, an experienced mariner. On his left was his young son, breaking in to responsibility at sea. His own thoughts may be assumed to have been where they were supposed to be, on the weather, the wind, the glass, the set of the tide and the voyage ahead.

There was one contingency, however, to which *Polly*'s commander had not given due weight, and it brought about the abrupt end of his voyage, as recorded briefly in the Vice Admiralty Court at Halifax:

POLLY, letter of marque ship, Joseph Forster, Master, 14 guns, 35 men, Cape Ann to Guadeloupe. Cargo: fish and lumber. Captured July 4th 1782, near George's Banks, by H.M. Frigate *Ceres*. Joseph Forster, captain of the *Polly*, confirmed the evidence given by the Prize Master. [10]

Captain and crew would have preferred to celebrate the sixth anniversary of the independence they were fighting for in circumstances more of their own choosing. When they were put ashore at Halifax, some redcoat or a Tory recognized the brusque and burly Yankee skipper and remembered his much-resented treatment of the men captured after the *Falcon* fight seven years back. The word went out, and Joseph Foster was drummed through the streets of the last remaining British stronghold in North America "in retaliation for a triumphal march through the streets of Gloucester, in which British prisoners, captured by him, had figured as victims." [11]

But British justice bore no grudges, and in the case of the captured Gloucester privateer's officers moved swiftly, verging on cordiality. Peace was in the wind. No prison hulks for them. Less than three weeks after he had fallen afoul of *Ceres*, Captain Foster, his two young mates and his doctor were jouncing over the forty miles of rocky road that twisted through the wilderness of the interior, and he had a parole in his pocket:

PROVINCE OF NOVA SCOTIA

These are to certify that the persons named in the margin being Prisoners of War and late belonging to the Rebel Letter of Marque ship the *Polly* have permission to reside at Windsor in the said Province, and have this day signed a Parole, stipulating to keep in the said Town or within two miles around it, and to behave themselves in every other respect as Prisoners of War ought and should do.

Given under my hand at Halifax in the Province afore-said the 23d July 1782.

H. Turnbull
Depy Coming Genl for
Naval Prisoners [12]

Polly's crew was accorded hospitality of a different sort, as related by Israel Trask in his petition to Congress, and the years did not dim the memory of it:

We were sent to Halifax and put on board an old and large ship with three decks, under which some hundreds of our countrymen had been entombed for three long years. The gloom of the ship, the cadaverous appearance of the prisoners, made death preferable to a lengthy abode in such a filthy Avernus. With spirits undepressed and energy unrelaxed, two of our intrepid seamen swam about two miles in icy cold water and brought from under the ears of a sentinel in a foggy evening two boats, the smallest of which I entered. Just as the guards disco-vered us we received one volley of about forty muskets without injury and made our escape in the fog, while the other boat was captured. After ten days suffering with cold and hunger we got on board a Salem privateer, and I reached my paternal home in just one month from the time I left it. [13]

Polly's officers were not in Windsor and the surrounding two miles long enough to suffer undue disenchantment with its charms. They may very well have been reunited with their rejoicing families by means of a cartel which arrived in Salem late in October. [14] They definitely were home for a gala wedding in Gloucester on the third of November, because *Polly*'s third mate was the groom. The lusty swain was eighteen, his bride twenty-three. Joe Foster, Jr., had wasted no precious hours after his release from the north woods in sweeping Miss Rebecca Ingersoll off her pretty feet. [15] Did Pastor Forbes (for it was he who wed them) bite his lip as he made it right and proper for this lamb of his flock to lie with the young Universalist lion?

As they had suspected on the Fourth of July, the three Fosters found confirmation on their return to Cape Ann that the game was gone out of the privateering. Soon after *Polly* struck to *Ceres,* Captain John Tucker and seventy-five good men and true had sailed in the new ship *Tiger*, sixteen guns, built in the spring chiefly by William Pearce, Winthrop Sargent and John Somes, with results both less and more inglorious: *Tiger* took a prize ... and then both were captured and escorted into Halifax. Of course, Captain John Beach, the flamboyant Englishman, must have a final fling and was off in November in a fourteen-gun privateer with the puzzling name of *Forty-five* ... possibly a converted prize taken, let's suppose, at latitude forty-five north and longitude forty-five west, which would be not far east of the Grand Bank and right in the North Atlantic track ... or, if you will, a political allusion of her master to Bonnie Prince Charlie's romantic, fruitless Jacobite rebellion in 1745.

In Paris the preliminary articles of peace were signed on November 30. Commissioner John Adams again showed himself a friend to Gloucester and the fishermen; a principal provision in the final treaty awarded to the United States the *right* to fish the traditional grounds off Newfoundland and Nova Scotia, and the *liberty* to dry and cure on the unsettled shores of Nova Scotia, Labrador and the Magdalen Islands in the Bay St. Lawrence. A century and more of contention over these rights and liberties and what they meant lay ahead, but for the first time ... and to all intents and purposes for the last ... the representatives of the Federal government paid heed to the pleas of the Gloucester fishermen, who as early as January of 1782 had importuned the General Court and the Congress to push for such protection as "of the utmost consequence, not only to this town, but to the State in general."

The final winter of the Revolution was quiet on Cape Ann. Came the spring, and on March 28, 1783, the Boston brig *Tybalt* prepared for sea, the last privateer commissioned in the war. Her commander was Captain Elias Davis of Gloucester. *Tybalt* perhaps had not yet sailed, when four days short of eight years after the march on Concord and Lexington for the provincial stores, the Congress of the thirteen United States declared the American Revolution at an end and ratified the provisional treaty of peace.

The news of the signing of the final treaty at Paris on September 3 was brought to Gloucester on October 22 by Gloucester's own Captain Sargent Smith in bold *Robin Hood*, no more a free-booting rebel privateer, but by the stroke of a pen the proud merchantman of a new nation.

Above the shore on Duncan's Point, where Joseph Foster had stationed his townsmen with their rusty swivel gun and their mantelpiece flintlocks to lay a fierce fire on Linzee's landing party, stood a lonely, gnarled and venerable oak tree, twenty-three feet by actual measurement around. It dominated the hill which is now crowned by the gabled stone studio of Gloucester's greatest artist, Fitz Hugh Lane. Wrote Babson:

> It had long been a cherished object, and a favorite resort for the people; and, when the news of peace arrived, the ancient oak was fixed upon as the place at which the joyful event should be celebrated. Its hollow trunk and leafless branches were brilliantly illuminated; and, though no living person could remember the grandeur of its maturity, all agreed that it could not have surpassed the splendor which it now exhibited in its decay. [16]

Thus ended the Revolution for Cape Ann, eight years of combat, and more than that of resistance, tension, suffering and sacrifice. No seaport in the colonies endured more, and more the wonder that out of the shambles she found the strength and will to fit out a single privateer. It was not a worthy enterprise in the opinion of her historian; Babson wrote with a feeling which one senses must have been communicated to him by the last living survivors of those terrible and inspiring times:

> A true history of our Revolutionary privateering would be a record of individual experience; of widows' broken hearts; of orphans' bitter tears; of the agonies of men struggling with the ocean, in the face of death; of physical

suffering in prison-ships; of wanderings in foreign lands, without friends, without money, and without health; and, worst of all, of the demoralizing influences of a practice which every enlightened conscience declares to be at war with the justice of God and the happiness of man.[17]

An eloquent condemnation, but in the light of a longer retrospect, perhaps unduly harsh. The Yankee privateers were all that stood between the struggling colonies and the might of the British Empire on the seas when there was no American navy, and it would be, as it proved to be, a war to the finish.

18

BUT THE REVOLUTION GOES ON

And it is the opinion of the most judicious and feeling hearts among us, that this man and his pernicious doctrines have been more damage to this town than the late war; for while this destroyed our interest, those have corrupted our morals in their first principles, broke up our peace, and deeply sowed the seeds of fell discord among us...

A number of the inhabitants
of the First Parish in Glocester,
October, 1785.

The American Revolution had been achieved. A grievance over a tax on molasses had gathered a momentum that plunged thirteen colonies into eight years of civil war from which emerged a new nation. It was an outcome few on either side had dreamed of when the issue was finally joined one April afternoon on Lexington Green.

Behind the ringing rhetoric about the rights of man, the larger struggle was, as usual, for power, a game of chess on an international board in which the Yankee pawns rose up and refused to play the part. Britain was bound to keep control of the North American seaboard and the unplumbed resources and markets which her colonies and their potential for westward expansion represented, and she impatiently regarded their libertarian sensitivities as the upstart meddling of children with the management of the imperial household. Allied against her were her old enemies in Europe, forever vying for empire, who saw it to their own advantage to assist the revolutionary offspring in breaking the apron strings and making of themselves an independent, and weak, new state.

England's most serious error, perhaps, was in the failure of her mercantile establishment to comprehend the colonial war in terms other than economic. King, ministers and the conservative majority in Parliament saw it as a contest for markets, resources, spheres of influence and the rights to fish in certain waters. They were too cynical, too European. They could not understand how much the politics of it mattered to their fellow Englishmen transplanted across the sea, who initially harbored no deep resentment against their colonial status and were indeed willing enough to accept as a matter of pride the sovereignty of the crown and the authority of Parliament...on the not outrageous condition that their provincial charters be preserved inviolate and that they retain the liberties and exercise the rights of all other English citizens.

Joseph Foster most certainly considered himself a loyal subject of George the Third, even as he schemed to circumvent his "ministerial" customs officers out of a subtle combination of self-interest and idealism. He and his countrymen maintained that strong, emotional, inherited and inherent fealty through the first year of fighting. He was heir to a family tradition of inflexible attachment to the property-based principles of representative government guaranteed by the Mother Country through the Massachusetts charter. He and the other Gloucester and New England merchants began by smuggling, in rebellion against discriminating duties and restraints imposed by a distant Parliament in which they were not represented, and events pushed them finally to independence. It was a wrenching leap into uncertainty.

Thus do events, once set in motion, take over. Boston, Gloucester and a growing cohort first sought redress within the system, by economic boycott and political persuasion; when these failed, war was thrust on them and the rest of the land, and on the western world. Once embarked, there was no turning back. What commenced with the limited objective of restoring the balance of political liberty in a parliamentary monarchy ended in the outline of the world's first true constitutional democracy.

How ironic, how odd, that with the Revolution two years behind them, the rights of the people salvaged, the great Massachusetts Constitution written and ratified...that after all they had suffered over a decade in the name of freedom, the First Parishioners of Gloucester should still be at it, hounding their Universalist townsmen more furiously than ever, badgering their preacher and raging quite madly that their views on damnation had wreaked more havoc on the town than all the ravages of war!

When the First Parish purged its Universalist heretics in September of 1778, all were not read off the rolls for some reason. Joseph and Lydia Foster were not among the fifteen who were suspended for absenting themselves from worship, and Foster kept the ownership of his pew in the Middle Street meetinghouse until his death. John Murray's followers quickly consolidated their ranks, and on January 1, 1779, sixty men and women, this time including the Fosters, signed the Articles of Association of the Independent Church of Christ. The preamble conveys a certain cheerful complacency which must have infuriated their Congregationalist neighbors from whose eyes the veil had not been lifted:

> Inasmuch as it hath pleased God of his great mercy, in every age of the world, to choose a people for himself; giving them his fear, and revealing to them his secret; and as this great Lord of heaven and earth, the Father of our Lord Jesus Christ, hath been pleased to reveal to babes, what he had hid from the wise and prudent: We the subscribers, gratefully affected with a sense of the divine goodness, in thus distinguishing us, who had nothing in us to merit his notice; think it our interest and bounden duty, to let our light shine before men, that they may see our good works, and glorify our Father which is in heaven...

In two significant passages the Universalists served notice of the coming battle:

> As dwellers in this world, though not of it, we hold ourselves bound to yield obedience to every ordinance of man, for God's sake; and we will be peaceful and obedient subjects to the powers that are ordained of God, in all civil cases: But as subjects of that King, whose kingdom is not of this world--we cannot acknowledge the right of any human authority to make laws for the regulating of our conscience in any spiritual matters...

> As believers living godly in Christ Jesus, we expect to suffer as much persecution as the laws of the country we live in, will admit of: But we resolve by the grace of God, none of these things shall move us to act inconsistent with our character as Christians. We will as much as possible avoid vain jangling, and unnecessary disputation; and should we be reviled, endeavor in patience to possess our souls.[1]

It would not do for an organized church to continue meeting in private homes, as they had through the war, and fourteen of the members raised a subscription to buy a piece of land and raise a house of worship on it, which they did, on the westerly corner of Spring and Water streets, and dedicated on Christmas Day, 1780.[2] There were thirty large, square pews owned by the builders in proportion to their investment; Winthrop Sargent's commitment to Universalism, and his wealth, are indicated by his thirteen, whereas Joseph Foster and nine others owned one each. To his thirtieth share Captain John Somes added the organ, spoil from an English prize taken during a privateering cruise. It was a handcranked instrument with three barrels which wheezed out ten tunes apiece, none of them hymns. So a fourth barrel of good Universalist psalm airs was made; it served round and round, and over and over, for about fifteen years, when it was replaced with a keyboard.[3]

Foster and the Sargents, Universalists, and Coffin and Whittemore, Congregationalists, were delegates to the constitutional convention in Cambridge that winter, and the May after the dedication of Murray's church Gloucester ratified the controversial document, with Foster and Sargent expressing but not voting dissent, probably over Article III of the Declaration of Rights authorizing towns to collect taxes for the support of public worship, religious societies and their teachers.

For two years the town assessors tried to collect taxes from the Universalists for the benefit of the First Parish and Mr. Forbes, arguing that they did not fall within the definition of an incorporated religious society and that John Murray failed to qualify as an ordained teacher of religion.

The Universalists refused to pay. They rebutted that both their church and their minister were entirely qualified for that tax support under Article III in their own right. The controversy came to a head in 1782. To test its claim, the First Parish seized for taxes some English goods belonging to Winthrop Sargent, silver plate owned by Epes Sargent and an anchor from one of David Pearce's vessels and sold them at auction; the assessors also clapped David's brother William in Salem jail briefly for refusal to pay. Two unsuccessful attempts at recovery were initiated in the courts by the Universalists before it became clear that a suit under the state constitution would have to be brought in the name of their aggrieved religious teacher. It was a year before Murray, who had always preached for his keep in lieu of a fee, would consent to be the plantiff.

The war was over and Foster was getting back to business when he joined with the Sargents, David Pearce, John Somes, and David and Joshua Plummer on February 3, 1784 in pledging to finance Murray's suit against the First Parish in proportion to their assessed taxes. Foster and David Plummer, who had made such waves over the latter's molasses in '68, were delegated to take charge of pressing the Universalist case "against a species of usurpation and tyranny which tho' sanctified by the greatest number, has for its object, not the good order of civil society, but the subversion of humanity and religious freedom." [4]

Some time that spring Colonel Foster decided to get back into politics. He ran for the General Court at the May town meeting against Peter Coffin, who had represented Gloucester off and on since Foster's last term in '76, and defeated him by a vote of forty-three to thirty in one of the rare contests for the office. Colonel Coffin had moved to Middle Street from his farm in West Parish during the war and was a pillar of the First Parish, but Foster's constituency certainly crossed doctrinal lines.

A few weeks before his election Foster, Jacob Allen and Captain John Smith were sued in the court of common pleas by one Jonathan Norwood, Jr. of Gloucester, who claimed through his lawyer, the now eminent Theophilus Parsons, that they had seized his sloop *Sally* in November of 1775, worth two hundred pounds with cargo, and never returned her to him. Parsons had notified the defendants of his intent to sue, and the matter came up at a special town meeting in September of 1783, evidently at Foster's request; apparently he hoped the town would intervene, for the warrant referred darkly to the occasion at issue as "when said Norwood brought the smallpox into town." But after much debate, which generated no light, "the town thought best to pass no votes respecting it." The case was deferred to the September 1785 term at Newburyport, when the court dismissed it and assessed costs against Norwood.

At this time Foster and Parsons found themselves adversaries on a second front. The First Parish retained the Federalist lawyer to defend it against the Universalist suit, which meant defending his own interpretation of Article III, whose language he was largely responsible for; his co-counsel was his former law teacher, now representing Newburyport at the General Court, Theophilus Bradbury. Not to be outlawyered, Foster and Plummer cast about and settled on another of Foster's colleagues in the legislature, the brilliant young Rufus King, a Newburyport man like the two Theophili, and in his own turn, a former student of Parsons. It was a notable line-up: Parsons and Bradbury would one day sit on the Massachusetts Supreme Judicial Court, while the more liberal King would be a distinguished congressman and senator and President Washington's Minister to Great Britain.

In the midst of these legal preliminaries, son Joseph's firstborn son, Joseph Foster III, died a month short of a year old, on July 5, 1784. Three weeks later Lydia Foster died. The Colonel's wife was fifty-two. She had borne her husband eight children who were baptized; seven were living. Sad that she left no mark of herself but her posterity. Mary, Lydia and Joseph had married and made their own homes. Sarah was twenty-two and still unmarried. Benjamin was fifteen and by now probably sailing before the mast in one of his father's vessels. Judith was the youngest, twelve, and in school.

The remembered beauty of the Fosters was Elizabeth. On her sixteenth brithday in 1782 her father gave Betsy a fine bureau made in Gloucester from mahogany which family tradition genteelly claims he brought over from England; more likely it came out of the hold of some prize. With her mother dead, Betsy's new domestic responsibilities put her in the way of a handsome beau, Captain Will Dolliver. A handed-down story has it that not long after death took his wife of twenty-eight years, the Colonel bid this daughter: "Betsy, put on your best bib and tucker and help me to entertain a young Bilboa captain who is in my employ. He is a fine fellow, I like him, and have invited him to spend this eve here."[5]

It may have been during the months after his wife's death that Foster built and moved into his mansion house at the head of the long lot on Front Street above his wharf. The exact date is not known, but it was an appropriate time in their lives for him to move with his four unmarried children down the block toward the waterfront and turn the homestead on Middle Street over to his eldest son, especially since Becca had presented her twenty-year-old husband with a second Joseph III on the second of August, not a month after the death of their first and only six days after her mother-in-law died.[6]

Rufus King was elected to Congress after preparing the Universalist brief and turned the case over to James Sullivan and William Tudor. Sullivan was a fellow congressman from Boston, a former probate judge and future governor of Massachusetts. Tudor and his adversary, Parsons, had been chums at Harvard. He went on to study law under John Adams, and the two became lifelong friends; he practised law in Boston.

Murray versus the First Parish came to a jury trial before Massachusetts Supreme Court Justices Francis Dana, David Sewell and Increase Sumner in Ipswich in June of 1785, a month after Colonel Foster had been reelected by Gloucester to the General Court. Sullivan summed up the arguments in a letter to Rufus King on June 25. He and Tudor had contended that Universalism was a sect distinct from Calvinism and that John Murray "professed to teach the Christian Religion, which we thought to be a moral system, and that the persons whose taxes were in consideration attended upon him as a teacher of morality."

Parsons and Bradbury, Sullivan wrote, countered that Murray's doctrines were "opposed to morality because he denied punishment in another world. To this we objected, that although we were obliged to prove him a teacher of morality, yet they would not go so far as to bring before a civil tribunal the question whether the motives of rewards and punishments in another world were such as would induce piety; for, should we at once launch into that inquiry, there would be no end to it."

Nevertheless, the court was against them, Sullivan reported, and "gave it as their full opinion that no teacher but one who was elected by a corporate society could recover money paid by his hearers to the teacher of the parish. This excludes, you will observe, the Episcopalians, Baptists, Quakers, Presbyterians and Sandemanians [or Glasites, a Scotch sect founded by John Glas and proselyted by his son-in-law, Robert Sandeman] from all benefit arising from the third article. The jury thought otherwise and gave us a verdict."[7]

But since the jury found against their instructions, the judges decided to review the case a year hence.

Other communities had followed Gloucester in establishing Universalist societies, and to devise "some plan to defeat the designs of our enemies, who aim at robbing us of the liberty wherewith the constitution has made us free," as Murray phrased it, they planned a conference at Oxford, Massachusetts, that September. As a talking point, the Gloucester society a week beforehand drew up a prototype "Charter of Compact" with the object of supporting their minister and church by voluntary subscription should the suit fail on review. Membership had increased in six years from thirty to eighty-five, and greatly diversified. Besides Fosters (Joseph, Jr., and Jeremiah were members now), Sargents, a Somes, Pearces, Norwoods, Pools, Gotts, Plummers...most of the town's leading family names...there was Richard Pew who signed with his "X" and Gloster Dalton, a freed African slave. And of all the people on Cape Ann, Jesse Saville...tar, feathers, cracked skull, contraband molasses, broken gun, frightened wife, lawsuits, customs and king forgotten in reconciliation under the umbrella of salvation held heavenward over friend and foe by the benign hand of Preacher Murray.

Having prepared for the worst, the Universalists carried their cause to the people (and prospective new jurors) with a pamphlet written by Epes Sargent entitled *An Appeal to the Impartial Public by the Society of Christian Independents, Congregating in Glocester*. It reveals some of the capabilities of the liberated New England mind. Sargent saw in somewhat new light the old sins of governments and men: dogma, bigotry, propaganda and compulsion.

> ...We are full convinced that our blessed Redeemer left no particular form [of worship] to his followers, but submitted all to their wisdom and prudence. We conceive that a voluntary agreement, in religious matters, ought to be departed from, the moment the individual who is party to it, conceives that he has done wrong; and where those religious forms have been established by laws...they have only tended to fetter the human understanding, and have been the unhappy means of substituting the form for the substance of religion.

> ...We conceived that all conviction must rise from evidence rationally applied to the understanding...We therefore concluded that confessions of faith with us, might do what we believe they have done in other societies, where those of human invention have been introduced, oblige men, either to submit their faith to the controul of others, and believe without examining, or to profess to believe that which they have never fully considered or understood.

...We are fully convinced, that by establishing articles of faith, we should only injure the cause of religion, and possibly might lay a foundation for persecution in a future day...So bigotted are men generally to their own religious opinions, that they have rarely failed to procure, where it could be done, the civil authority to compel others to profess a belief in their tenets.

...The idea that it is necessary to the good order of civil government, that the Teachers of Religion should thunder out the doctrine of everlasting punishment to deter men from atrocious crimes, which they may otherwise commit in secret, has long been hackneyed in the hands of men in power; but without any warrant from reason or revelation for doing it; for reason itself, without the aid of revelation, gave no intimation of a state of retribution...It was not till the Christian Church was illegally wedded to state policy, that men in power dared to hurl the Thunders of the Most High at those who offended against government; and even then, modesty forbid it, only as they arrogantly pretended to do it for the honor of God and the advantage of religion.

Sargent did not go so far as to deny in this treatise that Article III justifiably required nonProtestants to support Protestant public worship by taxation "for the sake of making men better citizens, and better members of the Common-wealth." The Universalists had no desire at all to fling the door wide open; they were as afraid of "Papism" as their sectarian enemies. Their battle was to open it a crack, to broaden the interpretation of Article III sufficiently to substitute Protestant-ism for Congregationalism as the sheltered religion of the state, the requisite for officeholding and the citadel against the dire danger of a Catholicism imposed from abroad and "illegally wedded to state policy." Sargent concluded with nice selective myopia that if it is wrong for the minority to be obliged to subsidize the worship of the majority, "then we are abused, unless one sect is in subordination to another, and religion is no longer a matter between the heart of each individual and his God, but a matter submitted to, and under the controul of a majority in society." [8]

—259—

Well, one step at a time.

Such cool reasonableness enraged "a number of the inhabitants of the First Parish," and they snapped up the bait with a voracity which prejudiced their case beyond salvation of any sort. The anonymous writer of their answering pamphlet in October opened by recalling the old suspicion of the "foreigner" Murray nursed by the dying Pastor Chandler, to whom he was a false prophet, and by Pastor Ezra Stiles, now president of Yale College, to whom he was "one of those ostentatious, obstinate, but subtle, delusory characters, with which it is best to have little to do...a Romanist in disguise, endeavoring to excite confusion in our churches."

Having destroyed John Murray and "his jesuitical designs" with the warmed-over contumely of two old Calvinistical divines, the *Answer* went after his followers, some of whom had displayed "a becoming zeal" during the Revolution, but as for the rest..."it is a well-known fact that all who were unfriendly to the American cause here, were in this separation...that their teacher was admired most by those that were most unfriendly to the American cause, not only in this town, but through this Commonwealth; and several who are of this Association would do nothing in defence of the cause but by constraint...Their Association is made up partly from other parishes, and partly of foreigners, and some of the most abandoned characters; in short, any body and any thing whom they could by persuasion or pecuniary consideration hire into their service." True, some of them "sustain fair moral characters, yet not without a strong tinge of enthusiasm" (which in the contemporary usage meant, invidiously, an extravagant display of religious inspiration), but as for the general run of them:

Such is their rage for proselyting, that they are forever disputing, and using every art of fascination; and upon those whom they cannot gain to their party by these means, they try the force of interest, promising those that come into town to seek employment that they will put them into business, promising them constant employment if they will go to their meeting; and threatening others, who are already in their employ, that they will turn them out unless they will be of their party; so that some, who have no affection for their system, attend their meeting sometimes, lest they and their families should want bread.

You may think yourselves less in danger, from the standard of impiety being erected in this small peninsula of Cape Ann, but the ill consequences may be sooner and more sensibly felt by you, than you are aware of. If this Association should be adopted, and this artful deceiver supported by law, we may expect that an hundred similar associations will soon be formed, and as many mushroom teachers spring up from the seculency [sic] of vice and laziness to take the lead of them, to the discouragement of peace and order, which will soon precipitate these infant free states into anarchy and confusion. We speak feelingly, from experience. This town, once the seat of peace and commerce, is now nodding on the brink of ruin, owing chiefly, if not entirely, to this Association, headed by this foreigner.

...If this Association should be supported by law, then any one, two or three families may form themselves into the same, and claim the same privileges. What then will become of our colleges, incorporated parishes and churches? All crumbled into parties, and buried in ignorance and superstition, we shall be left, too late, and with more reason to weep, with the Roman orator, O tempora! O mores! What can we expect, when a system is defended and supported by law, which destroys both the solemnity and validity of an oath, which are predicated upon the certain future punishment of perjury? What safety, either of our persons or our property, can we expect? Nay, may we not expect frequently to see Beadle's tragedy acted over again--suicide and murders committed from pure benevolence?

And what will become of our youth? Their natures already viciated, their morals corrupted by this wretched system of licentiousness, their opening minds uncultivated with erudition, and unimpressed with virtuous principles, they will enter the stage, after us, ignorant and vicious; and under the direction of the wild-fire of enthusiasm, will soon be swallowed up in the vortex of superstition.

You may say, this is only the uncertain flights of fancy. No, fellow-citizens, no. We feel it, we realize it every day; and it is the opinion of the most judicious and feeling hearts among us, that this man and his pernicious doctrines have been more damage to this town than the late war; for while this destroyed our interest, those have corrupted our morals in their first principles, broke up our peace, and deeply sowed the seeds of fell discord among us; our trade interrupted by a party spirit, our churches rent by divisions; nothing can be done in town-meeting but through strife and unfair dealings; and the offices of benevolence cease, or are confined to a party; and the contagious influence of this system has been sensibly felt in other towns through this and the neighboring states. [9]

John Murray replied in righteous outrage to the *vile calumnies* of his enemies in a broadside printed October 29. "O! if these good men could but obtain a law to erect a stake and faggots, how cheerfully their pious souls would join in doing God and themselves service by killing us!" He thought it "but common justice to inform the publick that there are a considerable number of that parish whose honest hearts despise and detest the base conduct of their mistaken brethren" whose hope, he supposed, was to influence the bench and jury by "personal abuse and a collection of infamous falsehoods" in order to gain the verdict at the approaching review of his suit. [10]

This occurred in June of 1786 before Massachusetts Supreme Court Justice Francis Dana and a jury. Justice Dana was a close friend of John Adams and a former congressman and late emissary of his country on a frustrating mission to gain the recognition of Catherine the Great of Russia, the most tangible result of which was a magnificent, snow-white, fur-lined overcoat of which he was judiciously proud.

Dana was an able jurist, capable of changing his mind. At the first trial he thought the Gloucester Universalists had no case.

Now he believed that "as the Constitution was meant for a liberal purpose, its construction should be of the most liberal kind," applicable to all religious bodies, whether corporate or not. This time it had been proved to his satisfaction that John Murray was a teacher qualified under Article III. "It is my opinion that Mr. Murray comes within the description of the Constitution, and has a right to require the money."

The jury agreed, and for the second time the constitutional right of Protestant dissenters to worship as they pleased, without discrimination, had been upheld by their peers.

Rejoiced John Murray: "I have been the happy instrument of which the God of peace and mercy has made use to give a death wound to that hydra, parochial persecution." [11]

But the heads of hydra were many.

Murray had married a number of his flock on the ingenuous assumption that he was legally qualified, as their religious teacher. His enemies seized on this nuptial naiveté and brought a test case before the Massachusetts Supreme Court, claiming that he was not a duly ordained minister and the marriage in question was illegal. The court agreed and fined him fifty pounds. Fearing bankruptcy if each of the granny knots he had tied were to cost him an equal penalty (not to mention the bastardy he might be fostering), the embarrassed controversialist petitioned the General Court for relief and then fled to England on a visit in January of 1788. The legislators, with many a snicker no doubt, passed a special act indemnifying him and squaring all the knots. Murray returned in triumph and married his patron Winthrop Sargent's daughter, Mrs. Judith Sargent Stevens (whose husband John had also fled the country--in one of her father's vessels--to escape his creditors--and was assumed to be dead), and then he was ordained once and for all by his loyal and loving Gloucester flock on Christmas Day.

Dying but still dangerous, the many-headed serpent of parochial persecution watched these happy scenes with hateful eyes.

Within an hour of his return to Gloucester from a preaching tour in the summer of 1790, John Murray was served with a writ claiming that a resident of a corporate parish (as all established parishes were, including the First Parish) could not divert part of his taxes for religious support to an unincorporated society. For some reason this action, which would have overturned the 1786 decision if it had succeeded, did not come to trial. But it did convince the battleweary Universalists that they should seek incorporation, which was granted by the General Court to David Pearce, Winthrop Sargent, Joseph Foster and forty-eight members of The Independent Christian Church in Gloucester on June 28, 1792.

For going on eighteen years Eli Forbes and certain members of his congregation had plotted to pry John Murray loose from Gloucester with every crowbar they could lay their hands on, from calumny to the courts. What were their *real* motives?

One who held some opinion was the Reverend William Bentley, pastor of the East Church in Salem, long on learning, religious liberalism and wit, and a dedicated diarist. When Eli Forbes died in 1804 Dr. Bentley assessed his ministry, making special note that during its entirety none of the other parishes east of Squam River had a settled pastor for any length of time, so that "since the war he has had the power of a Bishop in Gloucester, tho' he had no clergy under him." This sagacious observer thought Pastor Forbes possessed "agreeable manners, a sweet voice & a good person. He was not a man of letters as his controversy with the Universalists proves..."

Ever since Dr. Forbes has been in Gloucester he has had the whole Island under his command, excepting a society of Universalists who were formed by a Mr. Murray who long since left them & went to Boston...It is believed by many that Dr. F was content to have things as they are. But the present prosperity of the Parishes leads to expect the speedy resettlement of them all. The controversy of the Universalists convinces me, & my personal knowledge of both parties, that had Mr. Forbes discovered more prudence, or known more, he might easily have prevented the existence of that sect or any other in the Town & have obtained useful pastors in all the parishes. He was too much under the influence of particular men &

had too great jealousy to promote a generous regard to the public interest. He lost that influence by political indiscretions.12

That was the Salem minister's veiled view of Pastor Forbes, his weakness and his motives. What he meant by political indiscretion is amplified by his entry of May 23, 1802, that Mr. Forbes "by a decided part in the Hamilton interest, will unite to the Universalists all the republicans" in Gloucester, an implication that for some time the liberal Universalists had been tinged with Republicanism while their enemies up the street leaned to Federalism, conservative and authoritarian. The politics of Epes Sargent, author of the *Appeal*, may be an index; he was appointed by President Washington Gloucester's first collector of customs in 1789 and was replaced by William Tuck when John Adams defeated the Republican Thomas Jefferson for the presidency in 1796.

If Eli Forbes had "too great jealousy," John Murray exuberated in an excess of enthusiasm. The longer the face of the one, the broader the smile of the other. They did not mix.

Yet neither ideological differences nor clashing personalities alone account for the passion and vituperation of the orthodox attack. The war had been over three years when the Forbes party, in its frenzied reply to the even-tempered *Appeal* of Epes Sargent, unwittingly stripped off the theological mask to reveal the visage of hatred behind, an intense and bitter hatred which had very little to do with conjectures concerning degrees of damnation or the detergent merits of the blood of Christ. That fleeting revelation of whatever it was that was really bothering a number of First Parishioners exposed all those doctrinal cannonballs fired from the broadside of their meetinghouse; they were mere sabbatarian symptoms of the mundane, underlying suffering and strife and bitterness which broke through the torn fabric of Gloucester's life under the stress of war and uncertainty that crushed the town more agonizingly, perhaps, than any other in America.

Why such a fire was directed at John Murray and his people can still only be guessed at. Misery must have its scapegoat, more so than ever when the cause of it all lounges on a throne three thousand miles across the ocean. The Sargents and the Pearces, especially, added to their fortunes as Gloucester's principal outfitters of privateers. They presented a contrast, while all around them were suffering and privation. But that they profited at the expense of their townsmen, who shared in some of the prize money and spoils as well as in the losses, seems not an entirely justifiable conclusion. Not so, however, when the well-to-do Universalists withdrew their tax support for Mr. Forbes and in so doing threw the burden of their share onto the faithful who remained in his flock, while Mr. Murray nodded and smiled and dined with the Sargents. Now *that* was something to complain about.

There is no fight like a church fight, and the undertones and overtones of this one have long since faded and been forgotten. What has survived is the clear trace, in what is taken for granted today, of the constitutional chalkline at which the antagonists finally agreed to meet, toe to toe, and bloody it out in court. That line was on the issue of who was to get the benefit of whose taxes within the circumscribed context of the prevailing theology in Gloucester and New England. It was a Protestant family fight over whether the state should favor one sect over another, and its adjudication was a requisite preliminary step toward settlement of the larger question whether government should favor one religion above another, or any at all. By going to the highest secular court available to them, the adversaries agreed to disagree on one point of conflict--the limited liberalization of Protestant worship--and thereby they forwarded unintentionally the cause of the larger freedom. Furthermore, the enemies in the one conflict were comrades in the other, the common war for political and economic liberty which likewise was fought within the context of the commonly accepted qualifications on that very liberty such as property ownership (meaning economic status), sex, race and religion, factors which have still not been altogether eliminated from the American equation.

Joseph Foster's appalling role in one and perhaps two outrageously criminal assaults on an officer of the crown, and his prominent part in the persecution of a fellow citizen with whom he differed politically, are painful reminders that the concept of the dignity of the individual in pre-Revolutionary America was a frail seedling in unploughed soil. That he opened his mind to Universalism and embraced it, represented his town faithfully in the General Court, served his country as a soldier, nourished his intellect by contact with men of different political dimension, labored upon the constitution of self-government and at last welcomed the old enemy, Jesse Saville, to his company are further reminders that the seedling took good root and grew, when tended by those who had roots and were capable of growth themselves.

The 1786 decision of the Supreme Judicial Court of Massachusetts in the case of John Murray versus the First Parish of Gloucester was not the single fork in the way which separated church and state in America. That road split by degrees as this and other parochial battles loosened the grip of the old hydra of orthodoxy on town governments and the minds of citizens. The constitutional test which divided Gloucester's church taxes into two piles, where they had always before been lumped into one, was a major wedge, widening the separation but by no means completing it.

Three years later a permanent signpost was erected at that fork which still reads: "Congress shall make no law respecting an establishment of religion, or prohibiting the free exercise thereof." It is the First Amendment to the Constitution of the United States of America.

19

HE WOULD SUFFER NO IDLERS

If Joseph Foster went to sea again after that abruptly terminated privateering cruise in *Polly,* there is no record of it. From 1789 on, when the new Federal government began registering all American vessels in foreign trade, and he was entering his sixties, his name is not among the captains, although he is mentioned as an owner.

For New England, and particularly the fishing ports of Gloucester and Marblehead, peace did not bring with it prosperity. Their schooners had been burned or blown up or lay rotting at their rotten wharves. Britain imposed an absolute ban on Yankee fish in her West Indies, while making a point of encouraging the fisheries of the Canadian maritime possessions that remained to her. With the French, they were New England's major rivals on the banks. To compound the fishermen's hard luck, France and Spain, America's late allies, decided on protectionist policies of their own in the Caribbean.

For Cape Ann, the harvest of eight years of war was four more of depression. But by 1787 things were looking up. The fleet of small Chebacco boats in the shore fishery was large and increasing. They brought in a subsistence, anyway, and a few schooners were being launched, though in no great numbers by any means; Gloucester's fishing would not take the ascendancy for nearly another half a century, as Marblehead's declined. To help matters, France and Spain by 1790 were finding it to their advantage once more to welcome American trade with their

West Indian colonies, and ways and means were being discovered whereby Yankee skippers and British colonial officials each might smile and look the other way, while their duties went neglected.

No man in Gloucester was more resourceful than David Pearce. Finding his old markets in the West Indies under interdiction, he looked elsewhere to invest his privateering profits ... to whaling, for instance. Although the first recorded whaling voyage from Gloucester was that of his brig *Sea Horse* in 1788, Captain Pearce ran a spermaceti works above his wharf as early as 1786. That same year of '86 he sent Captain William Wyer, one of Colonel Foster's pre-war masters, on a far-ranging voyage in his new ship *Polly,* with Ignatius Webber as mate, which took them to the West Indies, then to South Carolina for rice, to Amsterdam, and St. Petersburg, Russia; homeward bound, *Polly* made it as far west as the Grand Bank, when a continuous succession of adverse gales forced her clear back to Spain, where she refitted and again headed for Gloucester, arriving finally after sixteen months out.

That was how David Pearce and his captains put Gloucester back in foreign commerce and into the trade with Surinam, or Dutch Guiana, which was from the outset virtually monopolized by the town, exporting cheap salt fish for the slave plantations and bringing back sugar, molasses, rum, spices and fine wares from Holland. It is not unlikely that restrictions on commerce with the West Indies induced Pearce to bypass them for the coast of South America and Surinam's port of Paramaribo.

On the crest of the wave, Pearce was reckoned the richest man ever to reap the sea from Gloucester, and yet it mattered little to him that a flood of disasters reduced his fortune from $200,000 to bankruptcy when he was seventy; he was not one, in Babson's admiring phrase, to "allow the loss of his property to tinge the evening of his life with the hues of sadness and discontent." [1]

Like cream in a pail of milk, the wealth rose to the top. There were a few farmers on Cape Ann, a few artisans, no middle class to speak of, no industry worth the mention beyond a few small operations that served the harbor or depended on it, such as Beach's ropewalk and Pearce's rum distillery. It was a small pail, and the milk of the sea was thin. The very existence of the war-ridden port depended on the ocean's whim and on the ability of a few capitalists to continue building and sending forth vessels. Few fishermen, seamen or shore workers ever were out of debt for long. So disparate were the life styles between the merchant class and the mass of the people that more than one scarred and pockmarked veteran limping home from battlefield and prison hulk wondered whether he had merely traded one clique of masters for another.

Democracy and self-government were much talked of, had been for twenty years, but when it came to definitions and guarantees, the Massachusetts Constitution of 1780 created the Senate frankly to represent the propertied class, and put a double-edged property qualification on the House of Representatives. This meant that in order to qualify for his elections in 1784, 1785, 1786 and 1788, Joseph Foster had to be the owner of a freehold, or landed estate, of at least a hundred pounds in value, or taxable property of no less than two hundred; and to vote for or against him for representative in town meeting, one must be a male, over twenty-one and the owner within the commonwealth of real property producing an annual income of at least three pounds or a whole estate worth sixty. The framers of the constitution advised those who had reached twenty-one but didn't yet own property to accept this suspension of their voting privilege gracefully until they did, rather than defer to "those whose idleness of life and profligacy of manners will forever bar them from acquiring and possessing property."

Not the least effort was made to dissemble the fact that it was, in the words of Samuel Eliot Morison, "a lawyers' and merchants' constitution, directed toward something like quarterdeck efficiency in government, and the protection of property against democratic pirates."[2] So naturally when postwar town meetings kept right on doing business and electing town and state officials in the same old way, by votes of a hundred and less in a population of five or six thousand, everyone knew the same establishment was running Gloucester that always had.

With two town houses, a large farm, many acres of salt marsh, his own wharf, warehouse, store and vessels, Colonel Foster was a man of property on Cape Ann, and property talked. But he remained as brusque and blunt as ever, and as ready to take the responsibility which he believed went with the ownership of property, be the task ever so humble. He continued to stand for such town offices as field driver, surveyor of highways, fire warden, clerk of the market, sealer of leather, and hogreeve, holdovers from colonial days. And he served on committees to see that town land adjoining the Stevens pasture be enclosed "with a good stone wall six feet high" and to view the road through the Kettle Cove woods from Manchester and to find a proper location for the militia training field. Occasionally he drew a special assignment fitting his experience, such as taking charge of the Fort at Watch House Point, with authority to prosecute encroachers.

The reaction of Colonel Foster the military man to the populist revolt of the western Massachusetts farmers whose products were begging for markets and whose lands were being foreclosed by the rich seacoast merchants in 1786 can be imagined. They found "neither advocates nor apologists in the people of Gloucester," is Babson's curt comment on the debtors' rebellion led by Captain Daniel Shays. The town raised a company in January of '87 to put the farmers to rout; they marched off with the Middle Essex regiment of Colonel Nathaniel Wade of Ipswich, Foster's son-in-law. "It was a victory of property over democracy," in Morison's view ... "of maritime Massachusetts over farming Massachusetts." [3]

Wade was a soldier's soldier. After Bunker Hill he served with the Continental Army through the Rhode Island and New York campaigns, and under Benedict Arnold at West Point. When Washington learned of Arnold's treachery on September 25, 1780, he put Colonel Wade in command of that strategic post until he was relieved by a general officer. [4] The thirty-mile forced march Wade led through a driving snowstorm during the campaign against Shays, he always said, was harder than anything he endured during the Revolution.

The Wades and the Fosters shared bereavement as they had happiness. Colonel Wade's wife Mary, Colonel Foster's daughter, died on Christmas Day, 1785. She was only twenty-eight and had given birth to their fourth child, Timothy, in September. He died at twelve weeks, and then his mother. The threat to infant and mother when midwives carried infection from one lying-in to the next was far more to be feared in these times than the smallpox. Fortunate was the mother who had not lost one child at least, and the twice-married widower was commonplace.

Some time within the next year or two (the date is not known), Lydia Foster Sargent followed her sister. She was about twenty-six. She and John Osborne Sargent had three children, Amelia, born in 1780, Frances in 1782, and Epes, on March 7, 1784. Many years later all Epes was able to say of his mother was that "I have been told she was a beautiful and very lovely woman, highly respected and esteemed by every one that knew her."[5] Colonel Foster's Sargent grandchildren had made their appearance with biennial regularity, leading to the conjecture that Lydia, as Mary probably had, died of the complications of childbirth.

In the large family, marriage was a palliative to death. Ben was twenty when he and Mary Ingersoll were wed in January, 1789. They called her Polly; she was almost nineteen, probably a first cousin of Becca Ingersoll, Ben's older brother's wife. Ben followed Joe to the Ingersolls, to the altar and to the quarterdeck, for a year later, when he was twenty-one, he had command of his father's brigantine *Polly*. It was no doubt the Colonel who had her built at Biddeford, Maine, in 1785, naming her perhaps for his last privateer; she was fifty-eight feet long, 128 tons burthen.

Betsy had long since given up entertaining that good-looking Bilboa captain on her father's account and had been doing so well on her own that a few months after brother Ben took the step, on November 25, 1789, she became Mrs. Bill Dolliver. This latest of the sons-in-law had been a firm Universalist for all of eleven years, since he was nineteen, and he had served in the army in the Revolution. The match pleased Colonel Foster no end, and he gave Betsy a fine set of imported plates for a wedding present. A wedding guest sighed to one of their grandchildren in her old age, "they were the finest looking couple of their day; he, tall and broad-shouldered, with clear, honest, blue eyes; she, small, brown-eyed and very beautiful." [6]

It was a happy epidemic, bringing one romance after another from bud to bloom, filling the void left by death with gayety and laughter, the clink of glasses, the rustle of brocade, the squeal of the lively fiddle, the dancing feet, and the promise of new lives to come.

Even Sarah was not immune, and high time, because the Colonel's oldest surviving daughter was twenty-eight, pushing the outer limit of eligibility. Perhaps Sally pushed too hard, as it turned out. Ben had gone to Joe's well for a wife, so Sally looked to Betsy's for a husband, and to add confusion to confusion, she captured William Dolliver's first cousin of the same name, William Dolliver III. They were married in August of 1790. It was an unhappy, childless union. Eighteen years later Sally's Bill referred to their "dissolution" in a letter to Judge Samuel Holten concerning his late father-in-law's estate: "I wish to be put to no farther trouble with her (the *said Sally*)...being so much injured by her." [7]

Betsy was the lucky sister. She and her broad-shouldered Bill had seven children and were dissolved only by his death after fifty-two years of marriage. The fates of the Foster girls at the hands of the two Bill Dollivers make one wonder if the cousins were the subjects of a forbidden ditty which the urchins of Gloucester two generations later screeched up and down the length of Front Street, at either end of which resided a Dolliver: "Bilboa Bill below the hill, and devil's Bill above!" [8]

At last the rash of nuptials among his children infected the father, and on October 30, 1790, a few weeks after Sally had departed his house with the other Bill Dolliver, Colonel Foster brought home his own bride. She was Mrs. Hannah Somes, the widow of his old friend Isaac Somes whom, in horror, he had watched disappear between lightning flashes with all his men that tempestuous night nearly nine years earlier. Lydia had been in her grave six years, and he was now sixty. Hannah was twelve years younger and had six Somes children of her own, the smaller ones in need of a father.

But there was something else besides romance behind Joseph Foster's remarriage. The husband of his dead daughter Lydia, John Osborne Sargent, had died months and perhaps only weeks before Mrs. Somes became Mrs. Foster. Only thirty-three, Sargent had left three small children orphans, Amelia ten, Frances eight and Epes six. Their Grandfather Foster and their new stepgrandmother took them into their home on Front Street to bring them up. These net additions of Someses and Sargents to his family as the result of marriage and death explain why the first Federal census of 1790 counted in the Foster household two males over sixteen including the Colonel, one male under sixteen, six females, and "one other" of elusive gender.

When Epes Sargent was a retired shipmaster living in Roxbury, he wrote an account of his life, in 1846, in a series of charming letters to his own grandson of five, Epes Sargent in Iowa. He remembered his feelings and some of his experiences as a boy in his Grandfather Foster's house in Gloucester:

I have but a faint recollection of my father [John Osborne Sargent]. The day he died I have a vivid recollection of, but child as I then was, grief doubtless soon gave place to the joys incident to children. My sisters no doubt felt our loss more keenly,. being several years older than myself. My father has always been represented to me as a man greatly beloved and highly respected. He lived in hard times and never had much opportunity to acquire property, and consequently died poor.

You now find me an orphan boy living with my grandfather. My grandmother-in-law was very kind to me and took as much care of me and my sisters as she could under the circumstances. Yet we could not help feeling the want of a mother's care. However, we were everything to each other. And my sisters being very good and kind, they in a great measure by their constant care of me supplied the place of a mother.

In due time I was sent to school to an old lady to teach me my letters etc. I do not think however that I made very rapid progress in learning. The schools were not so good in those days as they are now. At the age of about nine I was sent to a man's school to learn to write. The master's name was Rogers, a descendant from the martyr, John Rogers, that was burnt in Smithfield, and I verily thought he would have made a martyr of me.

The first day I went to school he furnished me with a pen, ink and paper, set me a copy of a book and without teaching me how to hold my pen, ordered me to write my copy. Well, I went to work and did the best I could, filled my paper with all sorts of queer-looking things, blotted my paper very much, and then being called for, took my copy up to my master. And what do you suppose he did to me? I will tell you. He called me a careless blockhead, told me to hold out my hand, which I was compelled to do, and receive a severe feruling on my bare hand which blistered it.

I was then ordered back to my seat, and without any instruction, ordered to try again, which I did, and with no better success. And how I finally learned to write I cannot tell...

During the time I had to live with my grandfather, I had to work hard. He was an industrious man and would suffer no idlers about him. I had however as much time for play, probably, as was necessary, and have no great reason to complain. Yet I often thought I should be much happier if I had a father and mother to care for me, encourage and cheer me through the days of my childhood. [9]

Memory is a fond deceiver, and one of Colonel Foster's great-granddaughters used to tell of hearing Betsy and Sally in their old age speak often of "the dear kind father," and how, when he "was laying in the winter supply in his home, as all provident New Englanders were wont to do in the olden time, he always put aside an extra barrel of flour and pork, a bag of coffee, etc., to be given to the poor, by any member of the family who was called upon."[10]

A gruff old sea captain who would suffer no idlers about him and allowed his small grandson no more time for play than was necessary may or may not have enjoyed, as his friends the Sargents certainly did, the famous Cape Ann conviviality which drew the convivial Reverend Bentley from Salem back to visit Gloucester at every opportunity. One might suppose, though, that if the wine flowed as free, and the fiddles were as felicitous at Colonel Foster's as in the neighboring mansion houses of Daniel Rogers, the Sargents, the Pearces, the Someses and John Beach, Dr. Bentley would have made approving note of it in his all-seeing diary, but he did not.

Joseph Foster was not an elegant fellow (nor was David Pearce, whom Bentley called "a primitive man"--except that Pearce had his rum distillery and was free with the production). There are no portraits of the Fosters by the fashionable John Singleton Copley of Boston, as there is a Gloucester gallery from his brush of the wealthy Rogerses, Stevenses, Ellerys, Allens and Sargents. All that survives is a lone silhouette of the Colonel in spare tribute to a man of no vanity.

By contrast, the Sargents were at the vortex of the social whirl and cultural excitement that were welcomed back by most of Gloucester's merchant class with the return of its prosperity (its upper prosperity) in the 1790's, reflected in glittering rounds of assemblies, parties, nuptials, and even theatricals such as the production in a private home of a play for which Mrs. Judith Sargent Murray, Gloucester's literary light of her day, wrote a witty epilogue. Mrs. John Stevens Ellery enthused over the event in a letter to her son dated January 17, 1790:

> The long expected play was acted last Thursday evening at Mr. Murphy's [probably William Murphy, a well-to-do merchant who resided on Front Street] to a very crowded audience. Your papa and I were present. The performers were greatly applauded; they far exceeded everyone's expectations. Mr. Row pronounced the Prologue and was loudly clapped; the scenes then followed; each went

through their part excellently well; Mr. Gorham Rogers pronounced the epilogue composed by Mrs. Murray, and very much admired; Sally shall copy it for you and send it. She was as much chagrined at not being at the play, the room not being half large enough to admit of half that would have been glad to be present; but it will be performed again next Tuesday, and then I hope she and many others will be gratified.[11]

Eighteen months after this soiree Dr. Bentley was at a church association meeting in Gloucester ("the preacher discoursed upon the doctrine of future punishment, the subject which since 1773 has kept the Town in confusion") and noted in his diary that "we were conducted to a Mr. Sergeants' at whose house music was prepared for the evening. There was a considerable number of gentlemen & ladies & very handsome entertainment. The instrumental & vocal music were well performed. We have nothing like it in Essex [County]. The conviviality is remarkable."[12]

The earthier side of Gloucester was the side that Foster was at home in, and nothing conveys the town's sense of earthy urgency in the closing years of the revolutionary century so vividly as its first set of by-laws, drawn up by the captain merchants Joseph Foster, David Pearce, William Pearson and John Somes, and David Plummer (of molasses fame but not a captain) and approved by the court of general sessions of the peace at Newburyport in 1795.

Seven of the twenty-two regulations had to do with fire, so fearful were such veteran wardens as Colonel Foster of a stray spark loose at the caprice of the wind in a seaport town built of wood. Hence, there may be no bonfires or other burning where it will endanger property; coopers shall not fire or burn casks except in a brick or stone chimney; no fire may be carried from one place to another unless in a warming pan or some covered and safe container to keep it from being scattered by the wind; no vessel with a fire in its stove may come within twenty yards of a wharf between ten at night and dawn; every regularly used "smoke" of every chimney in Harbour Parish between the Cut and the Head of the Harbor must be swept twice a year by a chimney sweep licensed by the selectmen; all wells and pumps must be kept in good order, "ready to deliver water for extinguishing any fire;" and no one, due to the danger of it, may light or smoke a "segar or pipe" in the open air after ten at night.

Traffic safety was another concern: every coach, chariot, sleigh, chaise, sled or other carriage must have bells on the horse or the vehicle when there is snow in the streets, as warning; all carts and sleds drawn by horses or horned cattle shall keep a foot pace or common walk in streets, lanes and alleys; "to prevent the dangers and mischief arising from galloping horses in the streets ... no persons shall at any time hereafter ride on a canter or ride or drive a gallop or other extraordinary travel or pace ... unless upon extraordinary occasions, particularly between the Cutt and the Head of the Harbour so called."

And public morals: "whoever shall presume hereafter to profane the Lord's day by swimming or skaiting or sailing about in boats in the Harbour of this town or publicly exercising themselves without necessity"--five shillings fine.

As for the public health: ducks and geese are not to go at large, to prevent their "voiding and dunging" in springs and watering places; it is forbidden to carry, cart or throw into the streets dust, dirt, dung, soot, garbage, carrion, shreds, shavings, filth, soil, oyster or clam shells or other rubbish "so as to discommode any inhabitant or inhabitants."

Other by-laws regulated dogs, taxes, the sale of rye meal and malt and the weighing of meat, prevented fraud in the sale of wood, frowned upon the discharge in public of guns, pistols, firecrackers and squibs, and funneled all fines for infractions to the poor fund.

It was a sign of the times that a port town which for a hundred and fifty years had managed to keep order with an elected constabulary now found it necessary to provide for the appointment of an inspector of police.

The youthful Captain Benjamin Foster had taken his father's brigantine *Polly* on at least four voyages (one, and possibly all, to the West Indies, since *Polly* is mentioned in the family accounts as home from Martinique in August of 1791) when the French Revolution burst upon the world. Joseph Foster by now had two vessels in a foreign trade which was growing riskier by the day. That same autumn of 1790 that launched her owner on the seas of matrimony with Mrs. Somes, *Polly* was joined by the new brigantine *Becca,* which he had built up the Merrimack River at Bradford. He named her for young Joe's wife and gave him the command of her. *Becca* was a foot shorter than *Polly,* fifty-seven feet nine inches; but she was broader and deeper to the extent of another twenty-two tons, and she was adorned with a figurehead, undoubtedly of Rebecca herself.

The proclamation of the French Republic in September 1792 was hailed with joy in America, somewhat chilled by the execution of Louis XVI the following January and France's declaration of war on England, Spain and Holland a few weeks later. President Washington was determined to keep the United States out of it and announced American neutrality. The British were equally set upon stopping American trade with the French West Indies and began harassing and seizing Yankee vessels in the Caribbean in 1793, which brought tensions to such a pitch that America's involvement in the war was a distinct possibility.

In this situation, Captain Joseph Foster, Jr., was sailing in the wake his chance-taking father had made through Carib's blue and green twenty-five years before him when he touched at the French island of Guadeloupe in *Becca* in the spring of 1793; from Pointe-à-Pître he included in a shipment home three barrels of sugar to his Becca of flesh and blood, care of the Colonel, as duly noted in the Foster accounts for July.

The Fosters were gambling their chips in a dangerous game. Early the next spring Captain Ben cleared Gloucester in *Polly* for the West Indies, probably with the usual cargo of cheap salt fish for the plantation slaves and a few thousand feet of lumber and miscellaneous products of New England country industry. He seems to have figured that he could slip by British cruisers and into Pointe-à-Pître, where his brother had made commercial contacts the previous summer, fill out his cargo and run back to Gloucester with it.

Ben miscalculated. On April 4, 1794, *Polly* was captured by an English frigate (*Siren* or *Sirius*), Captain George Engelton, from the fleet of Admiral John Jervis, Earl of St. Vincent, who was in the process of reducing Martinique, St. Lucia and Guadeloupe; the French surrendered the latter seventeen days later, on April 21. English possession of the island was of short duration. Guadeloupe was retaken by Victor Hugues and his force of liberated slaves on the second of June, but not before the chagrined young Gloucester captain had lost his *Polly* and twenty-two thousand gallons of molasses, eight thousand pounds of coffee, twelve thousand pounds of sugar, a hundred barrels of beef and pork, two bales of cotton and three casks of nails, fourteen hides, four thousand pounds of cordage and shrouding, and 380 dollars in cash--all amounting, including the value of *Polly* herself, to £ 6571.

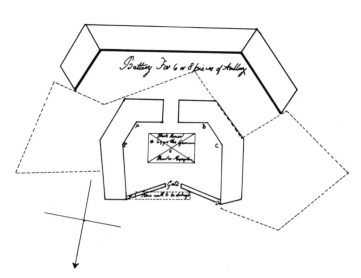

The dotted lines on Rochefontaine's 1794 plan for a new fort on Watch House Point mark the crumbling colonial earthworks.

The owner got his younger son back, later that summer, minus brigantine and cargo. Mayhap Ben arrived at Gloucester with some trepidation. *Polly*'s was one of a rising number of losses by seizure. War was so much in the air right then that Colonel Foster and others recommended ceding the earthworks on Watch House Point to the Federal government; this the town did, and they were rebuilt from plans by the French engineer Bechet Rochefontaine, who had been engaged to superintend the fortification of New England. A confrontation was averted, however, by the signing of Jay's Treaty in November, by which Great Britain, among other points of grudging concession, opened the West Indian door a humiliating crack to American vessels of seventy tons or less, provided they renounce such mainstay cargoes as molasses, sugar and cotton. The two nations further agreed to refer the question of allegedly illegal seizures of American vessels to a joint commission which ultimately awarded Joseph Foster and his heirs about $18,000 in compensation for *Polly* and her cargo.

Benjamin Foster, like his oldest sisters, was ill-fated. Not grudging *Polly*'s extremely damaging loss, his father gave him *Becca* for a voyage in January, 1795, probably to the West Indies again. Whatever happened to him on this passage is a mystery. The final mention of Benjamin in the Foster accounts occurs in June. On August 7 a Captain Marshall is identified as master of *Becca,* leaving the inference that Ben died by illness or accident. He was about twenty-six and left his widow and two children in Gloucester.

By signing away its differences with one combattant in the Jay Treaty, the United States infuriated the other ... while the French, heroes one moment with the Americans, made villains of themselves the next by the excesses of their revolution. Indeed, they so alienated their old allies that Pastor Forbes, for one, was goaded by a Jacobin-minded parishioner one sabbath into fulminating from the pulpit with such vigor "as to send his wig from his head and throw it whirling down into the deacon's seat below." [13]

It was a bad time for the former friends and comrades, and it would get worse as they came to real grief in the undeclared naval conflict which history calls the Quasi-War; but for now, the French Directory reacted to the Jay Treaty in kind, by passing the word to the naval vessels and privateers of the Republic to seize American merchantmen found trading with the English.

Into this precarious maelstrom of thrust and counterthrust the gambler in Joseph Foster sent forth *Becca,* evidently hoping to recoup *Polly*'s loss. He entrusted her for this chancy voyage to his stepsons, the Somes boys, John going master, with his younger brother Henry as mate. They sailed for Surinam--surely a neutral and safe destination--on October 6, 1796.

Within sight of the Surinam coast they were spoken by a sloop from Providence and given the news that the colony was under a British blockade. Since *Becca* was leaking, and they were short of fresh water, Captain Somes bore away for neighboring Demerara, which had already been taken by the British. They arrived there on November 16. For three months the governor interned *Becca.* Not until late in February, 1798, did Somes get his papers back; on the first of March he cleared Demerara for Gloucester with a cargo of coffee, cotton, sugar, rum and sherry.

They were plain unlucky. Five days out, *Becca* was chased and seized by the French privateer schooner *La Polline* near St. Lucia. Captain Amelien took Captain Somes and six of his Gloucester crew on board *La Polline,* leaving Mate Henry Somes and another man to assist his prize crew of eight Frenchmen under Captain Toussent Baudry in getting *Becca* to Guadeloupe, in company.

Finding that his prize kept falling to leeward (was Henry Somes up to Yankee tricks?), Captain Baudry shaped a course for the Virgin Islands, while *La Polline* kept on for Pointe-à-Pître.

Alors, sacre! The fortunes of war again. On March 8 the British sloop of war *Fury,* Captain Henry Evans, fell in with *Becca,* recaptured her on the claim that she was an enemy prize and took her to Tortola in the British Virgins.

Captain Somes, meanwhile, made his way from Guadeloupe to Tortola in time to hear the British Admiralty Court on April

24 award Captain Evans and the crew of *Fury* one-sixth of the value of his vessel and cargo as salvage in compensation for getting them back for him from the French ... that is to say, a sixth of the proceeds of their forced sale at auction.

By some time in May the Somes boys were home on Cape Ann, breaking the bad news to their stepfather and initiating the tortuous process of an international protest. *Becca*'s cargo, they reported to Colonel Foster, had shrunk mysteriously between her capture and her sale, and by the time lawyers, agents, officials and sundry others along the line had got their sticky fingers into the gross proceeds of £ 4780, there was only £ 3137 left to bring back to Gloucester.

Never say die, growled the old man, and went in quarter-shares with son Joe, nephew Jeremiah and Joseph Locke (a Boston merchant who a couple of years later married Ben's widow), in *Dispatch,* a square-sterned, sixty-foot sloop of sixty-eight tons, which they loaded for Surinam. Captain Andrew Davis sailed the nineteenth of May, 1797.

Three months later, and one day out of Paramaribo, *Dispatch* was captured by the British privateer ship *Harlequin* and sent into Martinique. Davis must have convinced his captors of his rectitude, for he was soon home in Gloucester, making what had by now become the familiar apologetic visit to Colonel Foster's doorstep. Joseph, Jr., and Jeremiah bought out the Colonel and Locke. The following June, with relations with the French coming apart altogether, Davis again embarked for Surinam in *Dispatch.* This time his luck ran out. On July 7 Congress terminated the alliance with France, and the Quasi-War got under way. *Dispatch* was captured by the French armed schooner *Victoire* on July 31 and brought to Cayenne, where she was condemned as a lawful prize.

Well, let the younger fellows scrap it out and carry on. He had lost a son and two good vessels and their cargoes by this endless fighting of the old enemies over the West Indies. The fields and the quiet up to the Beaver Dam Farm looked green and good to Joseph Foster, pushing his three score and ten.

20

BOUND HOME

The orphaned Sargent children had been sheltered for some nine years in their Grandfather Foster's house on Front Street that looked out over Gloucester Harbor when the old captain, who would suffer no idlers about him, made it plain to Epes that now he was fourteen, his formal schooling was over and he must find a respectable occupation.

It was the beginning of 1799. A century of upheaval and revolution was about to give way to one of slow resolution whose dawn would happen to coincide with Joseph Foster's seventieth birthday. He had had enough of the cares of commerce, politics and war in his more than fifty years of venturing and sending others upon waters which had never been anything but troubled and precarious.

And where was that elusive wisp, domestic bliss? Since Lydia's death at the end of the Revolution, some new loss of a son or daughter, or of one of their spouses, or of a grandchild, was alway being mourned. Or it was some new trouble.

There was Judith. In '93 he had married off his youngest daughter to Captain Thomas Bradbury Sanders, a son of his old comrade in the *Falcon* fight. Unlike her sisters, Judy was tall and large, no great beauty. It was her husband's second marriage. This match, like Sally's, soured. They separated, without children, and now Mrs. Sanders was back under her father's roof.

Living with his own family in the older mansion house up on Middle Street, Captain Joseph Foster, Jr., was serving the first of several terms as selectman. He was established and respected, and his father hankered to turn the business over to him, rid himself of family burdens and retire to the Beaver Dam Farm; he just wanted to tramp about his acres, mow his fields and leave the tides and winds to others to contend with.

This was the state of affairs when the boy Epes Sargent around the frosty New Year's Day of 1799 found himself poised on the edge of the nest. Grandfather, and all the weight of Foster and Sargent family tradition were shoving. "Being born and thus far brought up upon a small promontory nearly surrounded by the ocean and being accustomed to the almost incessant roar of the billows dashing upon the rock-bound coast," he wrote his Iowa grandson many years later, "my thoughts, almost instinctively, turned seaward."

At this time an opportunity presented for me to procure a berth as cabin boy on board a ship then fitting out in Boston for China. The captain being an acquaintance of our family, and the chief mate being a cousin of mine, my grandfather consented to my going, and took measures to engage the situation for me. The ship was to sail in a few weeks, and now you may imagine my making preparations for my departure.

The first thing to be provided was a "sailor's chest" to contain all my wordly goods, consisting of a good quantity of clothing suitable for such a voyage. There was what is called a till to the chest. This is a little compartment in one end used for the purpose of containing sundry little articles such as a sailor's palm and needles, marlin-spikes, fids, sail hooks, twine, palm irons, flints, steel tinderbox and tinder, matches, a roll of brimstone to make matches with. So much for the till.

Under the till was a workbag containing pins, thimble, tape, thread, buttons, scissors, etc., in short, everything useful for mending clothes. So you see I was well fitted with all things useful. In addition to what I have named, I had books, paper, quills, ink and wafers. So I had no excuse for not writing home whenever an opportunity presented.

My sisters made me a quantity of hard gingerbread, and I made me a little box to put it in. This I stowed away in my chest to regale myself with upon the mighty deep where there are "more kicks than coppers" and where coppers will not buy cake. Well, now I am all ready and the time has arrived for me to take my departure from all that is dear to me. This you may depend required a stout heart and a firm resolve.

Now picture to yourself a cold but clear morning in the month of February, the ground nearly covered with snow, a coach badly provided with the necessary means of making passengers comfortable, drawn up to the front door of our house; the driver blowing his fingers to keep them warm, engaged in strapping on the sailor's little red chest; and now the little sailor himself taking leave of his sisters at the threshhold of the door. And now he enters the coach. The door is closed. He waves a last adieu and the coach rolls rapidly upon its destined way.

After a cold and cheerless ride, I arrived in Boston quite late in the afternoon, found the ship and went on board, and the day following took my station as cabin boy of the ship *Eliza* belonging to Francis Amory, commanded by James Odell; supercargo, John Waley; first mate, Charles Lenox Sargent; second mate, Gilbert Gardner, with a crew and petty officers amounting to about thirty in number.

The ship was three hundred tons burthen, and mounted eighteen guns to protect us from French cruisers and pirates that infested the straits we had to pass through to reach the China Seas, and also those seas. [1]

Eliza sailed from Boston, bound for Canton, on March 6, 1799. One day out, a very seasick Gloucester boy observed but hardly celebrated his fifteenth birthday.

A year passed, more or less, and the richly laden *Eliza* was back, swinging at anchor in Nantasket Roads. Several of the crew were sick with scurvy, and the port doctor came on board and ordered them put ashore on Rainsford Island for treatment; this consisted of burying the poor fellows in fresh earth up to their chins, a form of therapy which had "the happiest effect," gathered Epes, who was now more man than boy, as Grandfather Foster had intended he should be. As soon as *Eliza* was permitted to come into dock at Boston the young mariner hustled on shore to buy himself a pair of superfine blue broadcloth pantaloons, a coat with gilt buttons and first-class white waistcoat to match. Then he was paid off and prepared to head home for Cape Ann, but first,

well, I am now going on board the *Eliza* once more for that "little red chest" and other things that I have on board, and if you please, you may go with me. Now we are on our way with a man and a hand cart to take my effects to the Gloucester stage office.

We have reached the ship. Take care, don't fall going up the side. We are safe on board. Slip into the cabin, there is no time to lose. Hand cart man, that is the chest. I will help you put it on the wharf. Be careful how you handle that box of china.

All is now safe on the cart. Perhaps you would like to go with me to the Gloucester stage office and see me safe off. Well, come along. Now we are there. Don't you see the "little chest" strapped on behind the coach? Well, all is now ready, and I am on my "winding way" for home.

After an interesting journey through Charlestown, Malden, Lynn, Salem, Beverly and Manchester, old Cape Ann appeared in sight and right glad was I once more to behold those venerable moss-covered rocks. And now old Eastern Point appeared in view, covered with its grove of stately oaks, and Ten Pound Island, the school boys' "tiny world" dedicated to fun and frolic, now attracts my eye and awakens the remembrance of "joys departed, never to return."

It is now near sunset. All is calm and quiet. The distance between me and my dear sisters is rapidly diminishing. And now the coach is at my grandfather's door. The happy faces of those dear objects of my love are the first to greet me with their smiles...

My old grandfather met me with silent, but powerful indications of joy. His heart seemed too full for utterance, and the tears of joy rolled down his furrowed cheek. I received a happy greeting, a cordial shake of the hand and welcome home from every one I met. [2]

Grandfather Foster had given the China hand an adventure of twenty-five Spanish dollars when he saw him off that frigid February forenoon, and he expected a full reckoning. Well, upon arriving at Canton, Epes had pooled his stake with his three months' wages of fifteen dollars and bought a store of silk handkerchiefs and ladies' parasols. Back home he found the parasols were in the height of fashion, and he sold them at "an immense profit" of a dollar and a quarter apiece over the fifty cents they cost him. [3]

Colonel Foster had launched *one* of his grandsons along the course that leads to the quarterdeck. Now, what about Joe's son, Joseph the third, only five months younger than Epes? Was it fair, was it just, to send one cousin away to sea (lucky lad on his fifteenth birthday) and leave the other home in Gloucester?

The answer, of course, was no, and about the same time in '99 that *Eliza* was heeling through the Straits with Epes Sargent trying to hand around the mugs and salt horse in the great cabin, Joseph Foster III was engaged in similar duties on board the grand ship *Massachusetts,* under the eye of Captain William Vincent Hutchings of Gloucester, a family friend, who had consented to see what could be done to make a man of the Colonel's namesake. He succeeded. *Massachusetts* was following by only a few months almost in the track of the ship *Franklin,* also of Boston, the first American vessel ever to visit Japan. Captain Hutchings brought his ship to Batavia, where he was engaged to take her to Japan under Dutch colors (the Dutch being allowed one vessel there a year). Her officers, crew and cabin boy spent the winter of 1799 and 1800 in Nagasaki Harbor aboard *Massachusetts,* the second ship in American history to sail to the islands of Japan.

This grandson, too, had some tales to tell his old grandfather and everybody else when he got back to Gloucester. And Joe, like his cousin Epes, wound up supping, instead of serving, in the captain's mess. [4]

Dr. Bentley, tireless excursionist of Essex County, had traveled from Salem to Gloucester over the bumpy road through the shore woods on the thirteenth of May, 1799, to visit his friend Captain John Gibaut for a tour of Cape Ann. By the time he arrived, there was still day enough left to go out to Wheeler's Point where they piled into a small boat and sailed out Squam River into Ipswich Bay. The preacher caught a few haddock, but when it breezed up he was seasick, and they returned, this time tacking up Mill River and disembarking at the mill dam at sundown. The next morning, in two chaises, the party of four started on their round-Cape circuit, halting in the Harbor to be shaved by Aunt Becky Ingersol, of whom Bentley thought "she shaves well, but has few attractions of her sex." Then they left the town and were trotting past Salt Island through The Farms, on the road by Beaver Dam to Sandy Bay:

> The roughness of the road is much less than formerly & at present not to be compared with Squam side. We passed Col. Foster & his son at work in the field about 2 miles from Sandy Bay. Their farm is a welcome object amongst the greatest rudeness of nature. Opposite to the pond we stopped in the road & passed to the right to view it. [5]

Colonel Foster at this time of early spring planting may not yet have forsaken the house on Front Street for Beaver Dam. But he was edging up to it, and perhaps the charms of the country were enhanced for him by the same disenchantment with the town which Dr. Bentley felt, as he mused about his visit:

> As Squam & Upper Town [the first settlement at the Green] have decayed, the Harbour has been enriched. The military character of Cape Ann is established. On a point of land, they can afford to employ the greatest hospitality towards all who visit them, and forming all their pleasures among themselves, they must be fond of all social institutions. They excell in their parties, in their clubs, & also in their military

parades...How unhappy it is that an air of dissipation should appear in so lovely a place in which they could give to themselves any manners they please without any danger of contamination from foreign influence & fashions...In no place which I have ever visited can they so easily combine for any social pleasure, in no place can they pursue pleasure with so little interruption and yet they have all the jealousies, competitions, & even enmities, belonging to little towns & human nature.[6]

Judith wanted independence after the failure of her marital experiment with Captain Saunders (she preferred the *u*).[7] She had returned to her father's house, and it is probable that she taught school in Gloucester for a time, perhaps with her friend Clementina Beach, an English niece of their eccentric neighbor, Captain John Beach; Dr. Bentley visited the Beaches and admired her as "a young lady of accomplishments." Colonel Foster admired his youngest daughter in the same vein. Judy was artistic and tasteful, and at the age of sixteen had fashioned a "memorial tribute" to a departed friend, likely one of the woven hair-work pieces which were the sentimental mode; her father had it encased in a gold setting as a family memento.

Judith and Clementina hit upon the idea of opening a girls' boarding school for Boston society, and they found the perfect location for it on the summit of Meeting House Hill in Dorchester, which offered a stupendous view of the whole sweep of Boston and the bay. They persuaded Colonel Foster to take a look. He approved, bought the land, and that summer of his seventieth birthday, 1800, built and presented to his daughter "Mrs. Saunders's and Miss Beach's Academy." It would be fashionable and famous for twenty years.

Amelia, the eldest of the three Sargent grandchildren he had raised in his house, reached her twenty-first birthday in 1801 and married Daniel Rogers, Jr., one of the twenty-one children of the wealthy merchant and shipowner who had died the previous year.

At long, long last the road to Beaver Dam was clear. Colonel Foster set the young couple up in the house on Front Street with Amelia's still unmarried sister Frances. And then he and Hannah moved out to the farm, where nothing much was heard but the gurgle of Alewife Brook back of the house, the breeze sighing through the trees, the gentle whisper of the surf on Little Good Harbor Beach some distance off, and the lonely mewing of the gull.

Amelia had been married a year when Epes Sargent, now eighteen, returned from a voyage to the news that his sister was dead. "Dear, sainted soul," he wrote his small grandson forty-five years later, "she was taken away from much sorrow to a blissful immortality. Many years, months, and days have passed since I suffered this sad bereavement, and the time is fast approaching when I trust in God, we shall meet again, never more to part."

Epes found Gloucester cold and lifeless to him in his grief. Frances had moved in temporarily with their Uncle Foster in the old Middle Street manse. His grandfather's other house on Front Street, where Epes had grown up and where Amelia and her husband had lived so briefly, was empty. He slept there alone for a night or two, but it was too depressing, and he wandered out to Beaver Dam Farm to see his grandfather. The old man welcomed his grandson warmly, and Epes tarried for a few more days, "but the place had no charms for me and I could not make myself contented there." Soon he returned to sea.

Along when Colonel Foster was still active in town affairs, ten years or so back, he took a leading part in trying to get Moses Bennett, who had bought Ring's mill, to open up his sluiceway at the Riverdale dam in the spring and fall of the year to let the spawning alewives through from the tidewater of Mill River to Alewife Brook and into that Cape Pond Dr. Bentley had paused to admire. Nothing came of it. Bennett was as stubborn as one of the Foster mules.

Then suddenly he came round, and in a wholly unexpected way. Moses made up his mind to sell out and join the other

Bennetts who had emigrated from Cape Ann to New Glouces-ter, Maine. Foster made a deal with him for his grist mill and the land that went with it, and gave him an advance of a thousand dollars to seal the bargain by way of an option.

There had been a sawmill there once, alongside of Bennett's grist works, but the sash saws had run out of work during the time of the worst of the Revolution.

That would be something, to get that old sawmill agoing again. It would carry a man back full cycle, so to speak, to when a small shaver of eleven did his first day's work for pay in Pa's mill over at Chebacco Falls.

It was not to be.

Epes Sargent returned from his voyage to be told that his grandfather had died at the Beaver Dam Farm on the tenth of December, 1804. "This was unlooked for, as he was in the enjoyment of firm health when I left home. He was between seventy and eighty years old and he having passed the age allotted to man, I was not so much surprised as grieved to hear of his death. His illness was short and he left this world without suffering."

Joseph Foster was in fact seventy-four years and five months old. His funeral was held in Gloucester on the thirteenth of December in the first Universalist church in America, which he had helped to found, and whose freedom he had fought for, as he had for a frequently misunderstood abstraction called liberty.

POSTSCRIPT

Joseph Foster was buried beside his first wife, Lydia, in Gloucester's oldest cemetery, the Bridge Street Burying Ground, off Centennial Avenue. He died intestate. Perhaps he preferred to leave it to the probate court to unscramble conflicts among his heirs which he saw as inevitable. The distributable balance of his estate in 1808 was valued at $20,046.18. Besides real property and securities, he left a rather spartan collection of household effects and farm utensils, and one yoke of oxen, five cows, six heifers, two "creatures" (probably horses) and one colt. Evidently he had sold out all his vessel interests.

Captain Joseph Foster, Jr., was administrator of his father's estate, and was the object of considerable animus on the part of his stepmother, Hannah Somes Foster, and his sisters, over his handling of it. A few weeks after his father's death, on January 8, 1805, he bought the Riverdale mill from Moses Bennett for $1200. He continued to go to sea off and on, as a master generally in the West Indies trade, and served in various town offices, including selectman from 1804 to 1807. He was a Republican, and his election barbecues at the Beaver Dam Farm were remembered for years.

In April, 1811, he was in financial trouble, possibly due to losses from the British embargo. He mortgaged the Riverdale mill and his pew in the Universalist Church to his son, Captain Joseph Foster III, and twenty acres of the Beaver Dam Farm, two acres of salt marsh behind Little Good Harbor Beach, the Foster wharf and cooperage and the old meetinghouse pew--all part of his share of his late father's estate--to Elias Davison. In May of 1813 he repossessed these properties, sold the mill to Zachariah Stevens for $1070 and borrowed $1100 from the Gloucester Bank on his one-year note. He defaulted on this note, and the bank obtained a judgment against him in the circuit court of common pleas in September, 1814.

On August 3, 1816, Captain Foster cleared Gloucester for Guadeloupe as master of William Pearce's sloop *William*. All aboard were believed to have been lost in a hurricane near the island about six weeks later.

Colonel Foster had been dead four years before his estate was allowed in 1808 by Essex County Probate Judge Samuel Holten, who had entertained him while a congressman in Philadelphia during the Revolution. Dr. Holten made a seven-way division of the real estate among the Foster children and their heirs.

The bulk of the Beaver Dam Farm was allotted to the children of Mary Foster Wade; in 1809 they sold it to Dr. John Manning, a physician of Sandy Bay who, like Colonel Foster, got the farm fever. Over the years he accumulated 182 acres which were sold at about the time of his death in 1841 to William A. Schenck, and eventually to Roger W. Babson.

The heirs of Benjamin Foster and Lydia Foster Sargent shared the house on Front Street which their father built and occupied before moving out to the farm. The two parts were soon sold, consolidated and passed through several hands before the house was purchased by Joseph and Lemuel Friend in 1852. Described as a three-stoy building at 148-152 Front Street, it burned to the cellar in the great fire which ravaged the waterfront and business district on the night of February 18, 1864.

Betsy Dolliver was apportioned the smaller house on the midsection of the Front Street property; the wharf and cooperage below it, with woodland and salt marsh at Beaver Dam and the Head of the Harbor, were awarded to Captain Joseph Foster, Jr.

The old mansion house at the corner of Middle and Hancock streets where the family lived before and during the Revolution was assigned by Judge Holten to Judith Foster Saunders, who was residing in Dorchester and running her girls' boarding school with Clementina Beach. Her brother, Joseph, Jr., was living in the house in 1808, and he may have stayed on with his family, renting, until his death in 1816. The lot immediately south, and the warehouse on it, went to Sally Foster Dolliver.

Fosters continued to live in the Middle Street manse. After the first edition of Joseph Foster IV's book about his family appeared in 1887 or 1888, a female cousin wrote him in reminiscence:

> I would be seated in the dear old parlor of the old house on Hancock Street. Such cuddling and petting, such bread and butter, apple-sauce, ginger-bread, etc., as I there received, with my feet upon the polished fender, before a cheerful wood fire reflected from tongs, shovel, hooks, bellows, sideboard and door-locks, made an impression upon my youthful mind, which years have not effaced.

> From the west chamber window I learned to count the hours from the old church clock just before that time-honored building was razed to the ground, before the eyes of a group gathered at that same window. In my mind's eye, I see almost forgotten churchgoers wending their way to the different places of worship, carrying coals in square or round foot stoves, to give some little warmth to their bodies during the services. [1]

The First Parish meetinghouse struck by *Falcon*'s cannon-ball was torn down in 1828 and replaced the same year with the Unitarian Church, now Temple Ahavath Achim, so Fosters were in their house then, watching at the window, and perhaps still there when Judith Foster Saunders sold it out of the family after seventy-eight years to Elbridge G. Friend in 1839, two years before she died in Dorchester.

Friend was a mason. During the half-century of his owner-ship he enlarged the rather small dwelling (it was twenty-eight feet square) with an extension on the east side built in two stages--half on the south, which left it looking like the Hardy-

Parsons House across Middle Street today, completed later with the north half. To make room for his son's dry goods store, he increased the ground floor toward Hancock Street with a lean-to addition. Elbridge Friend retired in 1886 and was a special judge of the Gloucester police court until his death in 1889. His family held on to the house for two more decades and sold it when it was 150 years old in 1909 to Charles F. Boardman.

The new owner wanted even more room for his sewing machine and piano business and attached the full-length addition with the flat roof onto the original front which once had a clear view over the harbor. When Gloucester's new City Hall was built after the Civil War (actually as a town hall, before the town turned city in 1873), an avenue was cut through between Prospect and Middle streets directly in line with the Foster-Friend-Boardman house and named for Dr. Ebenezer Dale, late owner of the three-story gambreled colonial home on the west corner of Hancock Street which years later was moved a dozen blocks northwest to Grove Street, where it still stands, to make way for the first YMCA. The creation of Dale Avenue placed his house, as Boardman soon discovered to his dismay, in some jeopardy--in double jeopardy in fact, as explained in *The Gloucester Guide*:

On the morning of September 26, 1913, apparatus of the fire department had assembled on Prospect Street and was thundering one piece after another down Dale Avenue and wheeling to the right onto Middle Street for a motion picture being filmed by the Gloucester Theater. Chief Crowe's car, the auto chemical, the steamer "going for all it was worth" and the hose carriage had careened around the corner, which was packed with vehicles and spectators, when the hook and ladder came clattering along with eight firemen aboard.

Somehow the driver lost control. They couldn't make the corner, and the momentum of the rig drove the two handsome bays right through the windows of Boardman's piano and sewing machine store on the street level of the

Foster House and catapaulted the man at the reins in on top of them. The driver was badly hurt; the other firemen and the spectators escaped, but the horses were so gashed by glass that the gutter flowed with blood, and back at the stable one of them had to be shot.

Some eight years later a man taking a driving lesson became so flustered by his instructor's directions coming down Dale Avenue -- whether to turn right or left -- that he did neither and again Boardman's windows were shattered. [2]

In 1929 came anther kind of Crash, and when the bottom dropped out of the piano market, too, Boardman converted his store to a whosesale confectionary. He died in 1939. The house was sold to Peter H. Ferron, stood vacant for five years, then was rented by Dr. Joseph W. Foley as his home and office until Dr. Reginald Courant, another dentist, purchased it in 1952. It contained an office and four apartments when its eighth owner, the Cape Ann Bank and Trust Company, acquired the Foster House from Dr. Courant on January 5, 1972. The bank restored the colonial appearance and remodelled the interior for its trust department, and reopened the 213-year-old home of Gloucester's Revolutionary leader in 1973.

NOTES

1. The Rasp of the Saw and the Song of the Sea

1. The setting of the Foster sawmill probably hasn't changed much in two hundred years. To find it, swing west on Route 22 at Essex center. Not far beyond the Town Hall on the left is Landing Road, which a short distance in spans the ravine where the tide of the Essex River dies out; this is where the Foster brothers are launched on their conjectured voyage to Ipswich Bay. Returning to Route 22 and continuing west a few hundred yards, turn left on Apple Street and immediately rejoin the stream, which flows narrowly under the low bridge and bends right sharply to parallel the road for a short way before veering off to the left and diving into the woods. The broad path above the stream is the original Apple Street before the bend was transected by the newer and straighter stretch of road. On a rise in the fork rests a comfortable old country clapboard house. It, or possibly its predecessor, is the probable birthplace of Joseph Foster. At the bottom of the gorge are the huge, mossy foundation stones of the sawmill that around 1875 was torn down (some say it fell down from the rattling of an Essex Branch freight train in the times when the track ran above the opposite bank). This mill was built by Perkins Story in 1837 on the site of the original operation, which had reverted to the Storys from the Fosters. After the mill went out of use the dam was knocked down to make it less of a jump for the alewives swimming upstream in the spring of the year.

The John Story who sold the mill to Jeremiah Foster was the grandson of William Story, who settled from Norwich, England, in 1637; William married Sarah Foster, Jeremiah's grandmother. John and his father, Samuel Story, were living in Norwich, Conncticut, at the time of the sale in 1724. Samuel acquired the mill from Jonathan and Thomas Wade in 1718. The stream rights were granted by Ipswich to a Jonathan Wade in 1656 or 1665; the records are unclear.

A third of a mile upstream during Joseph Foster's boyhood was another low dam providing a fall of water for Thomas Burnham's grist mill on one bank and a bark-grinding mill extracting tannin for a small tannery on the other.

2. One can only surmise that Jeremiah Foster quit fishing or coasting after he bought the mill. The first entry in the account book of sawing charges, which he kept until he died in 1769, is dated 1730.

3. Perkins Story's dam held back a deep pond. The fall was high enough to drive an overshot waterwheel at a rate that made the valley echo to the scream of his circular saw. The buzz saw didn't appear in America until 1814, so Foster needed only fall enough to turn the slow undershot wheel.

4. Jeremiah Foster's purchase included saws, "doggs and crows."

5. There was at least one other sawmill in the area, excluding the tidal operation which John Burnham is said to have run at a dam in the seventeenth century at "Saw-mill Island" in Chebacco's Haskell's Creek: this was the mill on Haskell's Brook in the West Parish of Gloucester, operated by William Haskell and his family from before 1690 well into the nineteenth century; the remains of the dam and pond are at Essex Avenue between Lincoln and Sumner streets.

6. Environmentalists point to the passing of the passenger pigeon as another lurid example of man the despoiler. It's just as possible that the species overpopulated itself out of existence, as man is trying to do.

7. Nathaniel Rust, Jr., was appointed schoolmaster of Chebacco in 1695 and granted six acres of pasture for support and a quarter of one to build his house on. He held classes here for a

few years on the Common, near the center, until he was elected a selectman and the parish built a schoolhouse in front of his place in 1702.

8. The six leaders of Chebacco's resistance were Wise, Robert Kinsman, Jr., John Appleton, John Andrews, William Goodhue and Thomas French. Kinsman was the son of Robert Kinsman, settler from England; he had been a selectman, and his father-in-law, Thomas Boreman, was an early deputy to the General Court, as he himself would be in later years. The younger Kinsman's daughter Joanna, Joseph Foster's grandmother, had married Master Rust two years previously.

9. This was, in fact, Chebacco's second fight over taxes in a decade. Fed up with the bother and hardship of journeying to Ipswich to church in all weather, the Chebacco people had organized the town's Second Parish in 1677 and asked its permission to build their own church. Not wanting to forfeit the taxes Chebacco had to pay for church support as long as the Ipswich parish remained undivided, the town refused. Two years later, three redoubtable matrons of Chebacco got their husbands to prefabricate a church on the sly, and then one day to trundle out the parts and assemble them near the center as a *fait accompli*. The ladies were briefly sojourned to jail but won their case. Chebacco completed its church, and hired John Wise.

10. Parrington's *Main Currents* I, 122.

11. Parrington, *ibid*, 123. In the view of this respected historian, Wise had "the keenest mind and most trenchant pen of his generation of New Englanders...The struggle for ecclesiastical democracy was a forerunner of the struggle for political democracy which was to be the business of the next century; and in founding his ecclesiasticism upon the doctrine of natural rights, John Wise was an early witness to the new order of thought." (124-125).

12. Babson's *History*, 318-319.

13. Aaron Foster and Daniel Giddings were seriously ill during the siege, as were many of the army, according to the journal kept by one of the members of Captain Foster's Chebacco company, Benjamin Craft ... so ill that when Jere-

miah Foster, Jr., and his cousin were given leave to return home on July 15, Aaron was too sick to go on board the ship; not until August 7 did Craft report him well enough to embark.

2. Out of Gloucester

1. A Captain Joseph Foster made several voyages to the Virginia and Maryland coasts, according to the Salem customs records, in the thirty-five-ton sloop *Speedwell* and later in the schooner *Dolphin*, fifty tons, between November 1750, and November 1754. It would be tempting to conclude that this is our man, in command of his own vessel at the age of twenty, except that a certain Joseph Foster of Beverly was lost on a return voyage from Virginia in March, 1755. Since the records furnish no further references to a captain of that name visiting the Chesapeake region, it appears that this earlier Joseph Foster was lost returning in *Dolphin* from the voyage for which he was cleared out of Salem for Maryland on November 13, 1754 --no trace of his arrival home.

2. The coincidence of two Joseph Fosters clearing Salem in two *Speedwell*s must be accepted as just that, unless the sloop was rerigged with a second mast as a schooner ... possible in view of their nearly equal tonnages.

3. Colonial Gloucester owned slaves. How did it come by them? Were they purchased by ones and twos in the West Indies, or along the Carolina coast, and brought home? No evidence has yet been uncovered that Cape Ann shipmasters ever directly engaged in the traffic. But the temptation was there.

4. Babson's *History*, 381-382.

5. *Ibid*, 491.

6. A search of court records at Salem and Boston has turned up no trace of this case.

7. The Salem customs identified *Sanders* as a brigantine rather than a brig, terms often confused. It may indicate that Foster substituted fore-and-aft sails for one or all of her main squaresails to improve her windward ability. The presence of *Sanders* in Gloucester at this time, incidentally, makes an exception to Babson's claim that up to the Revolution only two

squareriggers, owned by Epes and Winthrop Sargent, are known to have belonged to the town.

8. Babson, *Second Series*, 135-136.

9. Possibly *Polly and Betsey*.

3. Dowse vs. Thirty-three Hogsheads
of Molasses

1. *Essex Gazette*, July 25, 1769.

2. Jesse Saville was twenty-seven at the time of this attack on his home. His father, Thomas, was a cooper in Annisquam. Saville Lane remains a woods road along the ridge between Dennison Street and Bennett Street, the old abandoned town way to Squam. A barely discernible cellar hole in the woods off to the right of the lane may be Jesse's home site. Farther along, the location of his tanpit is easily spotted at the bottom of one of the deepest gorges on Cape Ann.

3. Paul Dudley Sargent was a son of Epes Sargent of Gloucester (1690-1762) by his second marriage.

4. From *Essex Institute Historical Collections* XLII (January 1906), 36-39. The author has corrected the least comprehensible spelling.

5. *Essex Gazette*, July 25, 1769 (datelined Boston, May 20).

6. *Ibid*, August 22, 1769.

7. Under the charter granted to Massachusetts (which at this time included Maine) by King William in 1691, the governor, lieutenant governor and secretary were appointed by the crown. The House of Representatives of the General Court was elected annually by the freeholders of the towns. The upper chamber, the Council of twenty-eight members, was elected annually by the General Court itself, subject to the approval of the governor. The charter gave the governor the power to veto the acts of the General Court, and the king might veto any law within three years of its passage. No law was to be adopted contrary to the acts of Parliament.

8. *Journal of the House of Representatives of Massachusetts Bay*, 139.

9. *Ibid*, 178-181.

10. Hutchinson's *History* III, 203-205.

11. Writing to an unidentified correspondent, from Boston on November 30, 1770, three weeks after the Gloucester slave's conviction, Hutchinson declared that Saville was "very intrepid... and in spite of all their menaces carried on a prosecution against one of the most criminal and convicted him." He had requested the customs commissioners "to show some mark of favour to this Saville, who behaves well, and they have given him an active place of 20 or 30 £ a year. I wish to encourage all who have courage to do their duty..."*Massachusetts Archives* 27, 61.

About the time George was in Salem jail awaiting trial, another black man, Titus, was putting all the distance he could in his shoeless state between himself and his owner, Thomas Jaques of West Parish. Jaques informed the watchful countryside in the *Essex Gazette* of July 19, 1769, describing his property as about twenty-one, of middling stature, missing part of one great toe, hatless and barefoot, clad in striped jacket, striped woolen shirt and sheepskin britches. "Stutters considerably when he speaks." Eight dollars reward for his return. The same who ran away on the first of June.

Titus was recaptured, but not his spirit, and on October 19 Jaques had to insert another card in the *Gazette*. This was his slave's third escape, and this time he took with him "a span of iron, with a chain fastned to it, on one leg; it is supposed he will change his clothing if he has opportunity, and get off the chain." The reward was reduced to six dollars.

Jaques was the son of the Reverend Richard Jaques, Harvard College class of 1720 and the second pastor of West Parish.

4. Storm Clouds to the Eastward

1. Babson's *History*, 459, 281.
2. Frothingham's *Warren*, 189.
3. *Ibid.*
4. Babson's *Second Series,* 139.
5. The old Babson cooperage was purchased by Roger W. Babson in 1931 and restored as the James Babson Museum, open summers and now operated by the Babson Historical

Association. At that time the Foster farmhouse stood between the cooperage and the road. The farmhouse is gone, along with a landmark granite barn nearby.

6. The vestiges of this 1642 dam can be inspected today in the woods off the Old Rockport Road, and the stream stained wine-red from the bog-iron rust trickles through as it did when the Fosters fished it.

7. Babson's *History*, 387.

5. With Heavy Hearts

1. The senior Epes Sargent had voiced his conservative views as early as 1768, when on September 19 Peter Coffin and Thomas Sanders, Jr., were elected delegates to a provincial convention in Boston after Governor Bernard refused the Boston town meeting's demand that he summon the General Court into session. The debate in Gloucester meeting was noted in the record that day, "Epes Sargent Esqr. desiring them to be careful of acting." The vote was unanimous but one.

2. Babson's *History*, 387.

3. Webber's usual exceptional memory must have failed him. This couldn't have been *Lively* coming in from England. She was moored at Marblehead all winter and had pounced into Gloucester Harbor only a month earlier, as noted. Instead, they might have spoken the sloop of war *Falcon*, which arrived at Boston on April 16.

6. War

1. Babson, *Second Series*, 144. Subsequently, Quincy's body was removed from Gloucester to the family lot. Mrs. Quincy had been prevented from fleeing Boston earlier in the month by the serious illness of their two children. Their only daughter died on April 13, thirteen days before her father. Their only son, Josiah, grew up to be a reforming mayor of Boston and president of Harvard College.

2. Nineteen-year-old Benjamin Webber was credited by James R. Pringle in his *History of Gloucester* (1892) with firing the shot that mortally wounded Major John Pitcairn, who had

led the British march on Lexington and Concord. According to Pringle, who got the story from a descendant, Webber picked off Pitcairn with "an old Queen's arm" he hiked from Freshwater Cove to Lanesville to procure; it had been lengthened with a section of barrel tubing brazed on. At the rail fence Ben spotted Major Pitcairn on horseback. " 'Do you see that officer on horseback?' remarked Webber to a comrade, 'Well, I am going to try and bring him down.' Raising on his knee, the young farmer took unerring aim, fired with deadly effect and Major Pitcairn fell mortally wounded." (74). History, however, credits Peter Salem, a freed slave in Prescott's regiment, with firing the fatal shot. (See Fleming's *Bunker Hill*, 280.)

A year after the battle William Ellery put in a claim for the coat the town owed his servant; Low petitioned for Callahan's wages "and anything else that belonged to him."

3. *Naval Documents* I, 828.

4. *Ibid*, 937.

7. Peregrine, Swooping from on High

1. *Naval Documents*, I, 703.

2. *Ibid*, 576-578. The account of *Falcon*'s depradations around the Elizabeth Islands and Martha's Vineyard is based largely on sources in *Naval Documents* I.

3. Sabine's *Fisheries*, 147.

4. *Naval Documents* I, 900.

5. Babson's *Falcon* centennial address of 1875.

6. Daniel Fuller states in his diary that *Falcon* sent in "a barge with fifty men." However, since her largest boat appears to have been a double-banked pinnace of about a dozen oars, his figure--half of the warship's complement--seems much too high. Besides, they must reserve room for the sheep.

7. Tradition credits Peter Coffin's man "Tailor" Robbins with roaring out the inspired firing command, if indeed any such ruse was employed that day. A William Robbins was ensign of the Third Company of Gloucester militia at the time, and one of Coffin's slaves is said to have been named Robin; after his manumission Robin took the name Robert Freeman and owned the house still standing on the Essex road at the

head of Little River. A more likely candidate is Samuel Robbins Bray of West Parish, who was probably Coffin's work boss. In his *Falcon* centennial address, Babson added to the lore of the occasion: "Two of the Major's party, Sam Bray, his overseer, and Sambo, one of his slaves, claimed the honor of the shot that hit the officer commanding the barge, and Black Rose, Sambo's wife, with true conjugal fidelity, maintained his claim long after he was dead. 'But,' said the aged widow of the Major to a grandson, from whom I had the story, 'it was a ball from your grandfather's rifle that compelled the British officer to return to his ship, though he was always willing that Sam Bray and Sambo should have the honor of it between them.' "

8. The Falcon Fight

1. The Duncan's Point rocks today lie buried under the new Coast Guard base. Sargent's Wharf is the site of the Quincy Market freezer on Rogers Street. Vincent's Cove was gradually filled during the early twentieth century; the entrance is under the freezer's truck lot. The State Fish Pier was built out over Five Pound Island in 1938. The flats on which the fleeing schooner grounded were dredged to navigable depth in the nineteenth century.

2. Babson's *Falcon* centennial address.

3. Before attempting to capture the grounded West Indiaman, Babson states in the *History* (394), Captain Linzee "sent in a boat, with a flag; and the Committee of Safety went on board of his ship, where they were detained till they promised to release the schooner. But the citizens would not suffer the schooner to be taken out." It is hardly credible that the committee of safety could have been induced thus to thrust its collective head into the lion's mouth, even supposing that Linzee already had the town in the sights of his gunners, or that the *Falcon* commander would not have held some or all of them hostage until he had retrieved his prize. Furthermore, if he did deliver such an ultimatum to Gloucester in an offer to avoid bloodshed--and if the townspeople refused to be bound by the pledge of their leaders (as they did, if such a pledge was ever made)--it would

have appeared in the record to Linzee's credit. But he made no mention of any such parley either in his log of the day or in his more detailed subsequent report to Graves; neither did contemporary newspaper accounts. And Babson, who did not identify the source of his statement, chose to omit it from the later version he presented in his centennial address of 1875.

4. Rose Bank has to be a contraction of "Rowe's Bank," the area around Rowe Square early owned by the Rowe family.

5. The supposed Dogtown cellar hole of Peter Lurvey's house is marked by boulder 25 in the brush east of the path known as Wharf Road.

6. A hundred years later the Daniel Sargent house was owned by James Mansfield. The site now is occupied by the new police station-courthouse. Around World War I the original house was razed, and much of the frame was worked by the late hotel man George O. Stacy into a house which stands at the south end of Niles Beach. The cannonball is displayed at the Cape Ann Historical Association.

7. The lodging place of the cannonball which struck the meetinghouse was discovered by a mason, Jonathan Sargent, who returned it to the hole it made coming through the outside wall, "as a monument of the divine care." The old church was replaced by the Unitarian Church, now Temple Ahavath Achim, in 1828, and the sacred ball hung on a chain in the vestibule for more than a century until it was removed to the Cape Ann Historical Association, where it too is on display.

The First Church had no settled pastor on the day of the bombardment. Samuel Chandler had died in the spring, and his successor, Eli Forbes, was not installed until June 5, 1776. Upon completion of the repairs, Mr. Forbes on February 13, 1792, delivered a sermon at the request of the committee in charge of the work (Peter Coffin, Daniel Rogers and Daniel Warner), remarking: "And has not God wonderfully preserved this house, when in imminent danger by a sacriligious attack made upon it by the *Falcon* sloop of war, commanded by Capt. John Lynzey, who, without orders, just provocation, or previous notice, cannonaded this defenceless place from one o'clock till five in the afternoon, directing the weight of his fire at this House of God, August 8, 1775 (which greatly injured and defaced the house)."

8. Babson's version of the day in the *History* (393-396) was based mainly on the account in Isaiah Thomas's *Massachusetts Spy* of August 16, published in Worcester, from which this passage is excerpted. The *Spy* ran the sole American report of the fight to which any credence at all can be given, entitled "A Letter from Gloucester" and dated August 13. Babson was unaware of the existence of *Falcon*'s log and Linzee's report to Admiral Graves dated August 10 from Nantasket Roads; otherwise the historian would have realized that frustrated and angry as he undeniably was, Linzee was less concerned with retribution against the town and the church than with diverting Captain Foster's marksmen long enough to give his trapped landing party a chance to get off.

Furthermore, Revolutionary ordnance was wildly inaccurate, and it is questionable if *Falcon*'s gunners could have hit the meetinghouse at a range of roughly fourteen hundred yards if they had aimed at it. The caliber of the average six-pound ball was 3.67 inches, approximately three-sixteenths of an inch less than the bore of the gun; with this much play, or windage as it was called, and with varying amounts of powder, there was no real telling where the ball might strike, except perhaps the hull of another vessel at point blank. The caliber of a half-pound swivel gun ball, incidentally, averaged 1.69 inches.

9. So claims family tradition. Foster's *Foster,* 46.

10. Captain Linzee's first-person account of the fight extracted in this chapter is from his report to Admiral Graves dated August 10, 1775, in *Naval Documents* I, 1110-1111.

11. The Reverend Daniel Fuller's version of the attempt to set fire to the town, from his *Journal:* "[Linzee's] boatswain likewise in attempting to set the town on fire by firing the train of powder to some combustible matter prepared, providentially the fire was communicated to the powder iron in his hand which occasioned an explosion and it is said he lost his hand if not his life."

12. Thirty prisoners are recorded in a list preserved in the Washington Papers, Library of Congress: "Robert Arnold, Master; Wm. Robert Broton, Midshipman; Philabeth Demett,

Midshipman; Justin Budd, Gunner; John Backster, Doctr's Servant; Hugh Hughes, Marine; Thomas Nash, Ditto; Jonathan Ellis, Do; Abraham Elliot, Do; Gyles Jones, Do; John Mechum, Do; William Allen, Steward; William Rickets, Capt of Forecastle; Hugh Jones, Sail Maker; Michael Love, Sailor; Thomas Taylor, Gunner Yeoman; William Mackey, Quarter Master; John McRady, impress'd -- released; Michael Flynn, since sick and remaining in Ipswich Gaol; Samuel Burd, impress'd; John Doyl, Sailor; Mathew Cornish, Marine; John Clark, Cook's Mate; Wounded -- John Warrick, Quarter Master -- Joseph Murray, Quarter Gunner; Killed -- John Molloy, formerly of Salem; Taken -- belonging formerly to Cape Ann -- and are now there -- Duncan Piper, William Putam, George Rigg, Jno Cleaveland." *Naval Documents* I, 1114.

The disposition of the original thirty-five prisoners is impossible to track down. All of the impressed Americans were said to have been released. Twenty-four were reported sent to Ipswich jail, and twenty of these were transferred to headquarters at Cambridge on August 14.

13. Determination of the exact number of *Falcon*'s boats captured is compounded by a confusion of counts and contemporary nomenclature. In his accounting to Admiral Graves, Captain Linzee reported only the loss of the pinnace and jolly boat, although he had sent in the long boat and evidently the skiff in which the wounded Thornborough was brought back to the ship, as well. The Gloucester version in the *Massachusetts Spy*, however, claimed capture of a "cutter," two "barges" and a boat, while Forbes in his 1792 sermon counted four boats and a small "tender."

14. *Naval Documents* I, 1164. August 17, 1775.

15. "Journal of the Siege of Boston, by Benjamin Craft of Manchester," *Essex Institute Historical Collections* III (April 1861), 51-57. Another garbled report found its way into the *New England Chronicle* of August 10 and thence into the *Boston Gazette* of August 14: "We hear from Cape-Ann, that a vessel bound in there from the West-Indies, being discovered off that harbour last Thursday, several of the inhabitants went off in a boat to assist in bringing her in. Soon after, about 30 armed

men, from the man of war commanded by Captain Linzee, boarded and took possession of the vessel; but she running aground on the Cape, was vigorously attacked by a number of men from the Town of Gloucester, who soon obliged the enemy to give up the vessel to the proper owners, and to surrender themselves prisoners. The whole number was immediately sent to Ipswich Gaol, in which 24 of them were confined. The rest (4 or 5 in number) were discharged, it appearing that they had been cruelly forced into the enemy's service. Lindzee was so enraged that he fired several cannon shot into the Town of Glocester, but did little damage."

16. Babson's *Falcon* centennial address.

Having left his large boats in the hands of the victors, Captain Linzee must have made hard going of it getting kedged or towed out the harbor against the wind. It may have been while he was making sail outside the Point, early on August 9, that he came upon a man and his son in a boat and impressed the father, William Moore, who lived above Freshwater Cove. Moore was never seen again; the boy rowed ashore and grew up to be the famous Gloucester teacher of navigation, Master Joseph Moore (1763-1845). The severely short-handed *Falcon* made straight for Nantasket Roads, where Linzeee stoically reported the bare details of his defeat to Admiral Graves. A fortnight later, *Falcon* and HM Sloop *Merlin* sailed in convoy with eighteen transports for the Bay of Fundy after cattle and forage.

On January 20, 1776 Captain Linzee embarked for England in *Falcon* with his wife, son and infant daughter. They returned to Boston in February 1792. Mrs. Sucky Linzee died in October at the age of thirty-nine; she had borne nine children. Linzee resigned from the British Navy, settled in America and died at his home in Milton in 1798 at fifty-six.

Irony of ironies, Captain Linzee's granddaughter, Susan Amory, in 1820 married William Prescott, grandson of Colonel William Prescott, who commanded the redoubt cannonaded by *Falcon* that day on Breed's Hill. Their eldest son was the historian William Hickling Prescott. The crossed swords of the enemies in the Revolution, who were reconciled in death by their progeny, hang at the Massachusetts Historical Society.

9. Their Spirit Seems Equal to Their Abilities

1. *American Archives,* Series 4, III, 320-321.

2. *Ibid,* 324.

3. Babson, *Second Series,* 145-146.

4. *Ibid,* 146.

5. The number and location of earthworks of lesser importance around the shores of Gloucester Harbor are a mystery. On August 20, 1757, for example, Samuel Chandler mentioned in his diary (Babson, *Second Series,* 45): "I visited at the fort of Eastern Point." The site is unidentified, but it is not the Eastern Point fort on the height of Fort Hill Avenue which was erected during the Civil War.

6. *Naval Documents* II, 226.

7. Babson's *History,* 397n.

8. *New England Chronicle,* October 5, 1775.

10. A Close Call

1. *Naval Documents* I, 297, 302.

2. *Ibid,* 568.

3. Timothy Newell's *Diary,* in *Naval Documents* II, 280.

4. *Naval Documents* II, 324-326.

5. *Ibid,* 374.

6. *Ibid,* 513-514.

7. A hundred years later, Babson in his *Falcon* centennial address made note of Mowat's expedition and of the fact that Gloucester was selected for destruction. Having no acquaintance with the British Admiralty records, he had to wonder, "why the design against Gloucester was not executed, we are left to conjecture." Graves's orders, *Canceaux*'s log and Mowat's report provide the answer.

8. *Naval Documents* II, 1155-1156.

9. *Ibid,* 859.

10. Currier's *Newburyport,* 609-611.

11. Crowell's *Essex,* 208-209.

12. The Massachusetts Legislature under the colonial charter had been "The Great and General Court." After General Gage

dissolved it in June 1774 the members met in defiance as the first Provincial Congress, which convened at Concord in October. Within a year this revolutionary body had reverted to the old form, General Court, meeting as the House of Representatives and Council, sometimes called Board, in "General Assembly."

13. *American Archives,* Series 4, III, 1255.

14. *Ibid,* 1500.

15. *Naval Documents II,* 1089.

11. Colonel Foster

1. Peabody's *Manley.*

2. A report in the *Boston Gazette* of December 4, 1775, dated November 26, raises the possibility that a third transport had crossed with the ordnance and powder ships, and had separated from them coming on the coast: "A large ship being near the light off Cape Ann was struck with lightning, which set her on fire, and burnt to the water's edge, 'till she sunk. A number of cannon were heard to go off, and 'twas thought at least a 20—gun ship; but we have an account from Boston, that it was the *Juno* [sic *Jupiter*] transport ship from London, laden only with hay for Burgoyne's heavy horse at Boston, which will soon become light, if forage fails at this rate."

3. Daniel Fuller noted in his diary that besides the ordnance ship, Manley "at the same time brought in a sloop in the service of the Ministerial Troops." None of the contemporary accounts, though, mentions a second prize.

4. *Naval Documents* II, 1199. "Mr. Palfrey" probably was Major William Palfrey, Washington's paymaster.

5. How her captors were able to conceal *Nancy*'s presence from any British warships which may have chanced by Eastern Point is something to speculate on. Freshwater Cove is shielded from view out to sea, south of Eastern Point, by Dolliver's Neck--somewhat less so east across the harbor over the very low isthmus of the Point made by Niles Pond and Brace Cove. The far interior of Freshwater Cove is a flat at low water, but there probably was depth at high tide for Manley's

prize crew to run *Nancy* aground barely inside the north shore of Dolliver's Neck; she could not have drawn less than ten or twelve feet. What about her top hamper, which would have been visible above the tree line to a sharp-eyed mastheadman on a warship passing Brace Cove or off the harbor? The solution would have been to send down *Nancy*'s topmasts, and if that didn't do the trick, to dismast her with an ax, and well worth it.

6. Peabody's *Manley.*

7. *Naval Documents* II, 1247.

8. *Ibid,* 1248. A very minor English poet, George Cockings, published "The American War" in 1781, with these lines:

> Laden with apparatus for the train,
> Thrice strove the *Nancy* Boston's port to gain;
> Oft as she came, the wind unfriendly grew
> (A rough opposing storm against her blew:)
> The *Cerberus* for her protection sail'd
> But in th' attempt the royal frigate fail'd;
> In darkness wrapp'd by tempest rudely tost,
> They parted, and the precious prize was lost;
> This through the loyal army spread a damp;
> And fill'd with pleasure the provincial camp.

(from *Washington's New England Fleet,* 16)

9. So nearly bare of cannon was Gloucester that one mistrusts the accuracy of the information in a letter home from the fleet in Boston, dated November 30, that "the *Nautilus* has been severely cannonaded by the Provincial batteries at Cape Ann; like military harlequins they attack us everywhere, God end this unnatural warfare." *Naval Documents* II, 1204. Possibly the writer referred to the bombardment *Nautilus* received from Beverly and Salem when she chased *Hannah* ashore on October 10.

10. *American Archives,* Series 4, IV, 1230-1231.

11. *Naval Documents* II, 1251.

12. Peabody's *Manley.*

13. *Naval Documents,* III, 194.

14. *Ibid* II, 1144.

15. *Ibid* III, 82.

16. Babson (*History,* 409) credits the schooner *Warren* with being "the first vessel that put to sea from Gloucester on a privateering cruise." However, she was not commissioned until the following August. *General Ward*'s home port may be in question, but not her initial ownership as a privateer; that was firmly in Gloucester in the persons of Foster and Parsons. The *Ward* may have cruised first out of Cape Ann, then shifted to Newburyport. Jewett's *Essex County* (328) states that *General Ward* sailed from Newburyport under Captain William Russell, one cannon and thirteen crew, and captured two brigs and a schooner.

17. It is impossible to know what to make of Maclay's statement in his *History of the United States Navy* (49) that on December 8 Manley in *Lee* captured three more English transports "and soon afterward she was chased into Gloucester by the cruiser *Falcon,* but by running close inshore inflicted considerable injury on her pursuer and escaped." In his article on Manley, Peabody claims *Falcon* grounded on Eastern Point chasing Manley some time around November 30. There is a total absence of documentation for either of these old accounts (1901 and 1909) among the vast amount of newly collected sources in *Naval Documents* and *Washington's New England Fleet.*

18. *Naval Documents* III, 151.

19. *Ibid,* 292. "Eastern Channel" may refer to Boston Harbor's North or South channels.

20. *American Archives,* Series 4, IV, 1362-1364.

21. *Ibid,* 1246-1247. The record does not reveal who received the nine votes in opposition to Foster for the colonelcy.

22. See Foster's orders to Lieutenant Lane, May 9, 1776 (Chapter 13) mentioning that the watch at "Chebacco side" was under his command.

23. *Naval Documents* III, 553-554.

12. The Difficulties We Labor Under

1. Babson's *History,* 397-398.

2. An inflationary omen in this entry is in the Gloucester selectmen's Day Book of March 9, 1776: "Jacob Allen by order

of Select Men wated on Captn William Person [Pearson] to return £ 60 thay borrowed of him, but as the money we had of him was harde he chose the Town should keepe it till thay was able to return it in harde specha again as it is on interess."

3. Eddy's *Universalism,* 180-181.

4. *Ibid,* 105.

5. *Massachusetts Archives* 138, 351.

6. *Naval Documents* III, 966, 991, 1075, 1247.

7. *Ibid* III, 1121-1122; V, 395.

8. *Ibid* III, 1043.

9. *Ibid* IV, 307-308, 317, 330. Babson's version of the *Stakesby* incident (*History*, 411) mistakenly has an unnamed brig chased ashore at Brace Cove by the frigate *Milford.* "Capt. Joseph Foster, with a company of minute-men, marched over from town to protect the vessel, in case the frigate should send a force to take possession of her. He got out some of the cargo; but, during the night, a boat's crew from the frigate boarded the brig, and set her on fire, by which she was destroyed."

10. Babson, *Second Series*, 149. This is one of only two letters written by Foster on record. He was misinformed in locating the fleet in Broad Sound, which is north of Boston Harbor and separated from Nantasket Roads by the outer islands.

11. *Naval Documents IV*, 537.

12. *Ibid,* 520.

13. *Ibid,* IV, 694. Sargent appended to this report a list of eleven names led off by "Kalep Whitten--Bad Man."

13. Yankee Heroes All

1. *Naval Documents* IV, 659.

2. *American Archives,* Series 4, V, 1303.

3. Babson, *Second Series,* 149.

4. *Naval Documents* V, 197-198.

5. *Ibid,* 338.

6. "Samuel Rust died Feb. 7, 1782, of small-pox caught from the hat of a sailor, who landed from a cartel from Halifax and stopped at his house at Little River." Babson, *Second Series,* 94.

7. *Naval Documents* IV, 658; V, 87-88, 266, 198.

8. *Ibid,* 691-692 (*Milford*'s log of the engagement).

9. At Nantasket Roads *Milford* transferred the prisoners from *Yankee Hero* on board HMS *Renown,* the flagship of Commodore Francis Banks, who, according to American reports, treated them with the utmost civility, while his surgeon took "the greatest care" of Captain Tracy and the other wounded. Commodore Banks was quoted as declaring that "no men could fight better than ours on board the *Yankey Hero,*" and that he would bend all his efforts through Halifax toward an exchange of prisoners. *Naval Documents* V, 491, 508.

The sick and wounded Americans, states Babson in the *History* (which gives an abbreviated account of the engagement, 399-400), were taken to Halifax, thence to a New York prison ship where several contracted smallpox. "Capt. Rowe, Lieut. Pool, and many others, were sent on shore, sick with this disease, to a hospital which the British had prepared on Staten Island. When they recovered, not being called for immediately to return to the ship, they let themselves to a sutler in the British camp, who used in his business a small sloop, on board of which they were employed. Being left with her on one occasion, they took the boat in the night, and escaped to the Jersey shore to the camp of the American Army."

Gott's *History of Rockport* (52) suggests that the *Hero*'s prisoners were more dispersed: "Some of the men were gone seven years; some were sent as prisoners to Halifax; others escaped on a raft while the frigate lay at anchor off Rhode Island; some were sent to New York."

10. A similar ruse around this time worked. The master of another English vessel coming on the coast thought he ought to have a pilot. He came upon Theophilus Lane of Gloucester, out fishing, and pressed him aboard. Lane "assured the captain that Gloucester was in the hands of the British and thus induced the latter to run into this port. Our people went off to her, and, being in sufficient number to overpower the crew, took possession of the vessel." Babson, *Second Series,* 148.

11. *American Archives,* Series 5, I, 273.

12. *Naval Documents* V, 436.

13. *Massachusetts Archives* 137. 93-96. The committee's

report was scrawled hastily and was not accompanied by a map locating the batteries.

14. *Naval Documents* V, 713.

14. Privateers and Privation

1. *Naval Documents* V, 658.

2. Gloucester's spirit was so far lifted by the shift in theatres of war that the Tyrian Lodge of Masons, which had not met since Lexington, assembled at Prentice's tavern on August 6 and voted not to disband, after all, but to elect officers regardless of "the confusion occasioned in this as well as other communities by the unnatural and cruel war in which we are engaged."

3. *Naval Documents* VI, 1053-1055.

4. Babson's *History,* 410.

5. *Massachusetts Archives* 166, 287-290.

6. *Massachusetts Privateers of the Revolution*, 310.

7. Precisely how John Beach fell in with *George,* and so to Gloucester, is a wonderment. Babson (414) described him as "principally distinguished for his wild pranks on convivial occasions." Years later, the Reverend William Bentley, who enjoyed *his* conviviality and his visits with Beach whenever he came to Gloucester, remarked in his *Diary* (II, 438, July 1, 1802) that "Beach is giving to his house uncommon elegance. He has added a third story in an octagon, which is surrounded by a dome which has an elegant effect. This eccentric man has great ambition & good taste." Beach's elegant house is today the original section of the Sawyer Free Library, pruned of its gingerbread.

8. *Life of John Murray,* 313-314.

9. Murray's opponents in the First Parish did not publicly identify these "great many enemies" to their country, as far as the record shows. Chief among them at this time, certainly, was the Loyalist Epes Sargent, Sr.

10. Committee of safety interrogation from Eddy's *Universalism*, 107-110.

11. *Life of John Murray,* 324.

12. Babson's *History,* 413.

13. *Ibid*, 425-426. *Civil Usage* was first commissioned in September 1776 to Captain Andrew Giddings, an in-law of Joseph Foster. It is not known how he fared with her.

14. Babson states (416-417), incorrectly, it is believed, that *General Stark* was chiefly owned by David Pearce, "who is said to have embarked a large portion of his capital in the enterprise," though sharing her with others, including some from Ipswich, and he gives her displacement as four hundred tons. This does not jibe with the ship's initial commission of August 14, wherein the *Stark* is rated at 220 tons...owners, Winthrop Sargent and others, of Cape Ann...bond, $10,000 Continental, £ 4000 Massachusetts...bonders, William Coas, principal; Winthrop Sargent and David Pearce of Gloucester, sureties. Babson also erroneously called her the *Starks,* a common slip; a brig, a brigantine and a sloop besides Gloucester's ship were commissioned *General Stark* at various times, and people frequently tacked on the *s*.

15. Six Small Cheezes & Part of a Pail of Butter

1. Babson's *History*, 151-152. The day Sargent died, January 7, 1779, his brother Winthrop and Joseph Foster and perhaps others, owners of the sloop *Union,* which had cruised with such success under Isaac Somes, had her commissioned to Captain Nathaniel Sargent.

Two or three years before his death Epes Sargent had made up his mind to join the hegira of Loyalists to Halifax, according to Babson (152). "But, on assembling his family for leave-taking on the evening before his intended departure, his spirits were so much oppressed with the pangs of separation, that he resolved to return to his home, and endure, as he best could, the fortune that might await him."

More light, and more mystery, are shed on Sargent's intentions by a report from the Newburyport authorities to the Massachusetts Council dated August 30, 1776 (*Massachusetts Archives,* 165, 232-233) to the effect that Sargent had been discovered and stopped in a plan to send his son (who was not identified by name) and one of his captains in a sloop bound from that port to Nova Scotia, where he had two or three vessels "we have reason to think has for some time past been employ'd in and under the protection of that government." The Newburyport committee intercepted a letter from Sargent to Captain Joseph Sayward, master of one of his vessels, dated Newburyport August 16: "Sir--I have only time to tell you that your family is well and that heaven must direct you in your movements. I cant get down. I beg you'd keep a good lookout. I cant say more. Your friend, Epes Sargent." After leaving Newburyport, the authorities there informed the Council, Sargent was said to have engaged a two-masted boat at Ipswich and sent his son off in her to Nova Scotia.

The Council summoned Sargent to appear before it on September 26 and explain his actions, but no further record of the affair can be found. Whether the individual mentioned was, in fact, his son, is questionable; both of Sargent's sons, Epes and John Osborne, were patriots and are believed to have remained in Gloucester throughout the Revolution.

2. Babson's *History*, 417, 424-425. Thomas Sanders returned to Gloucester, and the classroom. In 1795, during a mental depression, he threw himself into the well behind his house, where City Hall now stands, and drowned. Babson, *Second Series,* 75.

3. According to Emmons's *Navy* (140), this engagement was with the packet *Halifax* off the English coast, and she lost four killed and six wounded.

4. Babson erroneously transposed the brothers John and Isaac Somes in his account of *Wasp*'s two cruises *(History,* 423).

5. Babson, *Second Series,* 151. The story behind the shrinkage of Gloucester's fleet by three-fifths, three thousand tons in nearly five years of war, lies irrecoverably at the bottom of the sea. Occasionally a remmant washes up on the beach of time, as found in the log of HM Frigate *Milford*, August 22, 1776: "Cape Ann N 79 W 12 leagues--at 7 AM saw a sail--gave chase-- at 10 came up with the chace which proved to be a fishing schooner, burnt her." *Naval Documents* VI, 279.

6. Between 1775 and 1783 Nathaniel Tracy of Newburyport

was principal owner of 110 merchant ships, including twenty-three privateers, and twenty-four cruising ships. He had lost all but fourteen by the war's end, but his armed vessels had captured 120 enemy sail which, with their cargoes, he sold for $3,950,000 in gold. He gave away $167,219 for military and public purposes. Jewett's *Essex County,* 327.

7. If butter was short, Gloucester finally was long on guns after those lean and critical months of 1775. In an inventory taken on November 9, 1779, the selectmen toted up 2960 pounds of gunpowder in casks cached at eight locations around Cape Ann, twenty-five hundred musket cartridges, three thousand flints, six hundred pounds of musket balls, 294 twenty-four-pound shot, fifty-nine eighteen-pound shot, 513 nine-pound shot, 128 six-pound shot and ninety-one four-pound shot.

8. The account of this raid in Babson (44ln) omits mention of the prior visit of the women to the Beaver Dam Farm, related in Gott's *Rockport,* 50-51.

9. *Wilkes* was first commissioned on July 17, 1777, to John Foster Williams, then to William Pearce on December 28, 1779, finally to Job Knights on April 21, 1780. There is no reason to believe that this was not her last voyage under American colors before the capture which Babson declares occurred near the West Indies, but erroneously, it would appear, assigning her command to John Beach. The *History* (424) states that *Wilkes* made her first privateering cruise under Knights, was captured, retaken by Marbleheaders and brought back to Gloucester before her second capture under Beach. This does not square with the records of *Wilkes*'s commissions.

10. A number of *America*s received letters of marque during the Revolution, making for a confusion of identities further confused by the cryptic record in *Massachusetts Privateers* of her commissioning to John Somes on June 9, 1780...guns, men, owners unspecified. However, a ship *America* was next commissioned to Captain William Coffin of Newburyport, twenty guns, a hundred men, on October 12, and Babson (422) states that during a cruise whose date he fails to reveal she hailed from Newburyport under the command of Captain Somes.

11. *Essex Institute Historical Collections* XLII (October

1906), 375-376. Obadiah Parsons had been dismissed from the Annisquam pulpit the previous November after his exoneration of a crime, as Babson put it (365), "sufficient to degrade him for ever from his sacred office as a teacher of piety and morality." The historian spared his readers the details out of "a proper regard for decency," letting slip only that the person who charged him "repeated her accusation or complaint" before an investigating council of the church. In spite of its acquittal of Pastor Parsons, the council thought it best that he and his parish part company "considering the great alienation of affection." Nearly half had walked out on him. But apparently they let him hang around until he found a parish in Beverly, since the *America* entry was dated August 28.

12. The version of the *America* ordeal attributed to Nathaniel Allen is from a *Salem Gazette* of February 1839 extracted in Hurd's *Essex County* II, 1269-1270. It contains some minor discrepancies as to dates and details when compared with the contemporary account of Obadiah Parsons. Babson (89) adds a Witham to the crew which the 1839 article identifies as Aaron.

13. Statement of David E. Woodbury of Gloucester, 1906, accompanying the Parsons account (see note 11 above). Memorial services had been held for Captain Elwell, and his estate was under administration when he returned "like one being raised from the dead," according to Woodbury, who wrongly stated that the wanderer did not again go to sea.

16. Embrace the First Good Wind

1. To complete the record: in March, 1781, the schooners *Medium* and *Union*, four guns each, were commisioned to Captains Benjamin Witham and Daniel Parsons. *Union* is said by Babson to have taken a brig from Ireland with beef, pork and clothing.

2. John Higginson, Stephen's younger brother, had suffered capture at least twice. He was master of an American prize taken to Halifax, and returned to Salem in a prisoner exchange cartel in 1777. He returned to sea and was captured again, landing in Forton Prison. According to the diary of William

Pynchon of Salem, August 11, 1782: "Prisoners from England. Jno. Higginson et al come home, & say that all the American prisoners are released & sent home at the instance of the new ministry." Higginson's *Descendants*, 17.

3. Duncan Piper's only known privateer commission was dated August 9, 1781, as commander of the schooner *Industry*, seventy tons, twelve guns, fifteen men, owned by Captain William Pearson and Company of Gloucester.

4. Two lesser armed vessels also sailed from Gloucester this summer: Captain Thomas Sanders in his most formidable command to date, the schooner *Swift*, twelve guns, thirty men, in June; and Captain Daniel Young's schooner with the engaging name *Little Dan*, four guns, twenty-five men, August 9. Results unknown.

5. The bare account of this cruise is in Babson's *History* (422-423), with some slight confirmation from a statement in Emmons's *Navy* (140) that *General Stark* captured three large ships bound to Quebec from London, with cargoes valued at $400,000, and indicating somewhat ambiguously that the year was 1781. Babson supplies no date and adds to the melee by declaring at the beginning of his report of the cruise, on the one hand, that James Pearson was in command... while concluding with the murky statement: "Having been so fortunate on this cruise, Capt. Coas was induced to take command of her again." Pearson had been Coas's sailing master in the *Stark,* actually had the command of the ship once or twice, and they may have been together on the cruise in question, giving rise to some misinterpretation with the passage of time as to which was chief.

Three facts are indisputable: William Coas was commissioned to the *Stark* on July 3, Coles to *Brutus* on July 10, and *General Stark* was captured, with Coas in command, on October 8. As for the rest of the story, continued research may one day fill it out in more of its fascinating dimensions. Here is one more negative example of the extent to which the infinitely intriguing history of privateering in the American Revolution, in part due to its secretive nature, has eluded documentation. Still, enough remains to reward the diligent investigative reporter of the past with some great scoops.

6. Babson's *History*, 285. *General Stark* was renamed by the British *Antelope Packet*, according to Babson, and was wrecked at the Pelew Islands in the Pacific. All of his men did not go to the bottom with Captain Coas. Others arrived home at Gloucester in another cartel, some of them so sick that when they were landed in Harbor Cove they crawled ashore on their hands and knees. A third contingent of *Stark* prisoners from Halifax was embayed in a cartel during a blizzard on Ipswich Bay. "The men were sick, and the captain was a stranger in that place; so that the vessel would probably have been wrecked, if Capt. William Allen of Gloucester--who was then lying sick in his berth--had not offered, if he could be helped to the place, to stand in the companion-way, and pilot her over Squam Bar." (423)

17. To the Finish

1. *Robin Hood*'s papers do not specifically identify Isaac Somes's command on this voyage as *Favorite*, but the inference is clear. *Favorite* was commissioned to no one else from December 14, 1779, the date of his papers, to December 6, 1781, when Elias Davis took her over. Clearing Christiansand in early September, *Favorite* had ample time to arrive home and refit by early December under the push of hard-driving masters, and owners eager to keep such a swift brig in profitable service.

2. Babson's *History*, 426.

3. Foster's *Foster*, 88.

4. Babson's *History*, 426.

5. *Ibid.*

6. The same day that the prodigal Somes was spying about their waterfront, the Gloucester selectmen voted a trifle petulently to give Epes Sargent 195 pounds of gunpowder "which with 105 lb formerly paid him, is in full for 300 lb borrow'd of his father Epes Sargent Esqr. deceas'd, year 1775, and the obligations not given up." The elder Epes had complied with the town's request for his powder in January of 1775, although all the thanks he got for it were insults and ostracism three months later when he refused to recant his Tory views.

7. In a letter dated October 4, 1778, which appeared in the *Boston Post* of January 9, 1779, Captain Wingate Newman of the twenty-gun privateer brig *Vengeance* of Newburyport reported that "on the 17th of September, in Latt. 49 N. and Long. 20 West, fell in with the ship *Harriot*, packet of 16 guns and 45 men ... from Falmouth [England] bound to New York, which, after a small resistance, struck. I man'd her and ordered her for Newbury-Port." Had *Harriot* been taken and retaken previously? Not likely, but the name is unusual; on March 7, 1776, a store ship *Harriot*, bound from London to Boston with cole porter [sic] and potatoes ran aground on Nantucket Shoals and was captured by manned boats from Edgartown after an engagement during which her master, Captain Orrock, was wounded. *Naval Documents* IV, 281.

8. In his account of *Harriot*'s recapture (444-446) Babson unequivocally identifies *Betsey* rather than *Polly* as the heroine of the chase, while the news story in the *Salem Gazette* eleven days later just as positively names *Polly*. David Pearce was indeed an owner of *Polly*, as the *Gazette* states. His partner was Winthrop Sargent. For tax purposes the town valued *Polly* early in 1782 at £ 4.10 per ton, assigning 180 tons to Pearce and sixty to Sargent for a total assessment of £ 1080. Foster had plenty of time to take *Polly* to the West Indies at the beginning of January and return with a cargo at least a fortnight in advance of February 21, when she was commissioned to Isaac Lee, who could have completed a five-week cruise in her before a lay-up for refit at the end of March. Might Israel Trask (see note 13 below) have given Babson a wrong steer from the vantage of his old age? Trask confused *Polly* with *Betsey* and claimed erroneously that he was captured with Captain Foster in the latter vessel. Furthermore, a *Betsey* was commissioned out of Gloucester only once during the Revolution, to Philemon Haskell on February 2, 1781, more than a year earlier. All things considered, there is reason in this instance to favor the contemporary identification of Gloucester's swift huntress over our good historian's of eighty years later.

9. Babson's *History*, 445.

10. *Essex Institute Historical Collections* XLV (July 1909), 236. "Records of the Vice Admiralty Court at Halifax, Nova Scotia."

11. Foster's *Foster*, 84.

12. *Ibid*, 88.

13. Israel Trask mistakenly recalled Captain Foster's vessel as *Betsey*. After his escape from the prison hulk at Halifax and return to Gloucester in the summer of 1782, Trask signed with Captain Solomon Babson in the speedy Newburyport brigantine *Ruby* which had so handily outsailed a twenty-gun English warship when Ignatius Webber was aboard. They cruised twice to Guadeloupe before the war's end. Home in Gloucester after the peace, he returned to the sea, rose to the command of his own vessel, entered business profitably, married and raised a family, entered politics and was twice elected state senator. Babson admired him greatly, remarking on the scantiness of his formal education, and wrote: "By temperament and exercise, he preserved the advantages of a good hereditary constitution, and retained in a wonderful degree, to the end of his life, all the mental and physical faculties with which nature had endowed him. It was only a few days before his death that his erect form and agile step were missed from our streets. He gave much attention to intellectual cultivation, and could speak several foreign languages with fluency; but he is best remembered by his townsmen as a man of pure morals, of benevolent heart, and very courteous manners. He died Oct. 4, 1854, aged ninety." (283-284)

14. The *Salem Gazette* of October 31, 1782 noted the arrival of a prisoner cartel from Halifax a few days earlier, but provided no names.

15. Becca Ingersoll is not to be confused with Aunt Becky Ingersol, the barberess. Becca was the daughter of the widow Dorothy Ingersoll whose late husband, Medifer, died in 1759 while a prisoner of war, it was said, on a French ship.

16. Babson's *History*, 463.

17. *Ibid*, 427.

18. But the Revolution Goes On

1. Eddy's *Universalism*, 154-155.

2. The present site of the first Universalist meeting house is Goldman's, Inc., 199 Main Street.

3. The Somes organ was retired in 1826, when the present meeting house was twenty-one years old, and replaced with a standard church organ of two keyboards built by Thomas Appleton of Boston. The Appleton organ gave way in 1856 to a larger model made by Hook of Boston. Hook's was followed by the current organ, built by George Hutchings of Boston in 1893, rebuilt by C.B. Fisk of Gloucester in 1962. *Gloucester Daily Times* article by Barbara Owen, June 7, 1973.

4. Eddy's *Universalism*, 131.

5. Foster's *Foster*, 165.

6. Babson's *History* has Colonel Foster living in his Middle Street house at the close of the Revolution and some time later on Front Street. Joseph, Jr., occupied the Middle Street house at the time of his father's death.

7. Eddy's *Universalism*, 24-26.

8. *Ibid*, 133-152.

9. *Ibid*, 157-176.

10. *Ibid*, 177-185.

11. *Ibid*, 27.

12. Bentley's *Diary* III, 127-128 (December 15, 1804). Babson undoubtedly had no knowledge of Bentley's estimate of Forbes when he wrote of him in the *History* (405): "During all this contention, Mr. Forbes took the right position--that of silence and inactivity. The wise pastor was more solicitous to maintain the peace and harmony of society than to gather to the parish coffers a few grudgingly paid dollars; and, while he undoubtedly considered the seceding members to be in a condition of dangerous delusion, the only means by which he tried to win them back was a constant manifestation of kindness and regard, the memory of which has long outlived that of the ill feeling engendered by the occasion that called them forth." Such facts as we know do not bear Mr. Babson out.

19. He Would Suffer No Idlers

1. Joseph Foster's relative postwar economic standing among the Universalists can be assayed according to the subscription raised in 1788 to pay John Murray a hundred pounds a year so he could marry and support Mrs. Judith

Sargent Stevens in her Middle Street home in the style to which he had become accustomed. (This today is the Sargent-Murray-Gilman-Hough House, number 49, open to the public during the summers, built for Judith by her father, Winthrop Sargent.) The levies were to be "in such proportion as we pay the town or state tax the year immediately preceding." One hundred and three were assessed, in descending order beginning with David Pearce's £ 8.19.0, Winthrop Sargent £ 2.11.0 and Joseph Foster £ 2.2.8.

A less reliable indicator is the style in which one rode about the streets. When they were desperate for taxes in 1782, while the war was still on, the assessors examined the conveyances of the well-to-do, and for a yardstick valued the most elegant of the thirty chaises worth taxing at thirty-five pounds, a category occupied solely by Epes and Winthrop Sargent and Benjamin and John Somes. Captain Foster's rig was alone in the thirty-pound class. David Pearce's was assessed at twenty-five. The rest trailed at twenty pounds on down.

2. Morison's *Maritime History*, 28-29.

3. *Ibid*, 37.

4. During La Fayette's visit to America in 1824 he paused at Ipswich, where a collation was served. "When in the act of taking his second glass of wine, Col. Wade was introduced to him...The cordial embrace of these two veteran companions in arms was affecting beyond description...'But, my dear General, do you remember West Point?' General La Fayette: 'O my dear friend I do! and when General Washington first heard of the defection of Arnold, he asked, "Who has the immediate command?" On being told that it was you, he said: *"Colonel Wade is a true man, I am satisfied!"* General Green and myself immediately repaired to the garrison. Do you not recollect seeing me riding rapidly in from the northeast corner when we took the Division up to King's Ferry?' Here the feelings of the two Heroes became too strong for utterance; they hung upon each other." *Newburyport Union* (in Foster's *Foster*, 131-132).

5. *Letters of Epes Sargent*.

6. Foster's *Foster*, 165-166.

7. Essex County Probate Records 9928 (1808).

8. Brooks, *Gloucester Recollected*, 14.

9. *Letters of Epes Sargent.* Sargent mentions that his father, John Osborne Sargent, "commanded a vessel in the merchant service in the West India trade." J.O. Sargent made one privateering cruise, at least, during the Revolution, when he was commissioned commander of the ship *Gloucester Packet* on January 11, 1782.

10. Foster's *Foster*, 18.

11. "Letters of the Late Harrison Ellery," *Cape Ann Advertiser*, 1879 (undated).

12. Bentley's *Diary* I, 265-266 (June 14, 1791).

13. Babson's *History*, 406.

20. Bound Home

1. *Letters of Epes Sargent.*

2. *Ibid.*

3. Back in Gloucester after his first voyage, Epes had a chance for a berth on the small ship *Winthrop and Mary*, Captain James Collins, owned by a Gloucester company which included his uncle Joseph Foster, Jr., fitting out in 1800 for a voyage to Sumatra. His schoolmate James Pearson, Jr., son of the privateersman, was going in her, as was David Saville, one of Jesse's boys. Epes was sorely tempted to join his friends but decided to ship on a Boston vessel to which he had already tentatively committed himself. *Winthrop and Mary* reached Sumatra and was never seen again after embarking from there. It was concluded that she was lost in a hurricane with all hands, in the Indian Ocean.

4. Epes Sargent followed the sea as a shipmaster from Gloucester for some years, then turned to business, moved to Roxbury and died there in 1853. He had three wives and twelve children. His grandson, Epes Sargent, to whom he addressed his series of autobiographical letters, was the son of his son George Bernard Sargent, who emigrated to Iowa; the boy died at the age of sixteen. Two other sons of Captain Epes Sargent and great-grandsons of Joseph Foster achieved distinction, Epes (1813-1880), journalist, editor, poet and dramatist, and John Osborne (1811-1891), lawyer, journalist and author. John

Singer Sargent (1856-1925), the painter, was descended from Winthrop's line.

Joseph Foster III, Colonel Foster's other grandson who took to the sea, was master of a dozen vessels in the world commerce during his career of forty-four years afloat, including a privateer in the War of 1812, *Sword Fish*. He lived in Gloucester on Middle Street, several houses west of his grandfather's, and died on board his brig *Ventrosa* at Martha's Vineyard in 1843, homeward bound from Surinam. The tradition was carried on by his son, Joseph Foster IV, born in Gloucester in 1841; the family moved to Portsmouth, New Hampshire, in 1850; he rose to be a paymaster in the United States Navy with the rank of rear admiral, compiled the genealogy-biography of his great-grandfather which has served so usefully in the present work, and died at Portsmouth in 1930.

5. Bentley's *Diary* II, 305.

6. *Ibid*, 309.

7. Judith and Captain Saunders were separated after hardly more than four years, for they were married in 1793 and she had returned to her father's house at least as early as 1797. A suspicion of what went awry may be hidden in a verse entitled "Cheerfulness," by the English poet Mark Akenside, which she copied at Gloucester on August 16, 1800, a month after her father's seventieth brithday. The final lines:

> Fair guardian of domestic life,
> Kind banisher of homebred strife
> Nor sullen lip, nor taunting eye,
> Deforms the scene when thou art by.

Mrs. Saunders was granted an uncontested divorce by the Massachusetts Supreme Judicial Court in 1806.

Postscript

1. Foster's *Foster*, 17-18.

2. Garland, Joseph E.: *The Gloucester Guide*. Gloucester, 1973, 109-110.

ACKNOWLEDGMENTS

I acknowledge with pleasure the assistance of Thomas E. Babson, former president of the Cape Ann Historical Association, who informed me of the existence of the *Robin Hood* papers there and gave this manuscript a critical reading; Frederick P. Worthen, a direct descendant of Joseph Foster, who permitted me to extract from family copies of the Epes Sargent letters in his possession, and Adair Miller, who put me on to them; Carolyn Wonson Pattillo, who allowed me to quote from the manuscript *Journal* of her ancestor, Ignatius Webber, Jr.; Larry W. Sherman, Master, and Earle T. Merchant, Secretary, for their cooperation in providing access to the early record of The Tyrian Lodge, A.F.&A.M., Gloucester; Mrs. Dorothy M. Potter, Librarian of The Essex Institute, Salem, and her always helpful staff, especially Mrs. Irene Norton, Reference Librarian, and Miss Mary M. Ritchie, Assistant Librarian; the Cape Ann Historical Association and its knowledgable Assistant Curator, Mrs. Caroline Benham; Gloucester City Clerk Fred J. Kyrouz and his staff for their cooperation in my search of town records; Stillman P. Hilton and his staff at the Sawyer Free Library, Gloucester; Miss Janet Foster and John Foster, descendants of Joseph Foster, for the loan of family records; Luther Burnham and Dana Story for helping with Chebacco Falls and Story family background; the National Maritime Museum of Greenwich, England, for the plans of *Falcon* and permission to reproduce them; Peabody Museum of Salem; New England Historic Genealogical Society of Boston; Philip C. Bolger and Paul B. Kenyon, for their constructive perusal of the manuscript; John F. Heaps for his efforts in behalf of the book; and Richard V. Hunt, the skillful restorer of the Foster House, who planted the idea for this project.

I am under special obligation to Miss Frances H. McGrew, whose meticulous editing exposed a heinous horde of "horrors," grammatical and stylistic. Her pointed commentary and her sure knowledge of the language served me as a very much needed refresher course in composition.

CREDITS

MAPS: 1 (inside cover), from Department of the Navy's *The American Revolution Atlas*; 2, by John Mason, courtesy of City of Gloucester; 3, 4, 6, 8 & 9, by Barry Parsons and David Collins; 5, from Lossing's *Revolution*; 7, by the author.

ILLUSTRATIONS: 1 (frontispiece), by Margaret Garland Spindel; 2 & 3, courtesy The National Maritime Museum, London; 4, courtesy The Mariners Museum, Newport News, Va.; 5, 6 & 24, by Charles A. Lowe; 7, The Cape Ann Bank and Trust Company; 8, courtesy The Peabody Museum of Salem; 9 & 23, from Foster's *Foster*; 10, 16, 20, 21, 22 & 26, courtesy Cape Ann Historical Association; 11, 12 & 13, from Linzee's *Lindseie and Limesi Families*, courtesy Essex Institute, Salem; 14, by Martha Rogers Harvey; 15, Babson's *History* and Cape Ann Historical Association (cannonball); 17, courtesy Museum of Fine Arts, Boston, M. and M. Karolik Collection; 18, after a miniature in *Naval Documents of the American Revolution*, I; 19, private collection; 25, from Murray's *Life of Murray*; 27, by Thomas E. Babson; 28, courtesy Essex Institute, Salem.

BIBLIOGRAPHY

For the sake of both reader and writer, certain referential economies have been effected. In general, only extracted or quoted material is annotated, mainly with the exception of the Gloucester town records at City Hall, the numerous excerpts from which are identified in the text as such and by date. Since the early volumes of *Naval Documents of the American Revolution* published to date already make six peaks in a mountain range of primary material, much of it wholly new to the Cape Ann historian, most references are to the compilation in preference to the original sources. As a gesture of good will to the compositor--that She may Not in *this* Work, at Any rate, have to Contend with the age of Reason's irrational obsession with Random capitalization--the writer has knocked the extraneous upper case in extracted documents down to the lower, in the spirit of the levelling tendencies of the twentieth century.

Adams, John: *Legal Papers of John Adams*. L. Kinvin Wroth and Hiller B. Zobel, eds. Cambridge, 1965.

Allen, Gardner W.: *Massachusetts Privateers of the Revolution*. Massachusetts Historical Society, Boston, 1927.

American Archives. Peter Force, ed. Washington, 1837-1846.

Babson, John J.: "Address on the Centennial of the *Falcon* fight, August 8, 1875." *Cape Ann Advertiser*, August 13, 1875.

-----------*History of the Town of Gloucester, Cape Ann, including the Town of Rockport.* Gloucester, 1860. Reprinted by Peter Smith, Gloucester, 1972.

-----------*Notes and Additions to the History of Gloucester, Second Series.* Salem, 1891.

Babson, Roger W., and Foster H. Saville: *Cape Ann Tourist's Guide.* Wellesley Hills, 1945.

Beattie, Donald W., and J. Richard Collins: *Washington's New England Fleet.* Beverly, 1969.

Bentley, William: *The Diary of William Bentley, D.D.* Salem, 1905. Reprinted by Peter Smith, Gloucester, 1962.

Beverly Vital Records I & II. Topsfield Historical Society, 1906 & 1907.

Brooks, Alfred Mansfield: *Gloucester Recollected: A Familiar History.* Joseph E. Garland, ed. Peter Smith, Gloucester, 1974.

Brown, Robert F.: "Whaling Out of Gloucester." Typescript, 1972.

Chandler, Rev. Samuel: *Journal, 1751-1764.* In Babson, *Second Series.*

Clark, Victor S.: *History of Manufactures in the United States.* Carnegie Institution, Washington, 1929. Reprinted by Peter Smith, New York, 1949.

Coggins, Jack: *Ships and Seamen of the American Revolution.* Harrisburg, Pa., 1969.

Commonwealth History of Massachusetts. Albert Bushnell Hart, ed. New York, 1929.

Craft, Benjamin: "Journal of the Siege of Boston." *Essex Institute Historical Collections* III (April 1861).

-------- "Journal of the Siege of Louisburg." *Ibid,* (October 1864).

Crowell, Robert: *History of the Town of Essex from 1634 to 1868.* Essex, 1868.

Currier, John J.: *History of Newburyport, Massachusetts, 1764-1905.* Newburyport, 1906.

Dictionary of American Biography. New York, 1964.

"Early Coastwise and Foreign Shipping of Salem, 1750-1769." *Essex Institute Historical Collections* LXII-LXIX (1926-1933).

Eddy. Richard: *Universalism in Gloucester, Massachusetts.* Gloucester, 1892.

Edes, Peter: *His Diary While a Prisoner of the British.* Bangor, Maine, 1901.

Emmons, Lt. George F., USN: *The Navy of the United States from the Commencement, 1775 to 1853.* Washington, 1853.

Encyclopedia of American History. Richard B. Morris, ed. New York, 1961.

Encyclopedia Britannica. Eleventh edition. New York, 1910.

Essex County Courthouse records (Circuit Court of Common Pleas), Salem.

----------Probate Court records, Salem.

----------Registry of Deeds records, Salem.

----------Superior Court records. Office of the Clerk, Massachusetts Supreme Judicial Court, Boston.

Ewan, N.R.: "Up-and-Down Saw Mills," *The Chronicle of Early American Industries Association*, II, May, 1941.

Felt, Joseph B.: *History of Ipswich, Essex and Hamilton.* Cambridge, 1834.

Fleming, Thomas J.: *The Story of Bunker Hill.* New York, 1962.

Forbes, Eli: *A Sermon, Preached at the Desire of the Committee, appointed for Repairing of the Meeting-House, in the First Parish of Gloucester, from the Waste of Time, and the wanton Spoilations of Captain Lynzey in the Falcon Sloop of War, immediately after those Repairs were completed, On the 13th of September, 1792.* Salem, 1795.

Forbes, Esther: *Paul Revere & The World He Lived In.* Boston, 1942.

Foster, Joseph, Rear Admiral (S.C.) U.S.N. (Ret.): *Colonel Joseph Foster. His Children and Grandchildren.* (1888 or 1889). With appendix compiled by Elima A. Foster. Cleveland, 1947.

French, Allen: *The Siege of Boston.* New York, 1911.

Frothingham, Richard: *Life and Times of Joseph Warren.* Boston, 1865.

Fuller, Daniel: *The Diary of the Revd. Daniel Fuller.* Daniel Fuller Appleton, ed. New York, 1894.

Gloucester Selectmen's Day Book, 1775-1782.

Gloucester Town Records Books 3 & 4, 1753-1800 & 1800-1820.

Gloucester Vital Records I. Topsfield Historical Society, 1917; II & III, Essex Institute, 1923 & 1924.

Gott, Lemuel: *History of the Town of Rockport*. Rockport, 1888.

Greene, Evarts B.: *The Revolutionary Generation*. New York, 1943.

Higginson, Thomas Wentworth: *Descendants of the Reverend Francis Higginson*. 1910.

History of Essex County, Massachusetts. D. Hamilton Hurd, ed. Philadelphia, 1888.

Holten, Samuel, M.D.: "Journal," *Essex Institute Historical Collections* LV, (July 1919).

Hutchinson, Thomas: *The History of the Colony and Province of Massachusetts-Bay*. L.S. Mayo, ed. Cambridge, 1936.

Innis, Harold A.: *The Cod Fisheries*. Toronto, 1954.

Ipswich Vital Records I & II. Essex Institute, 1910.

Journal of the Honorable House of Representatives of the Colony of the Massachusetts-Bay in New England.

Letters of Members of the Continental Congress. E.C. Burnett, ed. Carnegie Institution, Washington, 1921. Reprinted by Peter Smith, Gloucester, 1963.

Linzee, John W.: *The Lindseie and Limesi Families of Great Britain Including the Probates at Somerset House, London, England, of All Spellings of the Name Lindeseie from 1300 to 1800*. Boston, 1917.

Lossing, B.J.: *Pictorial Field Book of the Revolution*. New York, 1850.

McFarland, Raymond: *A History of the New England Fisheries*. New York, 1911.

Maclay, Edgar S.: *A History of American Privateers*. New York, 1899.

Mann, Charles E.: *In the Heart of Cape Ann, or the Story of Dogtown*. Gloucester, 1906.

Massachusetts Archives. State House, Boston.

Massachusetts Soldiers and Sailors of the Revolutionary War. Commonwealth of Massachusetts, Boston, 1899.

Memorial of the American Patriots Who Fell at the Battle of Bunker Hill. City of Boston, Boston, 1889.

Miller, John C.: *Origins of the American Revolution*. Boston, 1943.

Morison, Samuel Eliot: *The Maritime History of Massachusetts 1783-1860.* Boston, 1921.

Murray, John: *The Life of the Rev. John Murray, written by himself, with a continuation by Mrs. Judith Sargent Murray.* Boston, 1869.

Naval Documents of the American Revolution I-VI. U.S. Navy Department, Washington, 1964-1972.

Naval Records of the American Revolution. Library of Congress, Washington, 1906.

Parrington, Vernon L.: *Main Currents in American Thought.* New York, 1930.

Peabody, Robert E.: *Merchant Venturers of Old Salem.* Boston, 1912.

----------"The Naval Career of Captain Robert Manley of Marblehead." *Essex Institute Historical Collections* XLV, (January 1909).

Pierce, F.C.: *Foster Genealogy.* Chicago, 1899.

Pringle, James R.: *History of the Town and City of Gloucester.* Gloucester, 1892.

Quincy, Josiah: *Memoir of the Life of Josiah Quincy, Jun.* Boston, 1825.

Rawson, Marion N.: *Little Old Mills.* New York, 1935.

"Records of the Vice Admiralty Court at Halifax, Nova Scotia." *Essex Institute Historical Collections* XLV, (1909).

Robin Hood Papers. Manuscript papers and documents of the privateer ship *Robin Hood,* 1781. Cape Ann Historical Association.

Rowe, John: *Letters and Diary of John Rowe, 1759-1762, 1764-1779.* Boston, 1903.

Sabine, Lorenzo: *Report on the Principal Fisheries of the American Seas.* Washington, 1853.

Sargent, Epes: *Letters* to his grandson, Epes Sargent, December 9, 1845 to September 17, 1850. Typescript copy.

Ship Registers of the District of Gloucester 1789-1875. Essex Institute, Salem, 1944.

Sibley's Harvard Graduates. Clifford K. Shipton, ed. Cambridge and Boston, 1873ff.

Standard History of Essex County, Massachusetts. C.F. Jewett, Boston, 1878.

Stickney, Lucy W.: *Descendants of Robert Kinsman of Ipswich, Mass.* Boston, 1876.

Trask, Israel: *Petition to Congress,* Feb. 6, 1844. (Cape Ann Historical Association).

Tyrian Lodge A.F. & A.M., Gloucester, records.

The American Revolution 1775-1783: An Atlas of 18th Century Maps and Charts. U.S. Navy Department, Naval History Division. Washington, 1972.

The Tyrian Lodge A.F. & A.M. Bicentennial Celebration 1770-1970. Gloucester, 1970.

Webber, Ignatius: "A Narrative First Written in 1802--The Journal of Ignatius Webber." Manuscript.

Winsor, Justin, ed.: *The Memorial History of Boston.* Boston, 1880.

Zobel, Hiller, B.: *The Boston Massacre.* New York, 1970.

Boston Evening-Post; Boston Gazette; Boston News-Letter; Cape Ann Weekly Advertiser; Essex Gazette; Essex Journal & Newburyport Packet; Gloucester Daily Times; Massachusetts Spy; Newburyport Union; New England Chronicle; Salem Gazette.

INDEX

—339—

Fourth Parish, 23; Second Parish, 24; admiralty court, 147; convention, 216

Jackman, Timothy, 148
Jamaica, 187, 188, 206, 239
Japan trade, 288
Jenny, 160, 168
Joanna, 21, 23
John, 164
Joseph, 32, 33, 37, 38, 41
Jumper, William, 89
Juno (HM), 203, 313

Kelly, Mathew, 147
King, Rufus, 255-257
King Philip's War, 17
Kinsman, Robert (great-grandfather), 14, 15, 301
Knights, Job, 213, 321
Knights, Parker, 46, 49
Knox, Gen. Henry, 161, 171

Ladies' Adventure, 208
Lady Juliana, 178, 179
La Fayette, Marquis de, 328, 329
Lane, John, 120, 123, 124, 143, 144, 151, 152
Lane, Joseph, 170, 171
Lane, Theophilus, 317
Langdon (PV), 186, 187
La Polline, 282
Lee (US), 140, 160, 163, 179, 315
Lee, John, 77
Lexington and Concord, Battle of, 82, 83, 93, 119
Liberty, 42, 92
Lightfoot (PV), 212, 244
Linzee, John, on patrol to southward, 92-102; attempts Coffin's Beach landing, 102-104; attacks Gloucester, 4, 5, 105-

118, 307-311; mentioned, 121, 129, 136, 193
Little, Col. Moses, 87
Little Dan (PV), 323
Lively (HM), 77, 79, 80, 87, 123, 166, 305
Locke, Joseph, 283
Louisburg Expedition, 17-23, 32, 301, 302
Low, John, 57, 62, 74, 77, 179, 180
Lowther, William, 43, 46, 49
Lufkin, Zebulon, 79, 80
Lurvey, Peter, 109, 117, 308
Lynch (US), 163, 179

Machias, 110, 131
Magaw, Major Robert, 121-123
Malaga, 38, 41
Manchester, 77, 152, 271
Manley, John, 139, 143, 162-164, 167, 194, 195, 199, 203, 313, 315
Marblehead, 21, 65, 77, 79, 122, 123, 131, 135, 139, 145, 146, 150, 155, 168, 170, 172, 179, 180, 181, 240, 268, 305
Margaretta (HM), 110, 128, 131
Marquis de La Fayette (PV), 243
Marrett, Philip, 72
Mars (PV), 238, 239
Martha's Vineyard, 94, 95, 150, 159
Martinique, 32, 209, 222, 235, 244, 279, 280, 283
Mary, 221
Mason, Major, 135, 136, 142
Masons, Tyrian Lodge of, 71-73, 318
Massachusetts, 288
Mather, Cotton, 16, 17
McKean, John, 65, 66, 157
McNeill, Hector, 194